The Economics of the
World Trading System

The Economics of the World Trading System

Kyle Bagwell and
Robert W. Staiger

The MIT Press
Cambridge, Massachusetts
London, England

This book was set in Palatino by SNP Best-set Typesetter Ltd., Hong Kong and was printed and bound in the United States of America.

Library of Congress Cataloging-in-Publication Data

Bagwell, Kyle.
  The economics of the world trading system / Kyle Bagwell and Robert W. Staiger.
    p. cm.
  Includes bibliographical references and index.
  ISBN 0-262-02529-9 (hc. : alk. paper)
  1. International trade. 2. Free trade. 3. General Agreement on Tariffs and
Trade (Organization) 4. World Trade Organization. 5. Foreign trade regulation.
6. Commercial treaties. 7. Tariff. 8. Favored nation clause. 9. Competition,
International. I. Staiger, Robert W. II. Title.

HF1379 .B326   2003
382.9—dc21   2002075372

to Reid
to Sally

Contents

Preface

If the world trading system has a constitution, it is embodied in the Articles of the General Agreement on Tariffs and Trade (GATT) and now its successor organization, the World Trade Organization (WTO). Since the late 1960s legal scholars have actively explored the logic of GATT principles from the perspective of international law. Until recently, however, the GATT/WTO has not been the subject of systematic and formal economic analysis. Our purpose in writing this book is to provide a formal economic analysis of the central features of the GATT/WTO.

It might be expected that a formal economic exploration of GATT principles could proceed from the familiar economic arguments for free trade. After all, fifty-some years of negotiations under the GATT/WTO have resulted in an impressive freeing of trade. Surely it can be argued that a large part of this liberalization is attributable to the desire of governments to reap the efficiency gains of free trade for consumers everywhere, and that GATT principles can be interpreted as harnessing this desire. Yet a pair of observations suffices to explain why the familiar economic arguments for free trade are not of much help in interpreting GATT principles.

A first and fundamental impediment in applying such arguments to the interpretation of GATT principles is that the familiar case for free trade is a unilateral case, and as such it leaves no role for the existence of a trade agreement of any kind. Hence, when viewed from this perspective, the economic logic of the GATT/WTO is immediately suspect. And even if the economic arguments for free trade were couched in reciprocal terms, there is a second impediment to the application of these arguments in interpreting GATT principles. The fact is that virtually every tariff that has ever been lowered by a government as a result of a GATT/WTO negotiation—a tariff "concession" in GATT parlance—has been lowered for a simple reason: some exporters some-where in the world valued the market access, and as a result their gov-ernments were willing to offer something of value to that government in return (i.e., export access to their own markets through reciprocal tariff concessions of their own). Hence the consumer gain that comes from freer trade is not the liberalizing force that has been harnessed by the GATT/WTO. Instead, the GATT/WTO is driven by exporter interests.

Many economists have interpreted these observations as implying that some form of mercantilist logic lurks at the foundation of the GATT/WTO. And as a result a common view among economists is that GATT principles are, indeed, economic nonsense. According to this view, the GATT/WTO deserves the support of economists, but not because its rules have any demonstrable merit on economic grounds. Rather, the GATT/WTO deserves economists' support simply because negotiations sponsored by and implemented under its auspices have led to remarkably "good" outcomes (i.e., a remarkable freeing of trade).

We describe in this book an alternative perspective according to which the central GATT principles do make economic sense. This alter-native perspective does not require the development of "radical" or "exotic" formal models. In fact we develop most of the material in this book within very standard general equilibrium models of the world economy. But this alternative perspective does require that one take seriously an old idea: trade agreements exist to enable governments to escape from a terms-of-trade-driven Prisoner's Dilemma. A central message of this book is that economists have been too quick to reject this idea as a legitimate basis from which to interpret and evaluate GATT principles.

By describing the key institutional features of the GATT/WTO and presenting a unified economic framework within which to explore the logic of these features, we hope that this book can serve several pur-poses. First, we hope to provide established researchers in this area with a simple way of articulating the underlying problems that GATT principles seem well equipped to address, and with a simple and general framework from which to approach the economic analysis of the GATT/WTO. Second, we hope to entice new researchers into this research area. These include, of course, graduate students of interna-tional trade, but we also hope that this book will convince industrial organization economists, contract theorists, and applied game theorists that the GATT/WTO is an institution well worth studying. And finally, we hope that this book will be useful for those who seek to understand the functioning of this important international institution. In particular, we have attempted to keep technical material to a minimum while emphasizing general results and key insights, in the hope that this book will appeal as well to a more general audience of economists, policy makers, and advanced undergraduates.

During the process of writing this book, we have benefited from the input of many people. In this regard we thank Susan Athey, Robert Hudec, Patrick Low, Robert Madelin, John McLaren, Guido Sandleris, and participants at various WTO, university and conference seminars for helpful comments. We are particularly grateful to Bernard Hoekman, Henrik Horn, Giovanni Maggi, Petros C. Mavroidis, and anonymous referees for detailed comments. We thank the NSF for generous financial support under grant SES-9905460. Staiger gratefully acknowledges financial support from the Center for Advanced Study in the Behavioral Sciences.

1   Introduction

The important role played in the world economy by GATT (and now its successor, the WTO) is widely accepted. Since its creation in 1947 the GATT/WTO has grown in membership from an initial set of 23 countries to a roster that now includes more than 140 countries.[1] The expanding GATT/WTO membership reflects the success that this organization has had in facilitating tariff reductions. Through the eight rounds of trade-policy negotiations that have been sponsored by GATT, culminating with the completion of the Uruguay Round in 1994 and the creation of the WTO, the average ad valorem tariff on industrial goods has fallen from over 40 percent to below 4 percent. In light of the significant impact that GATT has had on the world economy, it is therefore important to assess the progress that has been made toward providing a theoretical interpretation of GATT and its main features.

While the past success of GATT justifies in its own right a theoretical interpretation of GATT's main features, this task is perhaps even more important when the future of this multilateral institution is considered. A critical question in the coming years is whether the same set of principles on which postwar multilateral liberalization has been based can or should be applied under the WTO to a host of "new" trade-policy issues. These issues include the spread of preferential

---

1. The GATT (General Agreement on Tariffs and Trade) was created in 1947, and the WTO (World Trade Organization) was established on January 1, 1995, as a result of the Marrakesh Agreement (also referred to as the WTO Agreement) of April 1994. The WTO Agreement includes the text of GATT, and hence GATT continues to exist as a substantive agreement. The WTO Agreement includes as well a set of additional agreements that build on and extend GATT principles to new areas. For both of these reasons, understanding GATT is the key to understanding the WTO. Therefore the primary focus of this book is on GATT. Moreover since much of our discussion refers to GATT history, and to specific articles of GATT—as opposed to the additional articles of the WTO Agreement—we often make reference to GATT rather than the WTO.

trading agreements, the treatment of labor and environmental standards, the harmonization of competition policies, the subsidization of
agricultural exports, and the treatment of services, foreign direct
investment and intellectual property. An understanding of why
GATT's principles have worked well in the more traditional arena of
multilateral tariff liberalization for industrial goods can lay the foundation for answers to this critical question.

In this book we present research that speaks to the purpose and
design of GATT. The book proceeds in three basic steps. We first discuss
the major theoretical approaches to the study of trade agreements.
Next, we develop the institutional context for our study with a description of the history and design of GATT and the WTO. Finally, in what
constitutes the bulk of the book, we draw on the theoretical literature
in order to interpret and evaluate the institutional design of GATT.

We begin in chapter 2 with a review of the major theoretical
approaches to trade agreements. We organize this discussion around a
simple but basic question: What is the purpose of a trade agreement?
In asking this question, we seek a "problem" that would arise for
governments in the absence of a trade agreement and that could be
"solved" with the creation of an appropriate trade agreement. Suppose,
for example, that in the absence of a trade agreement governments
would set their policies in a unilateral fashion. The creation of a trade
agreement is then potentially appealing to governments provided
that an inefficiency (relative to governments' preferences) exists when
trade policies are set unilaterally.[2] Once the inefficiency is identified,
the purpose of a trade agreement can be understood as an attempt
to "undo" the inefficient behavior that arises under unilateral tariff
setting, so that all member governments may thereby enjoy higher
welfare.

Our review of the theoretical literature suggests that there are two
kinds of problems that a trade agreement might solve. The first possibility is that the trade-policy decisions of one government give rise to
an externality that affects the welfare of another government. This is
the possibility that is emphasized in the *traditional economic approach to*

---

2. We evaluate efficiency from the perspective of the welfare enjoyed by governments.
As we discuss below, the government welfare functions that we employ may include
political considerations, and as a consequence free trade need not be efficient. This
approach is appropriate, since the GATT/WTO is an organization that facilitates the
negotiation of trading arrangements that are mutually beneficial to its members (i.e.,
the member governments).

trade agreements. Under this approach a government (of a large country) is assumed to set its import tariff in order to maximize national welfare, while recognizing that some of the cost of the tariff falls upon foreign exporters whose products sell at a lower world price (i.e., at a diminished terms of trade). This "terms-of-trade externality" naturally leads governments to set unilateral tariffs that are higher than would be efficient. The purpose of a trade agreement is then to eliminate the terms-of-trade-driven restrictions in trade volume that arise when policies are set unilaterally, and thereby offer governments a means of escape from a Prisoners' Dilemma.[3]

An apparent weakness of the traditional approach is the seemingly unrealistic hypothesis that governments maximize national welfare. Real-world governments, after all, have both political and economic motivations. It is thus important to assess whether the purpose of trade agreements identified by the traditional approach is in any sense tied to the hypothesis of national-welfare maximization. To explore this issue, we follow the recent political-economy literature and allow that governments are also concerned with the distributional consequences of their tariff choices. We refer to this generalization of the traditional approach as the *political-economy approach to trade agreements.* While the inclusion of political concerns enhances the realism of the model, we show that it does not offer any separate purpose for trade agreements. Whether or not governments have political motivations, it is their ability to shift the costs of protection onto one another through terms-of-trade movements that creates an inefficiency when tariffs are selected unilaterally. In both the traditional and political-economy approaches to trade agreements, therefore, the purpose of a trade agreement is to offer a means of escape from a terms-of-trade-driven Prisoners' Dilemma.

---

3. The terms-of-trade externality is not the only possible "cross-border" externality, but it is the externality that has figured most prominently in the theoretical literature. For example, an international "environmental externality" can arise if the trade-policy decisions of one government affect production decisions that in turn alter the global environment and thereby the welfare of a trading partner. See also Flam and Helpman (1987) and Helpman and Krugman (1989), who point out that unilateral tariff choices can be inefficient in the presence of monopolistic competition, even in the absence of terms-of-trade movements. Further, as Ethier (1998a,b) argues, a "scale externality" may arise if production technologies exhibit international increasing returns to scale, in which case the value of a trade agreement to one government can be influenced by the volume of trade between other countries. Ethier (2000) considers the possibility of a "political externality" across countries.

A second kind of problem for a trade agreement to solve arises when a government is unable to make credible commitments to its own private sector. A government, for example, may wish to commit that in the future it will not protect a certain industry, or that it will undertake extensive regulatory reforms. Such a commitment is potentially valuable to the government, since it induces behavior (e.g., investments in cost reduction or in export sectors) from the private sector that the government finds desirable. A problem in this case is that if the private sector does not respond in the desired fashion, then it may not be credible for the government to follow through on its proposed plan. A trade agreement can potentially help a government solve its time-consistency problem, if the agreement enhances the credibility of the government's plan, by calling for some form of retaliation in the event that the plan is not executed.[4] The *commitment approach to trade agreements* thus identifies a distinct problem for a trade agreement to solve; however, the application of this approach to the study of GATT's institutional design is not yet well developed. While we describe recent insights that emerge from the application of the commitment approach, our primary emphasis is therefore directed toward the traditional economic and political-economy approaches.[5]

In light of our discussion just above concerning the traditional economic and political-economy approaches to trade agreements, our decision to emphasize these approaches can be viewed as well as a decision to adopt the position that the purpose of a trade agreement is to offer a means of escape from a terms-of-trade-driven Prisoners' Dilemma. Yet real-world trade-policy negotiators rarely if ever speak of the terms-of-trade consequences of trade-policy choices. They choose instead to emphasize the market-access implications of trade policy. What, then, is the real-world counterpart to terms-of-trade motivations? We pause in chapter 2 to consider this question, and provide

---

4. Of course, the retaliation threat is effective only if the trading partner has the ability to punish the domestic government. The obvious possibility is that the trading partner raises its level of protection, which harms the domestic government through the terms-of-trade externality. In this sense a cross-country externality, such as the terms-of-trade externality, lies at the heart of all of the major theoretical approaches to the study of trade agreements.

5. While these three approaches include most of the theories that have been offered for trade agreements, there are some contributions that do not fit comfortably within any of the three approaches. Among these, we discuss Ethier's (1998a,b, 2000) contributions in later chapters, wherein we consider possible alternatives to the political-economy approach and research that interprets and evaluates the central GATT rules.

a surprisingly simple answer: the terms-of-trade consequences of trade-policy choices can be expressed equivalently in the language of market access, and so the terms-of-trade consequences and the market-access implications of trade-policy choices are different ways of expressing the same thing. This equivalence is very important, as it provides a point of contact between the modeling approaches that we emphasize in this book and the concerns that dominate real-world trade negotiations.

The traditional and political-economy approaches indicate that a trade agreement can increase the welfare of member governments, if the agreement undoes the inefficient restrictions in trade volume that arise in the absence of an agreement. Governments can thus jointly benefit from a trade agreement that calls for a mutual reduction in the levels of protection. But this perspective raises a pair of further questions. First, how should the institution through which governments negotiate over trade policies be designed? Following the legal literature, we draw a distinction between "power-based" and "rules-based" approaches to trade negotiations. In a power-based arrangement, governments negotiate over tariffs in a fashion that is unconstrained by any previously agreed-upon rules of negotiation. The relative bargaining power of the negotiating governments is then an important component in the determination of the eventual tariff-negotiation outcome. By contrast, under a rules-based approach, the governments agree upon a set of rules or principles by which subsequent tariff negotiations must abide. In this case power asymmetries between governments can be expected to play a diminished role in trade-policy negotiations. We develop this distinction further in chapter 2.

Second, how is the trade agreement to be enforced? Enforcement is an important concern, since each government has a short-term incentive to deviate to a higher-than-is-efficient tariff, in order to obtain the consequent terms-of-trade gains. Governments are dissuaded from such opportunistic behavior only if the pursuit of short-term gains results in long-term losses, as when other governments retaliate in kind. Viewed in this way, it is clear that the tariffs that governments can achieve as part of a "self-enforcing" trade agreement reflect a balance between the short-term gains from protection and the long-term losses from retaliation. While the "most-cooperative" tariffs that governments can enforce are more efficient than the tariffs that would occur in the absence of an agreement, they may not be fully efficient. In chapter 2 we draw on the theoretical literature that directly addresses the enforcement of trade agreements and argue that a meaningful agreement must constitute an equilibrium of a repeated trade-policy game.

In chapter 3 we turn to the second step of the book and describe the origin and design of GATT and the WTO. We note that the origin of GATT can be traced to the disastrous economic performance that accompanied the high tariffs of the 1920s and 1930s. The design of GATT is rules based: GATT members accept a set of rules or principles that describe the manner in which any subsequent trade-policy negotiations may proceed. The primary enforcement task of GATT is then to ensure compliance with these rules. While there are a large number of specific articles in GATT, it is widely accepted that the pillars of the GATT approach are the principles of reciprocity and nondiscrimination.

Broadly speaking, mutual adjustments in trade policy conform to the principle of reciprocity if these policy adjustments bring about changes in the volume of each country's imports that are of equal value to changes in the volume of its exports. This principle arises as a norm of behavior when governments negotiate tariff reductions (i.e., "concessions") in a GATT round, as it has been observed that governments seek to achieve a "balance of concessions" in their tariff negotiations. The principle of reciprocity also appears as an explicit GATT rule when, for example, trading partners meet to renegotiate tariffs to higher levels. In this case, when one government withdraws a concession to which it had previously agreed, its trading partner is allowed under GATT rules to withdraw a "substantially equivalent concession" of its own. The principle of nondiscrimination is a GATT rule that requires (subject to certain important exceptions) that the import tariff selected by a government on a particular good cannot be higher for the exports of one GATT member than for those of another.[6]

With the creation of GATT, governments therefore constructed a rather elaborate set of rules with which to address their perceived trade-policy problems. But do these rules reflect an underlying economic logic? It is tempting to conclude that they do not. Putting aside the terms-of-trade externality mentioned above, standard economic theory holds that the optimal unilateral policy for a national-

---

6. Our description here focuses on the most-favored-nation (MFN) tariff obligation as the embodiment of nondiscrimination in the GATT/WTO. Nondiscrimination in the GATT/WTO extends as well to nonborder measures through the national-treatment obligation.

welfare maximizing government is free trade. From this perspective, the emphasis placed on reciprocity in GATT is surely mysterious. Why would one government be willing to help itself with a tariff reduction only if its trading partner made a similar "concession?" Indeed, according to standard economic reasoning, there is no reason for GATT to exist in the first place, and so any attempt to offer an "economic" interpretation of GATT is destined for failure. This view is regularly advanced, but it is perhaps stated most eloquently in Krugman's (1991, pp. 25–27) writings:[7]

There is no generally accepted label for the theoretical underpinnings of the GATT. I like to refer to it as "GATT-think"—a simple set of principles that is entirely consistent, explains most of what goes on in negotiations, but makes no sense in terms of economics. . . . The reason why GATT-think works is, instead, that it captures some basic realities of the political process.

By contrast, in what constitutes the third step of this book, we review a literature that suggests that GATT does, in fact, make economic sense. This literature places the terms-of-trade externality at center stage, and argues that the GATT/WTO may be understood as an institution whose central features assist governments—whether politically motivated or not—as they attempt to escape from a terms-of-trade-driven Prisoners' Dilemma.

We develop this argument in chapters 4 through 10, where we present various extensions of the traditional terms-of-trade model of trade agreements and interpret and evaluate GATT rules in the context of these extended models. We ask positive questions: Can GATT rules be understood as the means through which governments solve their terms-of-trade problem? Do the predictions that come from this perspective conform with GATT experience? And we also ask normative questions: If the terms-of-trade problem does account for the purpose of GATT, are the rules of GATT properly designed? Are the basic GATT principles well suited for application to the new trade-policy issues currently facing the WTO?

We begin the third step of the book in chapter 4, where we consider in some detail the principle of reciprocity. We then turn in chapter 5 to the other pillar of the GATT/WTO system and analyze the principle of nondiscrimination. As we discuss in these chapters, it is possible to understand reciprocity as a principle that "neutralizes" all externalities that travel through world prices, while the principle of

---

7. See also Krugman (1997).

nondiscrimination then ensures that no other trade-policy externalities arise across trading partners. Reciprocity and nondiscrimination thereby serve as complementary principles that assist governments in their bilateral negotiations to achieve more efficient trade-policy outcomes. These principles have as well a virtuous property when the welfare of nonparticipants is considered: together, reciprocity and nondiscrimination can help to ensure that a bilateral negotiation between trading partners does not alter the welfare of the government of a third country. Reciprocity and nondiscrimination thus limit the ability of negotiating partners to appropriate the welfare of nonparticipants. By the same logic, the ability of a third-country government to "free ride" on the nondiscriminatory tariff cuts negotiated by others is diminished when negotiations are also constrained to abide by the principle of reciprocity.

In line with the abstract discussion of power-based and rules-based approaches to trade-policy negotiations, we suggest further that the specific rules of reciprocity and nondiscrimination diminish the extent to which power asymmetries across countries influence trade-policy outcomes. More speculatively, we argue that the decision by governments to form a rules-based institution may have been motivated in part by a desire to encourage the participation of "weaker" countries. Recognizing that the governments of smaller countries might fear that they would eventually be "held up" at the bargaining table, the governments of powerful countries (i.e., the United States and Great Britain) effectively committed with a rules-based system not to exploit their weaker trading partners. From this perspective, the selection of a rules-based approach solved a commitment problem (across countries) that ensured participation, while the specific rules employed within this approach then served to solve the terms-of-trade problem. We also describe more broadly how this selection may have helped to diminish a variety of additional strategic concerns that could arise in a power-based system.

We return to the topic of enforcement in chapter 6. There, we note that the balance between the short-term incentive to protect and the long-term fear of retaliation can be altered when the trading environment changes; as a consequence, the most-cooperative tariffs that can be enforced may vary with underlying market conditions. Expanding on this basic viewpoint, we offer interpretations of some GATT rules and experiences. For example, we interpret the GATT escape clause, under which a government can temporarily raise its level of protection if it faces a surge in imports, as a safeguard provision that works to maintain cooperation within a self-enforcing agreement when the market environment is volatile. We also describe work that emphasizes enforcement limitations and interprets the gradual manner in which tariffs have been liberalized over the GATT/WTO's five-decade history.

In chapters 7, 8, 9, and 10 we further extend the basic model and consider four new trade-policy issues that currently face the WTO. We begin in chapter 7 with an evaluation of the potential implications of preferential trading agreements for the multilateral trading system. Preferential trading agreements, which take the form of free-trade areas or customs unions, are permitted under GATT Article XXIV as an important exception to the principle of nondiscrimination. In recent years preferential trading agreements have grown in number and significance. We frame our discussion of this topic around two questions. First, do preferential trading agreements compromise the effectiveness with which the principles of reciprocity and nondiscrimination can deliver efficient outcomes? Second, when WTO members are involved in preferential trading agreements, does the enforcement of multilateral trading agreements become harder or easier? After reviewing the literature, we answer the first question in the affirmative, while we suggest that the answer to the second question is ambiguous. At a general level, we thus conclude that preferential trading agreements may pose a threat to the existing multilateral trading system.

In chapter 8 we raise the issue of labor and environmental standards. This issue probes the limits of the ability of the WTO to promote global efficiency while respecting national sovereignty. Existing GATT/WTO rules speak to this issue only to the extent that market-access concerns are directly involved, as when one WTO member raises discriminatory tariffs against the exports of a second WTO member in response to the weak labor standards of the second member, or when a WTO member adopts a new environmental standard that has the effect of reducing access to its markets that another WTO member had previously negotiated. The national labor and environmental standards that member governments choose to adopt have never been the subject of direct GATT/WTO negotiations, but there is mounting pressure for this to change. A number of industrialized countries (with the United States taking a leading position) have recently advocated the adoption of a "social clause," in which a set of minimum international standards would be negotiated and then enforced with the threat of trade sanctions. Is the GATT/WTO's traditional preoccupation with market access misplaced when the issue of labor and environmental standards is raised? Should WTO member governments embark on negotiations within the WTO over their national labor and environmental standards? Should the WTO's limited enforcement ability be utilized to ensure that national labor and environmental standards are set in an appropriate fashion? We describe a literature that identifies conditions under which the answer to the first two questions is no and the answer to the third is a qualified yes. The broader suggestion is that GATT principles are potentially well-equipped to handle the issue of labor and environmental standards.

In chapter 9 we consider competition policy. The links between competition policy and the effectiveness of international agreements to liberalize trade have long been thought to be important. However, the GATT rules that apply specifically to restrictive business practices are quite limited, and introducing a more comprehensive set of competition policy rules into the WTO has recently received renewed attention. At an informal level, there are similarities between the issues raised by the existence of separate national competition policies of WTO member governments and the existence of separate national labor and environmental standards. It therefore might be conjectured, in analogy with the discussion of labor and environmental standards just above, that the GATT/WTO's traditional focus on market access could serve an important role in ensuring appropriate competition policy choices by its member governments. But, at a formal level, a discussion of competition policy must account for the existence of imperfectly competitive firms, raising the possibility of additional international externalities that could render a focus on market access inadequate. In chapter 9 we extend the basic model to allow for the presence of imperfectly competitive firms so that the links between competition policy and the effectiveness of international agreements to liberalize trade can be formally explored. And we argue that the analogy between labor/environmental standards and competition policy holds, at least in the important area of competition policy that deals with mergers: in principle, the traditional market-access concerns of the GATT/WTO can be harnessed to ensure that the independently chosen national merger policies of member governments are set in an appropriate fashion.

Next, in chapter 10, we consider agricultural export subsidies. The treatment of export subsidies in the GATT/WTO is perplexing and controversial. The official GATT rule is that export subsidies are prohibited; however, important exceptions exist. In particular, GATT has historically accommodated a range of export subsidization programs that is directed toward agricultural industries. The appropriate GATT policy toward agricultural subsidies emerged as a central point of conflict between the European Community and the United States in the most recent GATT round (the Uruguay Round), and the tension that surrounded this issue quite nearly derailed the entire round. How is the GATT/WTO policy toward export subsidies to be understood? We offer an interpretation in chapter 10. Our analysis suggests that the ongoing conflict regarding agricultural export subsidies can be interpreted from the standpoint of the strategic-trade literature, even though agricultural markets have competitive characteristics. More broadly, we conclude that the GATT rules against export subsidies in fact may represent a victory for exporting governments at the expense of importing government—and world—welfare.

Many economists are skeptical as to the practical relevance of the terms-of-trade approach to trade agreements. At the same time, in our attempt to interpret and evaluate the GATT/WTO in this book, we give primary emphasis to this approach (with modifications for political considerations). It is therefore important to consider directly some of the theoretical and empirical objections that are made against the terms-of-trade approach. In chapter 11 we describe these objections, and we argue that upon closer scrutiny, the objections are less compelling than they might originally appear.

We conclude in chapter 12. In this chapter we summarize the main lessons developed in the book, and we also propose new directions for future research.

A question that arises at the outset of this book is whether GATT rules that appear to be sensible from an economic perspective were, in fact, designed with this purpose in mind. There seems to be no presumption that evolutionary forces would select international institutions that deliver the best outcomes and whose features can therefore be interpreted "as if" they were designed to solve particular problems. So to the extent that GATT rules do appear sensible from an economic perspective, this may reflect wisdom, learning, or pure serendipity. Nevertheless, we may interpret and evaluate these rules with an open mind, and in this way identify the problems that GATT rules do seem well designed to address, without necessarily determining whether or not this design was purposeful. This is the approach we take throughout the book.

2   The Theory of Trade Agreements

Any theory of trade agreements must provide a reason for a trade agreement to exist. We thus begin by examining the purposes for trade agreements that are proposed in the literature. We also introduce in this chapter two additional issues to which we return in greater depth later in the book. First, we consider the broad manner in which governments might design a trade agreement, and we distinguish between power- and rules-based approaches. Second, we consider the means through which a trade agreement might be enforced.

2.1   The Purpose of Trade Agreements

We begin, then, with the most basic question: What is the purpose of a trade agreement? We develop the answers to this question that are offered by the three major theoretical approaches to the study of trade agreements. We first discuss the traditional economic approach, in which governments are assumed to set tariffs so as to manipulate their terms of trade with the objective of maximizing national welfare. Next we consider the political-economy approach, wherein governments are assumed to also place emphasis on the distributional consequences of their tariff choices. The final approach that we describe is the commitment approach, which stresses the difficulty governments may face in making policy commitments to the private sector.

We show that in response to the question raised above, the traditional economic and political-economy approaches answer in unison: the purpose of a trade agreement is to provide governments with an escape from a terms-of-trade-driven Prisoners' Dilemma. A distinct answer is provided by the commitment approach, which suggests as well that a trade agreement might be useful in helping a government make policy commitments to its private sector. Hence on this most basic question the literature provides two distinct answers and points the way toward two (possibly complementary) paths to the study of the GATT/WTO.

To facilitate comparison of the three approaches, we develop each approach in the context of a unified model of the underlying economic environment. In particular, we employ throughout a standard two-good general equilibrium model of trade between two countries. This model of the world economy is familiar, being analogous to those that can be found in any undergraduate international economics textbook. With the underlying economic environment captured in this fashion, we are then able to direct attention to the essential difference between the three approaches, namely, the modeling of government preferences. We begin by reviewing the general equilibrium model.

2.1.1 The General Equilibrium Model

The standard general equilibrium model of trade consists of two countries, home (no *) and foreign (*), that trade two goods. These are normal goods in consumption and produced in perfectly competitive markets under conditions of increasing opportunity costs. Let x (y) be the natural import good of the home (foreign) country, and define $p \equiv p_x/p_y$ ($p^* \equiv p_x^*/p_y^*$) to be the local relative price facing home (foreign) producers and consumers. The home (foreign) ad valorem import tariff is denoted as t (t^*), and we assume throughout that this tariff is not prohibitive. Defining $\tau \equiv (1 + t)$ and $\tau^* \equiv (1 + t^*)$, it follows that $p = \tau p^w \equiv p(\tau, p^w)$ and $p^* = p^w/\tau^* \equiv p^*(\tau^*, p^w)$, where $p^w \equiv p_x^*/p_y$ is the "world" (i.e., untaxed) relative price. The foreign (domestic) terms of trade is then given by p^w ($1/p^w$), and we interpret $\tau > 1$ ($\tau < 1$) to be an import tax (import subsidy) and similarly for τ^*.[1] Finally, to keep notation to a minimum, we henceforth use p to denote the function $p(\tau, p^w)$ and p^* to denote the function $p^*(\tau^*, p^w)$.

Within each country, production occurs at the point on the production possibilities frontier at which the marginal rate of transformation between x and y is equal to the local relative price. This allows domestic and foreign production functions to be represented as $Q_i = Q_i(p)$ and $Q_i^* = Q_i^*(p^*)$ for $i = \{x, y\}$. Consumption is determined by the local relative price, which defines the trade-off faced by consumers and implies

---

1. Under the Lerner symmetry theorem, trade taxes and subsidies can be equivalently depicted as applying to exports or imports in this two-sector general equilibrium setting.

the level and distribution of factor income in the economy, and by tariff revenue R (R^*), which is distributed lump-sum to domestic (foreign) consumers and measured in units of the local export good at local prices. Domestic and foreign consumption thus may be represented as $D_i = D_i(p, R)$ and $D_i^* = D_i^*(p^*, R^*)$ for $i = \{x, y\}$, where tariff revenue is defined implicitly by $R = [D_x(p, R) - Q_x(p)][p - p^w]$ or $R = R(p, p^w)$ for the domestic country and by $R^* = [D_y^*(p^*, R^*) - Q_y^*(p^*)][1/p^* - 1/p^w]$ or $R^* = R^*(p^*, p^w)$ for the foreign country. Given the assumption that goods are normal, each country's tariff revenue is an increasing function of its terms of trade. With tariff revenue now expressed as a function of local and world prices, national consumption in each country may be written as $C_i(p, p^w) \equiv D_i(p, R(p, p^w))$ and $C_i^*(p^*, p^w) \equiv D_i^*(p^*, R^*(p^*, p^w))$.

We next introduce notation for imports and exports so that the trade balance and equilibrium conditions may be expressed. For the home country, imports of x are denoted as $M(p, p^w) \equiv C_x(p, p^w) - Q_x(p)$ and exports of y are represented as $E(p, p^w) \equiv Q_y(p) - C_y(p, p^w)$. Similarly, for the foreign country, we denote imports of y and exports of x as $M^*(p^*, p^w)$ and $E^*(p^*, p^w)$, respectively. For any world price, home and foreign budget constraints imply that trade is balanced, so that

$$p^w M(p, p^w) = E(p, p^w) \quad \text{and} \tag{2.1}$$

$$M^*(p^*, p^w) = p^w E^*(p^*, p^w). \tag{2.2}$$

Making explicit the dependence of the local prices on the tariffs and the world price, we now determine the equilibrium world price, $\tilde{p}^w(\tau, \tau^*)$, by the requirement of market clearing for good y:

$$E(p(\tau, \tilde{p}^w), \tilde{p}^w) = M^*(p^*(\tau^*, \tilde{p}^w), \tilde{p}^w), \tag{2.3}$$

with market clearing for good x then implied by (2.1), (2.2), and (2.3). Thus, given any pair of tariffs, the equilibrium world price is determined by (2.3), and the equilibrium world price and the given tariffs determine in turn the local prices and thereby the production, consumption, import, export, and tariff revenue levels. Finally, we assume that the Metzler and Lerner paradoxes are ruled out so that $dp/d\tau > 0 > dp^*/d\tau^*$ and $\partial \tilde{p}^w/\partial \tau < 0 < \partial \tilde{p}^w/\partial \tau^*$.

2.1.2 The Traditional Economic Approach
The antecedents of the traditional economic approach to trade agreements can be traced back to the writings of Torrens (1844) and Mill

(1844), who discuss the role of terms-of-trade effects in determining optimal tariff policy. In a seminal contribution Johnson (1953–54) formalizes the terms-of-trade-driven inefficiencies that a trade agreement can correct by combining the hypothesis that governments use tariffs to manipulate the terms of trade with the separate hypothesis that governments seek to maximize national welfare. As exemplified by the work of Dixit (1987), recent research has exposited this argument in formal game-theoretic terms. The modeling strategy taken there is to represent the governments' "payoffs" (i.e., national welfares) in terms of their "strategies" (i.e., tariffs), in order to characterize the Nash equilibrium welfares and tariffs.

While this modeling strategy reflects the usual game-theoretic specification, we choose here to represent governments' objectives directly in terms of the local and world prices that their tariff selections imply. This representation highlights the inefficiency that arises when governments are motivated by terms-of-trade considerations. Using the notation developed above, we therefore represent domestic national welfare as $V(p, \tilde{p}^w) \equiv v(p, I(p, \tilde{p}^w))$, where v denotes the indirect utility function of the representative agent in the domestic country and I is domestic national income measured in units of good y at local prices.[2] The objective of the foreign government, $V^*(p^*, \tilde{p}^w) \equiv v^*(p^*, I^*(p^*, \tilde{p}^w))$, is similarly defined.

We now outline the rationale for trade agreements that the traditional economic approach provides. Figure 2.1 illustrates the main findings of this literature. The point labeled N depicts the noncooperative Nash equilibrium of the tariff retaliation and counterretaliation game as originally envisioned by Johnson (1953–54). At the equilibrium point N, the home (foreign) iso-welfare contour is vertical (horizontal), reflecting the fact that from this point neither government can improve its payoff with a unilateral change in its tariff policy. The outcome at N clearly represents an inefficient combination of tariff choices, as at this point the home and foreign iso-welfare contours are not tangent. Hence, as Johnson (1953–54) stresses, while neither country can improve its lot with unilateral trade-policy initiatives, each country could in principle be made better off under a trade agreement that called for mutual tariff adjustments.

---

2. Formally, $I(p, \tilde{p}^w) \equiv pQ_x(p) + Q_y(p) + R(p, \tilde{p}^w)$. As $\tilde{p}^w$ is a function of tariffs, it is apparent that the government's objective could also be represented as a function of tariffs, as in Dixit's (1987) model. Specifically, we could represent the government's objective as $F(\tau, \tau^*) \equiv V(p(\tau, \tilde{p}^w), \tilde{p}^w)$.

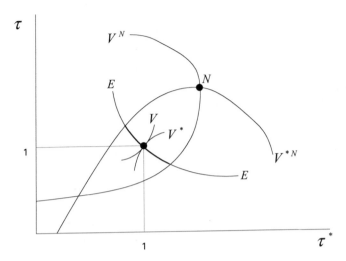

Figure 2.1

In subsequent work Mayer (1981) shows that the efficient tariff pairs in this setting satisfy the relationship $\tau = 1/\tau^*$, as these tariff pairs equalize local prices across countries and thereby achieve worldwide economic efficiency. Of course, reciprocal free trade (i.e., $\tau = \tau^* = 1$) is among the efficient tariff pairs, but there is in fact an entire set of efficient tariff pairs that involve one country taxing and the other subsidizing its imports. This set is depicted in figure 2.1 by the locus passing through the reciprocal–free-trade point and labeled $E \to E$, with each point on this locus representing an efficient tariff pair that is distinguished by the particular international distribution of income that the associated world price implies. The bold portion of the locus $E \to E$ corresponds to the contract curve (i.e., the tariffs that are efficient and yield greater-than-Nash welfare for each country). As pointed out by Johnson (1953–54) and later emphasized by Mayer (1981) and also Kennan and Reizman (1988), the contract curve need not include the point of reciprocal free trade if countries are sufficiently asymmetric. In the case depicted in figure 2.1, any asymmetries between countries are sufficiently small that the contract curve includes the point of reciprocal free trade.

While the government preferences associated with the traditional economic approach are simplistic, an attractive feature of this approach is that the potential role of trade agreements is quite clear: trade agreements provide governments with an avenue of escape from a terms-of-trade-driven Prisoners' Dilemma. To confirm this, we consider the hypothetical trade policy that each government would pursue if it ignored its ability to affect the terms of trade. For the home government, this would amount to setting its tariff to satisfy the condition $V_p = 0$, where here and throughout the book subscripts denote partial derivatives. Using standard properties of the indirect utility function, we then have that $V_p = t \cdot \tilde{p}^w \cdot v_I \cdot M_p(p, \tilde{p}^w)$, and so $V_p = 0$ implies that a domestic policy of free trade would be chosen.[3] In similar fashion $V_{p^*}^*$ $= 0$ implies that the foreign country would adopt a policy of free trade as well. Hence, according to the traditional economic approach, it is the pursuit of terms-of-trade gains—and this pursuit alone—that leads governments away from the efficient outcome of reciprocal free trade to the inefficient Nash outcome. The purpose of a trade agreement is then to remedy this inefficiency and guide governments back to a point on the contract curve.

The traditional economic approach offers a clear explanation for the creation of GATT, but many economists regard the practical relevance of this argument with some skepticism. As we discuss briefly below and in greater detail in chapter 11, this skepticism derives from several objections, and upon closer scrutiny the validity of some of these objections may be questioned. At this point, though, we simply note that the traditional approach ignores the manifest political constraints under which real governments operate. We therefore consider next the leading alternative, which adopts a political-economy perspective and emphasizes the political motivations that influence government preferences.

2.1.3 The Political-Economy Approach

The distinguishing feature of the political-economy approach is that governments may care about the political (i.e., distributional) as well as economic-efficiency consequences of the local-price movements that their tariff selections imply. When government preferences are generalized in this way, it may be expected that governments' economic incentive to manipulate the terms of trade again creates an inefficiency that a trade agreement can remedy. But does a separate political rationale for trade agreements arise as well? To address this question, we

---

3. Formally, we have that $V_p = v_I \left[\dfrac{v_p}{v_I} + I_p(p, \tilde{p}^w) \right] = t \cdot \tilde{p}^w \cdot v_I \cdot M_p(p, \tilde{p}^w)$, with the second equality following from Roy's identity and the efficiency of competitive production.

follow Bagwell and Staiger (1999a) and present here a general representation of government preferences that includes both the traditional case that governments maximize national welfare as well as the general possibility that governments are also motivated by distributional concerns.[4] We then consider whether governments' tariff selections would be efficient (relative to their own preferences) if they were to ignore their ability to affect the terms of trade.[5]

Government Preferences We begin with a description of government preferences. The objectives of home and foreign governments are represented by the general functions $W(p, \tilde{p}^w)$ and $W^*(p^*, \tilde{p}^w)$, respectively. We place no restrictions on government preferences over local prices. The only structure placed on W and W^* is that, holding its local price fixed, each government is assumed to achieve higher welfare when its terms of trade improve:[6]

$$W_{\tilde{p}^w}(p, \tilde{p}^w) < 0 \quad \text{and} \quad W^*_{\tilde{p}^w}(p^*, \tilde{p}^w) > 0. \tag{2.4}$$

The content of this assumption can be illustrated with the aid of figure 2.2. There an initial tariff pair is represented by the point $A \equiv (\tau, \tau^*)$, and this tariff pair is associated with a domestic iso-local-price locus, $p(A) \to p(A)$, and an iso-world-price locus, $p^w(A) \to p^w(A)$.[7] A second iso-world-price locus is also depicted, and along this locus the world price is lower than at point A, indicating an improved terms-of-trade for the domestic country. A reduction in the world price that maintains the domestic local price is thus achieved with the movement from A to B, corresponding to a higher (lower) domestic (foreign) import tariff. Condition (2.4) requires only that the international income transfer implied by the movement from A to B is valued by the domestic government.

In both the traditional economic approach and the leading political-economy approaches to trade policy, governments set trade policy as

---

4. The findings published in Bagwell and Staiger (1999a, 2001b) appeared first in a discussion paper (Bagwell and Staiger 1996).

5. Notice that the simple argument used in the previous subsection to confirm the efficiency of such tariff selections utilized properties of the indirect utility function and thus cannot be applied in the context of the more general representation of government preferences considered here.

6. Throughout, we also impose standard regularity conditions so that all second-order conditions are globally satisfied and all partial derivatives of W and W^* are finite.

7. Under the assumptions that the Metzler and Lerner paradoxes are absent, the iso-world-price locus has positive slope while the iso-local-price locus slopes down, as figure 2.2 depicts.

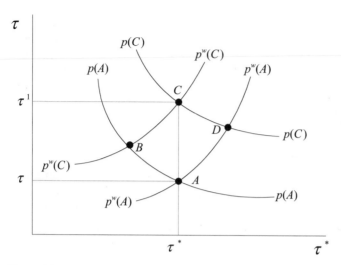

Figure 2.2

if they were maximizing a function of this form. With regard to the former approach, we note that the national welfare of a country improves when it experiences a terms-of-trade improvement. Within the political-economy literature, one possibility is that the government arises from a representative democracy. In this case, as Mayer (1984) shows, the government sets its trade policy to promote the interests of the median voter, whose utility can be represented as a function of this form. Alternatively, as Baldwin (1987) observes, the major approaches to the political economy of trade policy, as represented in the work by Olson (1965), Caves (1976), Brock and Magee (1978), Feenstra and Bhagwati (1982), Findlay and Wellisz (1982), and Hillman (1982), can all be represented in this way as well. Finally, the lobbying models of Grossman and Helpman (1994, 1995a) also fit within the framework developed here.[8]

A further possibility, suggested by Baldwin (1985), is that a government is motivated by autonomous ideological concerns that shape its general goals but faces a political-support constraint when setting trade policy to pursue these goals. A possibility of particular interest is that the home government is a "free-trader," whose ability to implement

---

8. Dixit, Grossman, and Helpman (1997) consider the influence of lobbies on government decisions for a general class of policy problems. They depart from the work of Grossman and Helpman (1994, 1995a), in that they do not restrict attention to quasi-linear preferences. The representation of government preferences that we consider in this book also includes this generalization (when applied to trade policy) as a particular case.

free-trade policies is hindered by the need to mobilize export support to offset political opposition to its liberalization efforts from import-competing sectors. To see that this possibility is included, let G represent the objectives of the domestic government and let the domestic government's political-support constraint be captured by the inequality restriction $S(p, \tilde{p}^w) \geq \bar{S}$. We may now form the associated Lagrangian, W, so that the domestic government ultimately seeks to maximize a function of the following form:

$$W(p, \tilde{p}^w) = G(p, \tilde{p}^w) + \rho[S(p, \tilde{p}^w) - \bar{S}],$$

where ρ, the Lagrangian multiplier, is also a function of p and $\tilde{p}^w$. It is thus evident that the problem facing a liberalizing government that must mobilize export support for its liberalization program can be represented within the modeling framework described here.

Unilateral Trade Policies   We consider next the unilateral trade policies that would arise in the absence of a trade agreement. Our general setup can be used to illuminate the motivations that influence a government's tariff selection in the various political-economy models of trade policy. As we are no longer limited to the familiar framework associated with the traditional economic approach to trade agreements, we now explain these motivations in greater detail.

To begin, we suppose that each government sets its trade policy to maximize its objective function, taking as given the tariff choice of its trading partner. These optimization problems generate home and foreign reaction functions, which are defined implicitly by

$$\text{Home:} \quad W_p\left[\frac{dp}{d\tau}\right] + W_{\tilde{p}^w}\left[\frac{\partial \tilde{p}^w}{\partial \tau}\right] = 0 \tag{2.5}$$

$$\text{Foreign:} \quad W_{p^*}^*\left[\frac{dp^*}{d\tau^*}\right] + W_{\tilde{p}^w}^*\left[\frac{\partial \tilde{p}^w}{\partial \tau^*}\right] = 0. \tag{2.6}$$

Letting $\lambda \equiv [\partial \tilde{p}^w / \partial \tau] / [dp/d\tau] < 0$ and $\lambda^* \equiv [\partial \tilde{p}^w / \partial \tau^*] / [dp^* / d\tau^*] < 0$, we may rewrite (2.5) and (2.6) as

$$\text{Home:} \quad W_p + \lambda W_{\tilde{p}^w} = 0 \tag{2.7}$$

$$\text{Foreign:} \quad W_{p^*}^* + \lambda^* W_{\tilde{p}^w}^* = 0. \tag{2.8}$$

As (2.7) and (2.8) illustrate, the best-response tariff of each government is determined by the combined impact on welfare of the induced local and world price movements.

The determinants of the best-response tariffs of politically motivated governments can be further illustrated by returning to figure 2.2. Starting from the initial tariff pair represented by the point $A \equiv (\tau, \tau^*)$, suppose now that the domestic government decides unilaterally to increase its tariff. Given the fixed foreign tariff τ^*, an increase in the domestic tariff from τ to τ^1 induces a new tariff pair, represented by point $C \equiv (\tau^1, \tau^*)$. This tariff pair lies on a new iso-local-price locus, given as $p(C) \to p(C)$, and also a new iso-world-price locus, represented as $p^w(C) \to p^w(C)$. Thus, by increasing its tariff, the domestic government induces a local price that is higher and a world price that is lower as compared to the prices associated with the original point A.

In analogy with (2.7), figure 2.2 can be used to disentangle the overall movement from A to C induced by a unilateral tariff increase by the domestic government into separate movements in the local and world prices, respectively. Consider first the movement from A to B. This movement isolates the change in the world price, and the corresponding welfare effect for the domestic government is captured in (2.7) with the term $\lambda W_{\tilde{p}^w}$, which is strictly positive by (2.4). Consider next the movement from B to C. This movement isolates the induced increase in the local price, holding fixed the world price, and the corresponding change in the domestic government's welfare is represented in (2.7) with the term W_p. The welfare implications of the local-price movement from B to C reflect the balance between the costs of the associated domestic distortions in production and consumption against any domestic political benefits. The welfare implications of the world-price movement from A to B, by contrast, reflect the benefits to the domestic government of shifting the costs of its policy onto the foreign government. It follows that, if the domestic government seeks to implement a local price corresponding to the iso-local-price locus $p(C) \to p(C)$, then a unilateral increase in the domestic import tariff shifts some of the costs of this outcome onto the foreign government. A similar interpretation applies for (2.8).

Consider now the Nash equilibrium that arises when both governments set tariffs unilaterally. A Nash equilibrium is a pair of tariffs, (τ^N, τ^{*N}), which simultaneously satisfy (2.7) and (2.8). We assume that the Nash equilibrium, which we take to be unique, represents the trade-policy decisions that governments would make if there were no trade agreement. The next step is to determine if these decisions are efficient for the governments.

The Value of a Trade Agreement   We assume that governments seek a trade agreement in order to achieve mutually beneficial changes in trade policy. Put differently, through a trade agreement, governments seek tariff changes that result in Pareto improvements beyond the Nash government-welfare levels achieved under unilateral tariff setting. A trade agreement entails *reciprocal trade liberalization* if the tariffs of both countries are lower than in the Nash equilibrium. Finally, an *efficient trade agreement* must rest on the efficiency frontier, which is defined by a tangency condition:

$$\left[\frac{d\tau}{d\tau^*}\right]_{dW=0} = \left[\frac{d\tau}{d\tau^*}\right]_{dW^*=0}. \tag{2.9}$$

As we confirm in appendix A, the efficiency locus can also be represented more concretely as the set of tariffs that satisfy

$$(1 - AW_p) = \frac{1}{(1 - A^* W_{p^*}^*)}, \tag{2.10}$$

where $A \equiv (1 - \tau\lambda)/(W_p + \lambda W_{\tilde{p}^w})$ and $A^* \equiv (1 - \lambda^*/\tau^*)/(W_{p^*}^* + \lambda^* W_{\tilde{p}^w}^*).$[9]

The efficiency of the unilateral tariff decisions of politically motivated governments may now be assessed. Following Bagwell and Staiger (1999a), we make three observations. We offer proofs of all three observations in appendix A.

A first observation is that the Nash equilibrium is indeed inefficient. This observation can be confirmed by using (2.7) and (2.8) and noting that the Nash tariffs fail to satisfy the condition for efficiency as given in (2.10). Intuitively, when governments set their trade policies unilaterally, they are motivated to shift costs onto one another through the change in the world price that their tariffs imply.

A second observation is that trade agreements among politically motivated governments must entail reciprocal trade liberalization. In

---

9. This characterization is provided in Bagwell and Staiger (1999a). Observe that $A \neq 0$ and $A^* \neq 0$ under our assumption that the partial derivatives of the welfare functions are always finite. As noted above, in the case that governments maximize national welfare, Mayer (1981) shows that the efficiency locus reduces to the form $\tau = 1/\tau^*$. In this case, along the efficiency locus, tariffs are adjusted so as to maintain equality in relative local prices between the domestic and foreign countries, with different tariff pairs along the efficiency locus simply resulting in different world prices and therefore different distributions of income across the trading partners. In the more general formulation of government preferences considered here, it is again true that the efficiency locus determines a relationship between domestic and foreign tariffs, but it need not be the case that this relationship equates relative local prices across trading partners.

other words, both governments can experience welfare gains relative to the Nash equilibrium only if both governments agree to set tariffs below their Nash levels.[10] The intuition for this observation is also clear. When governments set their trade policies in a unilateral fashion, they are led to set tariffs that are higher than is efficient, since they each recognize that some of the costs of a higher tariff can be passed onto the trading partner, through the consequent changes in the world price. Thus, if both governments are to gain through a trade agreement, it is not surprising that each must lower its tariff to a level that is below that which it chooses in the Nash equilibrium. In light of the broad generality of our representation of government preferences, this observation indicates that the incentive for governments to enter into trade agreements that result in mutually lower tariffs is quite general, and in particular is in no way limited to the hypothesis that governments maximize national welfare.

A remaining question concerns the exact nature of the inefficiency that explains the appeal of a trade agreement under the political-economy approach. Clearly, the terms-of-trade externality is one inefficiency that can be remedied with an appropriate trade agreement. But are there additional "political externalities" that might be remedied as well? To establish conclusively that the terms-of-trade externality is the only inefficiency that a trade agreement can remedy in this environment, we proceed as in the previous section and consider a hypothetical world in which governments are not motivated by the terms-of-trade implications of their trade-policy choices.[11] If unilateral tariff choices would be efficient in such a world, then we may conclude that the terms-of-trade externality is the *only* rationale for a trade agreement under the political-economy approach. To this end, we define *politically optimal tariffs* as any tariff pair (τ^{PO}, τ^{*PO}) that satisfies the following two conditions:[12]

---

10. A reduction in tariffs from the Nash level, however, is not sufficient to guarantee mutual welfare gains. For example, as we noted above, Johnson (1953–54), Kennan and Reizman (1988), and Mayer (1981) show that a large country may be better off at the Nash equilibrium than with free trade if the countries are sufficiently asymmetric.

11. We do not assume that governments fail to understand the terms-of-trade effects of their tariff choices. Rather, we wish to consider the hypothetical situation in which governments are not motivated by these effects. In terms of (2.7), governments understand that $\lambda < 0$, but we now suppose their welfare functions were such that $W_{\tilde{p}^w} \equiv 0$. We wish to identify the tariffs that would be selected by governments with these hypothetical preferences and then evaluate the efficiency properties of these tariffs with respect to actual government preferences.

12. We assume further that a unique set of politically optimal tariffs exists.

Home: $W_p = 0$ (2.11)

Foreign: $W^*_{p^*} = 0.$ (2.12)

When governments set politically optimal tariffs, it is as if they throw any welfare gains that are attributable to changes in the world price "back into the ocean." In the special case where governments seek to maximize national welfare, politically optimal tariffs correspond to reciprocal free trade, as we establish in section 2.1.2. More generally, government objectives may also reflect political considerations, and in this case there is no expectation that politically optimal tariffs correspond to reciprocal free trade.

A third observation can now be made: politically optimal tariffs are efficient. This observation may be confirmed using the definition of politically optimal tariffs given in (2.11) and (2.12) and the characterization of the efficiency locus presented in (2.10). To gain some intuition for this finding, let us suppose that the terms-of-trade motivation has been removed from the trade-policy decisions of each government. In this case each government sets its trade policy so as to achieve its preferred local price. With tariffs thus set at their politically optimal levels, consider now a small increase in the tariff of the domestic country. This change has three effects. First, it induces a small increase in the local price in the domestic country. This effect, however, has no first-order impact on the domestic government's welfare, since the domestic government initially has its preferred local price. Second, the domestic tariff increase induces a small reduction in the local price of the foreign country. But this effect has no first-order impact on the foreign government's welfare, since the foreign government also initially has its preferred local price. Finally, the small increase in the domestic government's tariff generates a corresponding reduction in the world price. The world-price reduction cannot generate an efficiency gain, however, as it represents a pure international transfer in tariff revenue. It thus follows that, once the terms-of-trade motivation is eliminated from the trade-policy choices of governments, there is no further scope for Pareto improvements.

Further intuition can be gained with reference to figure 2.2. Suppose that tariffs are initially at point A, and then the domestic government considers a tariff increase that would result in the tariff pair associated with point C. If the domestic government is motivated by the terms-of-trade consequences (i.e., the movement from D to C) of its tariff selection, then it recognizes that some of the costs of achieving the higher local price at C can be shifted onto its foreign trading partner, as a result of the reduced world price. Mindful of its ability to shift costs in this fashion, the domestic government finds the higher tariff especially attractive, and as a consequence Nash tariffs are always inefficient, with tariffs (trade volumes) that are too high (low). On the other hand, if the domestic government were not motivated by the terms-of-trade implications of its trade policy, then it would prefer choosing the higher tariff to induce point C if and only if it also prefers point D to point A. In this case the potential appeal of point C to the domestic government is separate from any cost-shifting benefits that may be associated with the consequent change in the world price, and so the domestic government has the "right" incentives when deciding whether to raise its tariff.[13] If both governments were to choose tariffs in this fashion, then a resulting consistent set of tariffs is politically optimal and efficient.

These three observations regarding the political-economy approach can be summarized with figure 2.3.[14] In line with the first observation reported above, notice that the Nash tariffs (point N) lie off of the efficiency locus as characterized by (2.10) and depicted by the curve $E \rightarrow E$. The figure also represents the Nash iso-welfare curves for the domestic and foreign governments, and these curves illustrate the second observation reported above: a trade agreement can increase the welfare of both governments beyond that received in the Nash equilibrium only if the agreement results in a reduction in both tariffs. Finally, as the third observation made above requires, the politically optimal tariffs (point PO) lie on the efficiency locus. Notice that iso-welfare curves are tangent at every point along this locus, including the politically optimal point. The novel feature of the politically optimal tariffs is that the iso-welfare curves at these tariffs are also tangent to the iso-world-price locus (the locus p_{PO}^w). The bold portion of the efficiency locus corresponds to the contract curve.

---

13. A willingness to move from point A to point D in figure 2.2 induces no externality through the terms of trade, but it will cause a change in the foreign local price. If the foreign government also selects tariffs that are politically optimal, however, then a small change in the foreign local price will have no first-order effect on foreign welfare.

14. In drawing this picture, we assume that a unique Nash equilibrium exists, a unique political optimum exists, and that the political optimum lies on the contract curve (i.e., it is on the efficiency locus and yields greater than Nash welfare for each government). The latter assumption is satisfied provided that countries are sufficiently symmetric.

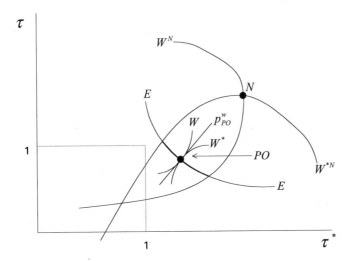

Figure 2.3

Figure 2.3 clarifies the basic task facing politically motivated governments who seek to design a trade agreement. In the absence of any attempt at cooperation, governments would set trade policies unilaterally, leading to the Nash outcome N. A trade agreement is then appealing to governments as a means to cooperate and move the tariffs from the inefficient Nash point to some alternative tariff pair that rests on the contract curve. Among the tariffs that lie on the contract curve, the politically optimal tariffs are quite focal, as these tariffs remedy the terms-of-trade inefficiency in a direct fashion. As figure 2.3 illustrates, when governments have both political and economic objectives, the efficiency locus need not pass through the point of free trade. While governments' political concerns affect their preferences over tariffs (e.g., the location of the efficiency locus), however, it is the terms-of-trade externality that creates a problem when governments set tariffs unilaterally that an appropriately designed trade agreement can solve.

In light of the prominence of terms-of-trade considerations in both the traditional economic approach and the political-economy approach to trade agreements, it may be useful at this point to ponder two further questions. First, can the terms-of-trade externality be interpreted in a more practical manner that might suggest greater relevance for understanding real-world trade agreements? And second, how might "political externalities" be injected into the political-economy approach? We consider each of these questions in sequence.

The Interpretation of the Terms-of-Trade Externality   At the broadest level, the discussion above confirms a simple notion: governments
can gain from trade-policy cooperation, if each would otherwise
attempt to shift costs onto the other, resulting in inefficient unilateral
policies. The terms-of-trade externality is then simply the means
through which such cost shifting would occur.

Yet, as mentioned in section 2.1.2, many economists are skeptical of
the practical relevance of the terms-of-trade argument for trade agreements. In part, this skepticism derives from the abstract manner in
which the traditional theory is usually interpreted. This interpretation
stresses that trade is fundamentally a process in which the home
country exchanges its exports for those from a foreign country, and the
government of a large home country can thus ensure that a given
volume of its exports commands a greater volume of foreign exports
(i.e., improve its terms of trade) if it imposes an import tariff (so that
the foreign export is abundant on world markets) or an export tariff (so
that the home export is scarce on world markets). This interpretation
is, of course, theoretically valid; however, it emphasizes a logic that
would not likely weigh heavily in the practical minds of policy makers.

At the same time, the terms-of-trade theory may be interpreted in
other manners, which suggest greater practical relevance. First, from a
partial-equilibrium perspective, cost shifting occurs via the terms-of-
trade externality if foreign exporters bear some of the *incidence* of the
import tariff. Then unilateral tariffs are inefficient for an intuitive and
plausible reason: the domestic government does not internalize the
harm to foreign exporters that its import tariff implies.[15] In most economic settings the natural presumption is that producers bear some of
the incidence of a tax, and we argue in chapter 11 that strong empirical support for this presumption exists in the trade context as well.
Second, when the home government raises its import tariff and thereby
shifts in its import demand curve, the consequent "price effect" (i.e.,
the home country's terms-of-trade improvement) has a corresponding
"volume effect" (i.e., the foreign country's reduction in access to the
home market). From this perspective it is natural that real-world trade-
policy negotiators emphasize the *market-access* implications of trade
policy.[16] Indeed, we may interpret "cost shifting," "terms-of-trade

---

15. This interpretation is developed further in Bagwell and Staiger (2001b), where we
derive the three observations mentioned above in a partial-equilibrium model.
16. This emphasis is well exemplified by the following excerpt from a GATT panel
report concerning a dispute between the United States and the European Community

gain," and "market-access restriction" as three phrases that describe the single economic experience that occurs when the domestic government raises its import tariff and restricts foreign access to its market.

This linkage between the terms of trade and market access can be formalized with a few definitions. For a given world price p^w and domestic tariff τ, the *market access* that the domestic country affords to the foreign country is defined by the domestic import demand function, $M(p, p^w)$.[17] Similarly, given a world price p^w and a foreign tariff τ^*, the market access that the foreign country affords to the domestic country is defined by $M^*(p^*, p^w)$. We may now say that a government *secures additional market access* from its trading partner through negotiations if there exists a world price such that the trading partner's negotiated policy changes provide additional access to the trading partner's market (i.e., if the trading partner's import demand curve shifts out for at least *some* world price). Given this definition, if the domestic government were to *fail* to secure additional market access from its foreign trading partner through negotiations, then the foreign import demand curve would shift in (weakly) at all world price levels. Assuming that the Marshall-Lerner stability conditions are met, such an inward shift in the foreign import demand curve would contribute toward a (weakly) higher equilibrium world price, $\tilde{p}^w$. Therefore, if the domestic government were to fail to secure additional market access from its foreign trading partner through negotiations, then the foreign country's agreed-upon tariff changes would contribute toward a terms-of-trade loss (weakly) for the domestic country.

---

over the EC domestic subsidies for oilseed producers: "... the main value of a tariff concession is that it provides assurance of better market access through improved price competition. Contracting parties negotiate tariff concessions primarily to obtain that advantage." (as quoted in Petersmann 1997, p. 168)

17. Notice that we define the level of market-access commitments in terms of the position of a country's import demand function. In particular, we do not define the level of market access as synonomous with equilibrium trade volumes. This distinction is well-represented in the legal interpretations of GATT rules. For example, the GATT panel report on oilseeds observed that "... It is of course true that, in the tariff negotiations in the framework of GATT, contracting parties seek tariff concessions in the hope of expanding their exports, but the commitments they exchange in such negotiations are commitments on conditions of competition for trade, not on volumes of trade." (as quoted in WTO 1995a, vol. 2, p. 666). When a government agrees to bind an import tariff in a GATT negotiation, it is committing to a particular competitive relationship between imported and domestic products, which can in turn be interpreted in the formal setting considered above as positioning its import demand function.

With this linkage established, the findings developed above can be interpreted in terms of market access. For instance, it may be confirmed (see Bagwell and Staiger 2001a) that the essential inefficiency arising in the Nash equilibrium can be described as one of insufficient market access. Hence, the terms-of-trade externality provides a rationale for why negotiators would emphasize the market-access implications of trade policy. In fact, as we confirm in appendix A, the second observation raised above can be re-stated as follows: beginning at the Nash equilibrium, each government must secure additional market access from its trading partner in order to reach a mutually beneficial agreement. It may thus be seen that, upon closer scrutiny, the terms-of-trade externality provides a rather direct theory of the market-access concerns that dominate real-world trade-policy negotiations.

Political Externalities   How might "political externalities" give rise to a theory of trade agreements? As we discuss above, in the political-economy approach it is the terms-of-trade externality that creates a problem when governments set tariffs unilaterally which an appropriately designed trade agreement can solve. The political-economy approach thus does not provide an answer to this question. Yet there is a strong intuitive appeal to the belief that "politics" is what trade agreements are "really" about. Here we consider possible ingredients in constructing such a theory.

In order to identify the possibility of a separate political motivation for trade agreements, it is natural to take as a starting point the assumption that all countries are "small," in the sense that no country can alter world prices with its tariff choices. As is well known, if it were assumed as well that each of the governments of these small countries were national-income maximizers, then their unilateral tariff choices would correspond to free trade, and there would be nothing for a trade agreement among them to accomplish. However, if it is assumed that these governments also pursue political/distributional goals with their unilateral tariff choices, then their unilateral policies need not correspond to free trade. As our review of the political-economy approach makes clear, though, this alone is still not enough to give a reason for trade agreements to exist. If politically motivated governments of small countries are to have something to negotiate about, an additional assumption is essential.

One possibility is to place a constraint on the trade-policy instruments that governments have at their disposal. A potentially promising avenue is to combine the assumption that governments seek, for political reasons, to help their *exporters*, with the additional assumption that export-promoting policies (e.g., export subsidies) are not available to governments. The apparent motivation for this additional assumption is the institutional design of GATT (see chapter 3), which places significant constraints on the use of export subsidies.

At the same time, as a building block for a theory of trade agreements, the assumption that export-promoting policies are unavailable has important limitations. After all, governments do routinely grant subsidies that are either explicitly offered to exporters (e.g., the export credits provided by the US Export–Import Bank, or the agricultural subsidies offered under the US Export Enhancement Program) or which have the effect of subsidizing exports, and these governments would clearly do so to a greater extent were it not for the constraints placed on them by GATT.[18] There is thus a risk of circularity in building a theory of trade agreements on the basis of a constraint that is motivated by its appearance in actual trade agreements (i.e., GATT).

Putting this concern to the side, we note that this additional assumption is still not quite enough to explain the appeal of a trade agreement for a small country. In particular, if there is a single export sector, then a government can replicate the effects of an export subsidy to this sector with an appropriate choice of import subsidies (Lerner's symmetry theorem). This suggests two alternatives: restrict the theory to apply to cases where each government has two or more export sectors that it wishes to help, or introduce the second additional assumption that exporters are not cognizant of the general equilibrium effects of trade-policy intervention (i.e., they cannot be made to understand Lerner's symmetry theorem). To our knowledge, the first alternative has not yet been formally analyzed in the literature. The second alternative, however, is the approach taken in a recent paper by Ethier (2000).

Ethier's (2000) model of political-externality-driven trade agreements stands in stark contrast to other attempts in the literature to model trade agreements.[19] We return to examine some of the implications

---

18. For example, the United States has recently been compelled to make revisions to the US Foreign Sales Corporation scheme, which provides tax breaks for certain export-related sales, in an attempt to bring its policy into conformance with WTO rules relating to export subsidies. See, for example, Magnusson (2000).

19. A second paper that provides a theoretical analysis of trade agreements between the politically motivated governments of small countries is Grossman and Helpman

of his approach in later chapters, where we consider in detail research that interprets and evaluates the central GATT rules.

2.1.4 The Commitment Approach

A third approach to the study of trade agreements is the commitment approach, which emphasizes the difficulty governments may face in making policy commitments to the private sector and suggests that trade agreements may provide one way to enhance policy credibility.[20] In contrast to the traditional economic and political-economy approaches reviewed above, the commitment approach redirects the focus of analysis from the game between governments to the game between each government and its private sector, in which the government chooses its trade policy and agents in the private sector make some production or investment decisions. A credibility problem may arise when a government has too much flexibility in setting trade policy.

This problem can be captured in a game between the government and its producers, in which the government sets its trade policy *after* production decisions are made. In this case the government may have incentive to surprise producers with a level of protection that it would not choose ex ante, when producers' decisions are still unsettled. The government's preferred ex ante and ex post tariff selections differ, since, once producer decisions are determined, the government recognizes that its tariff choice only affects consumer decisions. Of course, if producers understand the government's incentives, then they alter their production decisions in anticipation of the government's actions, and production decisions are therefore distorted. This production distortion is the real cost of trade-policy flexibility, and the identification of this cost suggests that a trade agreement could increase (ex ante) government welfare if it enables the government to commit to its (ex ante) preferred tariff.

(1995b). There, too, an assumed limitation on the trade-policy instruments available to help exporters plays an essential role in making a (free-) trade agreement potentially attractive to its member governments. We exclude from the present discussion papers that focus on commitment issues, which we review in the next subsection.
20. Papers focusing on credibility problems associated with the use of trade-policy instruments include Carmichael (1987), Staiger and Tabellini (1987, 1989, 1999), Gruenspecht (1988), Lapan (1988), Maskin and Newberry (1990), Matsuyama (1990), Tornell (1991), Brainard (1994), Mayer (1994), McLaren (1997, 2002), Grossman and Maggi (1998), Maggi and Rodriguez (1998), Krishna and Mitra (1999), and Mitra (1999).

Formally, the commitment approach introduces a distinction between a government's ex ante preferences, which we may represent by the functions $W(p, \tilde{p}^w)$ and $W^*(p^*, \tilde{p}^w)$ defined above, and its equilibrium ex post preferences, which differ from its ex ante preferences only in that they (and their arguments) are defined with production levels that are predetermined at their equilibrium values. We may therefore represent equilibrium ex post preferences by the related functions $Z(p, \tilde{P}^w)$ and $Z^*(p^*, \tilde{P}^w)$ where $\tilde{P}^w$ denotes the market-clearing world price as a function of domestic and foreign tariff levels when all outputs are fixed at their equilibrium levels.[21] The basic observation of the commitment approach to the study of trade agreements is then that tariff decisions determined by a government to be optimal according to its ex post preferences are suboptimal when gauged by its ex ante preferences. Therefore, if a trade agreement can help a government commit to tariff choices which better serve its true (ex ante) preferences, then a possible commitment role for trade agreements is identified.

The commitment role for a trade agreement is distinct from terms-of-trade considerations. This can be seen by observing that the elimination of terms-of-trade motivations in government tariff setting would now yield tariffs defined by $Z_p = 0 = Z^*_{p^*}$, and such tariffs in general do not deliver governments to the efficiency frontier characterized by (2.10). Rather, to ensure that the efficiency frontier is achieved, the elimination of terms-of-trade motives must now be combined with a solution to each government's commitment problem, which would then yield efficient tariffs defined by $W_p = 0 = W^*_{p^*}$. Hence the commitment approach identifies a second problem that a trade agreement might solve.

Maggi and Rodriguez (1998) offer an interesting formalization of the commitment approach. They focus on a small-country model so that the terms-of-trade argument for a trade agreement is eliminated, and

---

21. More specifically, denoting the (rationally) anticipated domestic and foreign tariff choices by $\tilde{\tau}$ and $\tilde{\tau}^*$, respectively, we may define equilibrium output levels in the home country by $\tilde{Q}_x \equiv Q_x(p(\tilde{\tau}, \tilde{p}^w(\tilde{\tau}, \tilde{\tau}^*)))$ and $\tilde{Q}_y \equiv Q_y(p(\tilde{\tau}, \tilde{p}^w(\tilde{\tau}, \tilde{\tau}^*)))$, and similarly for the foreign country we may define $\tilde{Q}_x^* \equiv Q_x^*(p^*(\tilde{\tau}^*, \tilde{p}^w(\tilde{\tau}, \tilde{\tau}^*)))$ and $\tilde{Q}_y^* \equiv Q_y^*(p^*(\tilde{\tau}^*, \tilde{p}^w(\tilde{\tau}, \tilde{\tau}^*)))$. Then with $\tilde{P}^w(\tau, \tau^*)$ denoting the market-clearing world price as a function of domestic and foreign tariff levels when all outputs are fixed at their equilibrium levels, we let $Z(p(\tau, \tilde{P}^w(\tau, \tau^*)), \tilde{P}^w(\tau, \tau^*))$ represent the equilibrium ex post preferences of the home government, defined over local and world prices when all outputs are fixed at their equilibrium levels. An analogous interpretation holds for the equilibrium ex post preferences of the foreign government, denoted by $Z^*(p^*(\tau^*, \tilde{P}^w(\tau, \tau^*)), \tilde{P}^w(\tau, \tau^*))$.

they allow that one of the two sectors can form a lobby. The government values national welfare and contributions from the lobby as in the Grossman-Helpman (1994) model. In this case the political process can distort the equilibrium allocation of resources: the politically organized sector may be larger than it would be under free trade, as firms invest in this sector in order to enjoy the protection that their contributions induce. This distortion in turn can give the government an incentive to commit to free trade, and it is assumed that the government can accomplish this by joining a pre-constituted free-trade agreement. To the government the benefit of this commitment is that the investment distortions are forestalled, while the cost of this commitment is that political rents (lobby contributions) are lost. The particular features of the political process are thus relevant for determining whether the government chooses the free-trade commitment: a commitment to free trade is most valuable when the government's bargaining position vis-à-vis the lobby is weak (as then the government cannot extract large rents through the political process) and when the government's responsiveness to contributions relative to national welfare is neither too low (as then the investment distortions are in any event modest) nor too high (as then the government is reluctant to forgo political contributions).

More broadly, there are a variety of commitment problems that a government might face, whether or not the government is politically motivated. For example, in line with Matsuyama's (1990) model, a government might seek to eliminate protection of an industry once the industry invests sufficiently in cost reduction. It may be, however, that the government would maintain protection if the investment does not occur. A commitment problem then arises, as the private sector may foresee the government's dilemma and decide not to undertake the investment, effectively ensuring that the government's ex post incentive is to continue the protectionist policy. If the government is unable to commit to withdraw protection on its own, it may then look to a trade agreement as a means to make credible the liberalization initiative. A trade agreement can serve this purpose if trading partners credibly threaten to retaliate (e.g., by imposing tariffs on the domestic export product) should the liberalization process not occur. This threat can alter the government's ex post incentives such that it prefers to liberalize even if investment is not undertaken, which in turn ensures that the private sector does undertake the desired investment.

2.1.5   Comparison of Approaches

Having reviewed the three major approaches to the study of trade agreements, we now summarize our findings. A comparison of figure 2.3 with figure 2.1 reveals the essential difference between the traditional economic approach to the study of trade agreements and the political-economy approach. By allowing that governments have political motivations, the political-economy approach "frees up" the efficiency locus to correspond to a richer set of potential outcomes than simply free trade. This represents an important advance over the traditional economic approach, in that it allows an interpretation of why free trade is so rarely the goal of trade agreements. But aside from this rescaling, the political-economy approach adds nothing to an understanding of the essential purpose of trade agreements based on traditional economic arguments. Under both the traditional economic and the political-economy approaches, trade agreements provide governments with an avenue of escape from a terms-of-trade-driven Prisoners' Dilemma. By contrast, the commitment approach identifies a distinct role that trade agreements may play, by suggesting that such agreements could help governments make commitments to their private sectors. With regard to the purpose of trade agreements, the literature therefore divides naturally according to which of two distinct roles the trade agreement is seen to fulfill. Strikingly, while many observers feel that "politics" is at the heart of understanding trade agreements, fundamental to neither role is the presence or absence of political considerations.[22]

This may be interpreted in either of two ways. On the one hand, if political considerations do explain the creation of GATT, then the existing models have failed to capture the relevant political ingredients. If this interpretation is adopted, then the immediate implication is that a political explanation for the existence of GATT requires a new modeling approach (possibly along the lines considered by Ethier 2000). On the other hand, one might conclude that either the traditional terms-of-trade externality or a commitment problem (or some combination of both) is indeed the central problem that GATT is designed to solve. From this perspective the political-economy approach described above captures the essential terms-of-trade externality in an augmented

---

22. While the political-economy approach does not offer a separate reason for the creation of a trade agreement (i.e., for a divergence between Nash tariffs and the efficiency frontier), models of this form can deliver new predictions concerning the extent to which tariffs will be reduced in a trade agreement (i.e., concerning the extent of the divergence).

framework that allows for broader political motivations. This conclusion carries with it a fundamentally different modeling implication as it suggests that the (politically augmented) terms-of-trade and commitment theories provide the necessary building blocks for a modeling framework with which to interpret and evaluate GATT and its features.

In this book we adopt the latter interpretation. In fact, while the commitment approach may play an important eventual role in this regard, there are as yet only a few papers that use this approach to interpret and evaluate certain features of GATT. For this reason most of our discussion will center on research that adopts the traditional economic and political-economy approaches.

2.2   Rules versus Power

Let us suppose that the purpose of a trade agreement is to provide an escape from a terms-of-trade-driven Prisoners' Dilemma. A fundamental question then is: How might governments structure their negotiations? Here we consider possible negotiating approaches by which governments might move from an inefficient Nash equilibrium, such as that depicted by the point N in figure 2.3, to a point on the contract curve. We highlight above a particular point on the contract curve, the political optimum, because politically optimal tariffs remedy the Nash inefficiency in a very direct way. But, in general, there is no a priori reason to expect that governments would choose the political optimum over any other point on the contract curve, and indeed the outcome ultimately depends on the structure of negotiations. In broad terms, we can distinguish between two approaches to the negotiation of trade agreements. We refer to these approaches as "power-based" and "rules-based" negotiations (e.g., see Jackson 1997a, pp. 109–12).

To illustrate the issues involved, we refer to figure 2.4, where the contract curve from figure 2.3 is depicted in welfare space, with W measured on the vertical axis and W^* on the horizontal axis. The origin measures the "disagreement" (i.e., status quo) welfare for each government, which we take to be the Nash welfare levels denoted by W^N and W^{*N}, and the political optimum (labeled PO) lies on the frontier as depicted, with the corresponding welfare levels denoted by W^{PO} and W^{*PO}. The slope of the contract curve in welfare space is easily calculated, and at the political optimum it is given by $W_{\tilde{p}^w}/W^*_{\tilde{p}^w}$, as displayed in the figure.

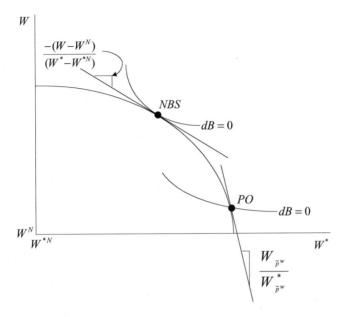

Figure 2.4

When seeking a reciprocal trade agreement, governments require an approach to negotiations that serves to move tariffs from the inefficient disagreement point to the contract curve. One possibility would be a power-based approach, in which governments bargain over tariffs in a direct fashion that is not constrained by agreed-upon principles of negotiation. Consider, for example, the tariffs that would be implemented if negotiations were characterized by the Nash bargaining solution. This solution generates a point on the contract curve that maximizes $B \equiv (W - W^N)(W^* - W^{*N})$. In figure 2.4 this point is labeled as *NBS*, and it corresponds to the point on the contract curve with slope $-(W - W^N)/(W^* - W^{*N})$. The welfare levels for each government associated with the Nash bargaining solution can then be achieved with the corresponding tariffs from figure 2.3. Notice that the Nash bargaining solution induces the political optimum only in the "symmetric" case where $(W^{PO} - W^N)/(-W_{\tilde{p}^w}) = (W^{*PO} - W^{*N})/W_{\tilde{p}^w}^*$ with all derivatives evaluated at the political optimum. If the domestic country were the relatively more "powerful" of the two, in the sense that $(W^{PO} - W^N)/(-W_{\tilde{p}^w})$ $< (W^{*PO} - W^{*N})/W_{\tilde{p}^w}^*$, then (as depicted in figure 2.4) the Nash bargaining solution would favor the domestic country relative to what it would receive at the political optimum.[23] As such, a power-based approach to the negotiation of trade agreements would lead to negotiated outcomes on the contract curve, and any divergence in these outcomes from the political optimum could be understood to reflect existing "power asymmetries" across negotiating partners.

While a power-based approach can serve to move tariffs from the inefficient disagreement point to the contract curve, this is not the approach to trade negotiations taken by GATT. The approach to negotiations embodied in GATT can be more aptly termed rules based.[24] Under such an approach governments identify and agree upon certain principles by which subsequent negotiations must abide. Jackson (1997a) describes the difference between these two approaches:

In broad perspective one can roughly divide the various techniques for the peaceful settlement of international disputes into two types: settlement by negotiation and agreement with reference (explicitly or implicitly) to relative power status of the parties; or settlement by negotiation or decision with reference to norms to which both parties have previously agreed.

For example, countries A and B have a trade dispute regarding B's treatment of imports from A to B of widgets. The first technique mentioned would involve a negotiation between A and B by which the most powerful of the two would have the advantage. Foreign aid, military maneuvers, or import restrictions on other key goods by way of retaliation would figure in the negotiation. A small country would hesitate to challenge a large one on whom its trade depends. Implicit or explicit threats (e.g., to impose quantitative restrictions on some other product) would be a major part of the technique employed. Domestic political influence would probably play a greater part in the approach of the respective negotiators in this system, particularly on the negotiator for the more powerful party.

On the other hand, the second suggested technique—reference to agreed rules—would see the negotiators arguing about the application of the rule (e.g., was B obligated under a treaty to allow free entry of A's goods in question?).

---

23. In the case of national-income maximizing governments, this measure of relative "power" reduces to a cross-country comparison of each country's national-welfare gain in moving from a trade war to reciprocal free trade (e.g., see Johnson 1953–54; Kennan and Riezman 1988; Mayer 1981; Syropoulos 2000). Our discussion assumes, for simplicity, that neither country is in a position to "win" the tariff war, so that $W^{PO} \geq W^N$ and $W^{*PO} \geq W^{*N}$, but the remaining cases can be handled as well.

24. In drawing a distinction between power- and rules-based approaches, we do not mean to suggest that GATT rules such as nondiscrimination are sufficient in practice to completely neutralize power asymmetries across negotiation partners. As Mavroidis (2000) argues, smaller countries may suffer a disadvantage under GATT/WTO rules, in that countermeasures may be less effective for such countries. We do suggest, however, that power asymmetries across negotiation partners are diminished by the presence of GATT/WTO rules. See also note 16 to chapter 4.

During the process of negotiating a settlement it would be necessary for the parties to understand that an unsettled dispute would ultimately be resolved by impartial third-party judgments based on the rules so that the negotiators would be negotiating with reference to their respective predictions as to the outcome of those judgments and not with reference to potential retaliation or actions exercising power of one or more of the parties in the dispute.

In both techniques negotiation and private settlement of disputes is the dominant mechanism for resolving differences; but the key is the perception of the participants as to what are the "bargaining chips." Insofar as agreed rules for governing the economic relations between the parties exist, a system which predicates negotiation on the implementation of those rules would seem for a number of reasons to be preferred . . . [In] international economic policy, we find that the dichotomy between power-oriented diplomacy and rule-oriented diplomacy can be seen. We have tried to develop rules, in the context of the International Monetary Fund and the GATT. (Jackson 1997a, pp. 109–111)

Of course, to understand the outcomes of trade negotiations within the GATT/WTO, it is necessary to appreciate the specific rules by which member governments must abide. Indeed, if the GATT/WTO as an institution has an impact on the trade policies that governments adopt, it may be largely through the particular set of rules by which the conduct of member countries is judged. A central question is then whether GATT rules can serve to reduce, or even eliminate, existing power asymmetries across negotiating partners. From the perspective of the (politically augmented) terms-of-trade theory, this question may be put more starkly: Do GATT rules serve to induce large countries to behave as if they were small countries, and thereby guide the outcome of trade negotiations toward the political optimum? In chapter 3 below, we describe the core features of GATT's rules, and this description provides the basis for our subsequent evaluation and interpretation of the GATT/WTO as an institution. But before turning to a description of the rules of GATT, we maintain the broader theoretical theme of the present chapter and consider how the outcome of negotiations, once agreed to, is enforced.

2.3 Enforcement

If a trade agreement is to provide an escape from a terms-of-trade-driven Prisoners' Dilemma, how is the agreement to be enforced? After all, the cost-shifting temptations that governments face when making trade-policy decisions do not simply go away once an agreement is signed. On the contrary, each government has a short-term incentive to deviate to a higher-than-is-efficient tariff in order to reap the consequent terms-of-trade gains. For example, a government facing renewed political pressure to protect an import-competing sector would be tempted to provide a greater level of import relief than would be efficient, if it thought that it could get away with shifting part of the cost of this relief onto its trading partners. As there is no "world jail" into which government leaders can be thrown if they are shown to have violated a trade agreement, governments are likely to be dissuaded from such opportunistic behavior only if the pursuit of short-term gains results in long-term losses, as when other governments retaliate in kind. Looked at in this way, it is clear that the tariffs that governments can achieve as part of a "self-enforcing" trade agreement reflect a balance between the short-term gains from protection and the long-term losses from retaliation. The "most-cooperative" tariffs that governments can enforce are more efficient than Nash tariffs; they may not, however, be fully efficient. Moreover a balance once achieved may subsequently be upset as underlying features of the trading environment change, and attempts to "rebalance" the agreement may then come in to play.

As McMillan (1986, 1989), Dixit (1987), and Bagwell and Staiger (1990) emphasize, the enforcement issues that are associated with trade agreements may be formally analyzed using the theory of repeated games. In particular, we may view the static framework described in section 2.1.3 as the "stage game" of an infinitely repeated game. As governments attempt to cooperate toward lower tariff combinations that approach the contract curve, they move below their reaction functions—as defined by (2.7) and (2.8) above—and consequently each government could benefit in the short-run from a unilateral tariff increase. However, if each government is concerned that such a deviation, once discovered, could undermine the entire agreement and ultimately drive countries back to the inefficient noncooperative Nash point, then this concern may serve as an effective deterrent, provided that the short-run temptations to cheat do not become too large. In this way, some cooperation can be sustained.

In chapters 3 and 6 we consider the issue of enforcement in greater detail, but we note here that the formal approach to enforcement taken by the repeated-game literature is broadly consistent with the views expressed within GATT itself concerning the nature of the enforcement challenges it faces. For example, in discussing the challenges governments faced as they sought to enhance GATT's dispute settlement procedures as part of the Uruguay Round of GATT negotiations, Croome (1995) quotes GATT's then-Director General Arthur Dunkel:

> Dunkel summed up his view from the GATT Secretariat in a speech in London in March 1991. He concluded that governments were being restrained from a substantial slippage towards protectionism only by "a kind of balance of terror": a fear that if they resorted to trade restrictions these would evoke retaliation, as well as undermining the trading system as a whole. Dunkel argued that this situation was untenable. The system could not cope with the pressures generated by rapid economic change, the debt difficulties of developing countries and other factors unless it could rely on a secure and reliable basis, which would not be achieved without a "concerted effort to establish momentum in the right direction." He added that he was "not unhopeful that such an effort will be made."
> Dunkel's hopes were founded primarily on his judgment that, acute though the differences of view among GATT member countries might be, all were acutely worried by the drift and deterioration in trade relations, and by the clear risk that the GATT itself—the rule of law in international trade—would be so undermined and bypassed that it would lose all credibility and effectiveness. He also had a more immediate and concrete reason for hope. A number of governments had told him that they would allow a frank assessment of the trading system's difficulties, and launch new efforts to overcome them. (Croome 1995, pp. 11–12)

There is thus a broad consistency between the formal theory of repeated games and the expressed views of GATT officials concerning the means of restraining governments from engaging in opportunistic behavior. This suggests that limits on enforcement power may shape the kinds of agreements that can be negotiated within the GATT/WTO, much as the literature on self-enforcing trade agreements would indicate. But it also raises additional issues regarding the role of the GATT/WTO as an institution, such as the purpose that the GATT/WTO dispute settlement procedures can actually serve in maintaining the "balance of terror." We return to these and related issues later in the book.

3   The History and Design of GATT and the WTO

Having summarized the theoretical approaches to the study of trade agreements, we now turn our focus to the world's major international trade institution and present an overview of the history and design of GATT and now the WTO. This overview provides an institutional context that guides our analysis in subsequent chapters.

3.1   The Origin of GATT and the WTO

The origin of GATT can be traced to the trade-policy choices made by governments in the 1920s and 1930s. Trade barriers became increasingly restrictive in the aftermath of World War I, and they reached extreme levels when the United States enacted the Smoot-Hawley Tariff Act in 1930. Under this act, average U.S. tariffs rose from 38 to 52 percent. Not surprisingly, many U.S. trading partners were quick to respond, and in the following months tariffs were raised in Canada, Cuba, France, Mexico, Italy, Spain, Australia, and New Zealand. Other countries, including Great Britain, joined the retaliatory outburst shortly after. Ultimately, retaliatory tariffs were imposed in an almost universal fashion, and the post–Smoot-Hawley tariff rates for the major powers were generally on the order of 50 percent.[1]

According to Hudec (1990, p. 5), "the postwar design for international trade policy was animated by a single-minded concern to avoid repeating the disastrous errors of the 1920's and 1930's." In the context of figure 2.3, we may think of the "tariff war" associated with

---

1. For further discussion of the origin of GATT, see, for example, Culbert (1987), Dam (1970), Enders (1997), Hoekman and Kostecki (1995), Hudec (1990), Jackson (1997a), Low (1993), Pomfret (1997), Rhodes (1993), and Trebilcock and Howse (1999). Coneybeare (1987) provides a comprehensive discussion of the Smoot-Hawley tariff wars.

the Smoot-Hawley tariffs as corresponding to the Nash point N.[2] The task before governments was then to implement a more cooperative trade-policy relationship, such as depicted in figure 2.3 by the locus of efficient tariffs.

Actually there were many multilateral attempts during the 1920s and 1930s to reverse the rising levels of protection and achieve such a cooperative trade-policy relationship, with the World Economic Conference of 1927 being a prominent example. As described in a League of Nations (1942, p. 101) report on commercial policy in the interwar period, however, this period is strikingly paradoxical: while there were frequent international conferences and committees in which governments proclaimed their intentions to pursue "freer and more equal trade," it is also true that "never before in history were trade barriers raised so rapidly or discrimination so greatly practiced." The causes of these failures are complex and varied. An important feature of the period is that in theory, many governments recognized the potential gains from cooperative trade policy; however, in practice, they interacted in an environment of mutual mistrust and tension so that each was hesitant to liberalize on the assumption of an enduring and reciprocal response from the other.[3] The problem was described by the League of Nations report (1942, p. 120) in this way:

... trade was consistently regarded as a form of warfare, as a vast game of beggar-my-neighbour, rather than as a co-operative activity from the extension of which all stood to benefit. The latter was the premise on which the [inter]-war conferences based their recommendations—a premise accepted by all in theory but repudiated by almost all in practice. It was repudiated in practice because, as the issue presented itself on one occasion after another, it seemed only too evident that a Government that did not use its bargaining power would always come off second-best.

As these failures illustrate, a general awareness among governments that mutual gains from cooperation were possible did not, on its own, ensure the spontaneous emergence of cooperative behavior. Notably, the interwar proclamations failed to provide a set of rules under which

---

2. In fact Whalley (1985, p. 246) argues that the tariff rates that prevailed among the major powers after the Smoot-Hawley Tariff Act were close to those that would be predicted in the Nash equilibrium for a computable general equilibrium model.

3. It should also be mentioned that in the 1920s, some countries, and perhaps especially the United States, were skeptical as to the national benefits that mutual tariff reductions might bring. The US position changed markedly in the 1930s, under the leadership of Secretary of State Cordell Hull, as discussed below.

governments could conduct negotiations, understand clearly their obligations under these negotiations and enforce compliance with these obligations. In the absence of such an institution, the initial multilateral efforts among governments, while well intentioned, failed to solve the underlying Prisoners' Dilemma problem that these governments evidently believed to characterize their trade-policy relationships.

Over the interwar period, the most important step toward a more cooperative trade-policy relationship was spearheaded by US Secretary of State Cordell Hull, who emphasized bilateral trade-policy negotiations and whose efforts led to the US Reciprocal Trade Agreements Act of 1934. Hull proposed that the United States offer import tariff reductions as "concessions" in exchange for reciprocal reductions in the import tariffs of a foreign trading partner. Hull's approach also included a multilateral component: the US tariff reduction achieved through a bilateral negotiation would then extend without discrimination to all trading partners that had been granted MFN status by the United States.

As Rhodes (1993, p. 56) argues, the Reciprocal Trade Agreements Act was important, as it marked the first time that the principles of reciprocity and nondiscrimination were united as fundamental components of US trade policy. It is interesting to remark further on the rationales that were offered for this approach. In light of the disastrous economic performance that accompanied the Smoot-Hawley tariffs, Hull argued that an expansion in international trade was vital for global economic recovery and prosperity. At a national level it was also recognized that an increase in US exports was incompatible with a reduction in US imports. With these economic relationships in mind, Hull proposed that the United States take the lead in negotiating reciprocal tariff reductions with its trading partners.[4] At the same time, it was also understood that a policy of reciprocal tariff liberalization had an appealing political by-product: the export-sector support for a reduction in foreign tariffs would serve as a political counterweight against the complaints that would arise from the domestic import-

---

4. Hull eventually persuaded President Roosevelt to approach the Congress with this plan. In a message to the public on February 28, 1934, Roosevelt presented the case for reciprocity in the following manner: "Full and permanent domestic recovery depends in part upon a revived and strengthened international trade. . . . American exports cannot be permanently increased without a corresponding increase in imports." This quotation is found in Hull's memoirs (1948, p. 357) and in Rhodes's book (1993, p. 57).

competing sectors. The principle of nondiscrimination then served to provide breadth and speed to this liberalization program. In effect, with this principle, bilateral reciprocal tariff reductions could be "multilateralized."

By the 1940s the US experiences with the bilateral trade agreements reached under the Reciprocal Trade Agreements Act had been quite successful, and the lesson that reciprocal tariff reductions could promote mutual gains had been learned. The United States thus sought to establish a multilateral institution that would build upon the essential components of the Reciprocal Trade Agreements Act. In 1946 negotiations began concerning the establishment of an International Trade Organization (ITO). The ITO would specify the rules under which multilateral negotiations would proceed, as well as the manner in which these rules would be enforced. Tariffs were to be lowered in reciprocal and mutually advantageous agreements, and the reduced tariffs would then be extended to all member countries through the nondiscrimination principle. In 1947, an interim agreement was reached. This agreement was known as the General Agreement on Tariffs and Trade (GATT), and it was drawn directly from ITO principles. While GATT was intended as an interim agreement, the ITO was never ratified by the US Congress, and so subsequent multilateral negotiations were carried out within the GATT framework.[5]

As the Preamble of GATT states, the objectives of the contracting parties include "raising standards of living, ensuring full employment and a large and steadily growing volume of real income and effective demand, developing the full use of the resources of the world and expanding the production and exchange of goods." The Preamble further states the participants' belief that "reciprocal and mutually advantageous arrangements directed to the substantial reduction in tariffs and other barriers to trade and to the elimination of discrimina-

---

5. Under the intellectual leadership of James Meade, Great Britain was also an active proponent of a multilateral trade institution. In fact, as Culbert (1987) explains, Meade drafted a proposal for an "International Commercial Union" in 1942. While Meade also endorsed the principle of nondiscrimination, he was less doctrinaire in this matter than was Hull. In particular, Meade favored the inclusion of a clause that allowed, at least to a moderate degree, the continuation of the preferential trade agreements to which Great Britain already belonged. This desire of Great Britain to maintain such agreements was strongly contested by the United States. Ultimately, as explained below, preferential trade agreements were permitted through Article XXIV as an exception to GATT's principle of nondiscrimination.

tory treatment in international commerce" would contribute toward the realization of these goals. It is notable that "free trade" is nowhere mentioned as the objective of GATT. Rather, the emphasis is on reciprocal tariff reductions extended in a nondiscriminatory fashion in order that participating countries could mutually benefit from the resulting increase in income. This emphasis on "reciprocity" and "nondiscrimination" has been maintained over GATT's five-decade history.

Since GATT's creation in 1947, there have been eight rounds of trade negotiations. The earlier rounds focused primarily upon the reduction of import tariffs on goods. By the mid-1980s import tariffs had been considerably reduced on most goods. Still, important problems remained. First, there were some goods, such as agriculture and textiles, for which the liberalization process had moved slowly. Second, the treatment of many "new" trade-policy issues—preferential trading agreements, labor and environmental standards, competition policies, agricultural export subsidies, and services, investment, and intellectual property—is inadequate in GATT, and these issues were seen as increasingly important for the global economy. Finally, GATT is an interim agreement, which "limped along for nearly fifty years with almost no basic constitution designed to regulate its organizational activities and procedures" (Jackson 1997a, p. 42). The participating governments thus sought to return to their original quest with the ITO and develop an official international organization.

These problems (and others too) were addressed in the GATT Uruguay Round, an ambitious and contentious round that lasted from 1986 to 1994. In this round governments achieved some success in the liberalization of agricultural and textile goods, and they ventured into a number of new issues, including those mentioned above. The Uruguay Round also resulted in the 1995 formation of the World Trade Organization. This organization embraces the rules and agreements made in the preceding GATT negotiations.[6] But it is also a full-fledged international organization, with an explicit organizational charter that defines various committees, bodies, and councils, as well as the duties of and relationships between these groups. As we discuss further below, an important innovation associated with the WTO is a unified dispute-settlement system.

---

6. The WTO charter states in Article XVI: 1 that the WTO "shall be guided by the decisions, procedures and customary practices followed by" GATT 1947.

3.2   The Rules of GATT

As we observe above, GATT is not simply the codification of the tariff
levels negotiated by its member governments. Rather, membership
in GATT carries with it an obligation to abide by a set of rules under
which future negotiations can occur and future conduct will be judged
(authoritative references on GATT rules and procedures include Dam
1970, Hudec 1990, and Jackson 1997a). While these rules are laid out
in a series of 39 articles, it is often observed that the pillars of GATT
are the principles of reciprocity and nondiscrimination (MFN), while
enforcement mechanisms form the heart of the GATT system. We now
interpret these core concepts with reference to the rules of GATT. We
divide our discussion of these rules into three basic elements: substantive obligations, permissible exceptions to those obligations, and
dispute settlement procedures.

3.2.1   Substantive Obligations

As Jackson (1997a, pp. 51–52) explains, the substantive obligations
contained in GATT may be grouped into three categories: tariff commitments (Articles II and XXVIII bis), most-favored-nation (MFN)
treatment (Article I), and a series of other commitments that together
represent a "code of conduct" regarding government behavior in the
international-trade arena (Articles III through XVII).[7] At the broadest
level, these provisions amount to an obligation to concentrate national
protective measures into the form of tariffs (and possibly subsidies), to
apply them on an MFN basis, and to honor any tariff ceilings that are
agreed to as "concessions" in a GATT negotiation. We focus here on
the rules associated with tariff commitments and MFN.

Tariff commitments made under GATT are in the form of "bindings,"
with the actual tariff not to exceed the bound duty rate. As the discussion above suggests, MFN treatment requires further that, for any
member country and given good, the member country does not discriminate with its import tariff between exporters from different
member countries (and any tariff applied to exporters from nonmember countries cannot be lower); in addition all tariffs of each member
country must conform to MFN regardless of whether these tariffs have

---

7. This includes national treatment (Article III), anti-dumping and countervailing duties
(Article VI), customs valuation and procedures (Articles VII, VIII, and X), marks of origin
(Article IX), quantitative restrictions (Article XI), subsidies (Article XVI), and state-
trading monopolies (Article XVII).

been bound in a GATT negotiation. There are also specific obligations that accompany a tariff binding that are meant to ensure that the binding cannot be undone by other government measures, such as non-tariff charges, new subsidies, or new methods of classifying or valuing goods. Tariff bindings can be altered through time, and indeed GATT provides for its members to sponsor "rounds" of negotiations to lower the general level of tariff bindings "from time to time." Within any such round a government offers a reduction in its binding on a completely voluntary basis, with the presumed goal of securing a mutually advantageous arrangement through a reciprocal reduction in the tariff bindings of its trading partners.

3.2.2 Exceptions

While the substantive obligations of GATT represent an attempt at the international level to restrain incentives for trade intervention that may exist at the national level, countries are not held rigidly to these "obligations." Instead, GATT provides for various exceptions that can be invoked in certain circumstances. Broadly speaking, exceptions can take two forms. First, an exception can be granted to a country for an "original" action. For example, GATT rules permit exceptions to tariff commitments that are associated with opportunities for (1) the renegotiation and modification of tariff schedules (Article XXVIII), (2) the suspension of concessions under the escape clause (Article XIX), and (3) the protection of human, animal or plant life or health (Article XX). GATT rules also permit an exception to MFN treatment for the purpose of negotiating preferential trade agreements (Article XXIV) and the imposition of antidumping or countervailing duties (Article VI). We discuss the specific provisions associated with each of these possibilities in more detail in subsequent chapters.

The permissiveness with which GATT grants exceptions for original actions by member countries suggests that GATT "obligations" are not what they might appear, and indeed they are not. Dam (1970, p. 80) explains the rationale for the inclusion of such exceptions:

The GATT has a special interest in seeing that as many agreements for the reduction of tariffs as possible are made. Enforcement of bindings is important in the GATT insofar as such enforcement gives contracting parties the confidence necessary to rely upon tariff concessions offered by other contracting parties. But because of the economic nature of tariff concessions and the domestic political sensitivity inherently involved in trade issues, a system that made withdrawals of concessions impossible would tend to discourage the making of concessions in the first place. It is better, for example, that 100 commitments should be made and that 10 should be withdrawn than that only 50 commitments should be made and that all of them should be kept.

Exceptions for original actions thus act as "safeguards" that are designed to encourage tariff commitments and confidence in the GATT system.[8]

Of course, exceptions for original actions must be subjected to some disciplining structure; otherwise, governments might abuse the permissive posture and claim exceptional circumstances on too frequent a basis. GATT rules therefore also permit a second kind of exception, which is granted to member countries for "retaliatory" actions. For example, when a government seeks to modify or withdraw a previous concession, GATT rules recognize the consequent cost borne by the trading partner that is the "principal supplier" of the relevant good. If this trading partner is unable to negotiate satisfactory "compensation" (e.g., the government may offer to compensate for its original action by reducing the tariff on some other good), then it is allowed to achieve that compensation through retaliation; in other words, the trading partner can then reciprocate by withdrawing a concession of a "substantially equivalent" nature. Thus, as a general matter, the temptation that a government may have to request exceptions for original actions is tempered by the permitted responses of its trading partners, who are allowed to seek compensation by retaliating with reciprocal adjustments of their own.[9]

Taken together, GATT's substantive obligations and its permitted exceptions to those obligations define a set of rules under which GATT members are expected to abide. Within this set of rules, it is then up to

---

8. Ostry (1997, p. 68) reaches a similar conclusion. She explains the purpose of exceptions as follows: "These exceptions were considered essential as a means of promoting liberalization, for in the absence of legitimate 'escapes,' governments would be reluctant to undertake any significant reduction of trade barriers."

9. Opportunities for compensatory withdrawal or suspension of concessions are explicitly provided in the Article XIX and XXVIII exceptions mentioned above. In the case of the Article XX exception, there is no presumption that compensation will be offered by the government who takes the original action, and so as Jackson (1969, pp. 741–42) notes, the practical protection against the misuse of this exception rests on the utilization of GATT's Article XXII and XXIII clauses on "nullification or impairment," which we discuss in section 3.2.3. The WTO includes an agreement on Sanitary and Phytosanitary Measures, which elaborates on the rules for the application of certain specific exceptions contained in Article XX, but utilization of the (WTO) nullification-or-impairment clauses is still the essential check against misuse of this exception (as is true also of the above-mentioned Article XXIV exception).

each member government to decide whether and when to engage in negotiations with any other member government, and any bargains struck are implemented subject to these rules. We consider next the manner in which these rules are enforced.

3.2.3 Dispute Settlement Procedures

When a government makes a tariff commitment as part of a GATT negotiation, is it then compelled under its domestic law to honor that commitment? As Jackson (1997a, pp. 79–105) details, the relationship between international and domestic law varies from country to country. In the United States, the authority to enter into trade agreements is granted by the legislative to the executive branch, and the conditions under which this authority is granted influence the domestic legal standing of the corresponding trade agreement. According to Jackson (1997a, pp. 96–97), the key parts of GATT and also the WTO agreements reached in the Uruguay Round appear not to be "self-executing," which is to say that such agreements do not have full standing as domestic law without further governmental acts. As Low (1993, p. 48) explains, this has the practical implication that "nothing in US domestic law . . . prevents the president from subsequently violating US tariff commitments under GATT. . . . In practice, this means that the status of the GATT and associated agreements under US law gives virtually limitless potential in US trade policy for noncompliance with GATT."[10] This discussion raises an obvious, but fundamental, question: By what means are GATT commitments enforced? As no external enforcement mechanism exists to punish GATT violations, meaningful commitments must be self-enforcing, with violations deterred by the credible threat of subsequent retaliation. The general argument is nicely summarized by Dam (1970, pp. 80–81):

The best guarantee that a commitment of any kind will be kept (particularly in an international setting where courts are of limited importance and, even more important, marshals and jails are nonexistent) is that the parties continue to view adherence to their agreement as in their mutual interest. . . .

Thus, the GATT system, unlike most legal systems, . . . , is not designed to exclude self-help in the form of retaliation. Rather, retaliation, subjected to established procedures and kept within prescribed bounds, is made the heart of the GATT system.

---

10. For further discussion of the domestic legal standing of GATT commitments, see also Dam (1970) and Hudec (1990).

The dispute settlement and enforcement provisions that are contained within GATT itself are thus essential to the functioning of the multilateral trading system.

The central components of the GATT dispute settlement system evolved through GATT practice with reference to the provisions contained in Articles XXII and XXIII. Article XXII calls for bilateral consultations when disputes arise, while Article XXIII ("Nullification or Impairment") is the real centerpiece of the GATT dispute settlement process, as it defines the circumstances under which the actions by one country serve to "nullify or impair" the benefits expected under the agreement by another country. Nullification or impairment has been interpreted to include actions taken by one country ". . . which harmed the trade of another, and which 'could not reasonably have been anticipated' by the other at the time it negotiated for a concession" (Jackson 1997a, p. 115). As Petersmann (1997) details, a nullification-or-impairment complaint may take several forms. A "violation complaint" occurs when a country is alleged to have failed to carry out its GATT obligations (as when a tariff binding is broken), while a "non-violation complaint" occurs when there is no claim that the harmful action is itself inconsistent with GATT rules (as when a production subsidy is offered to domestic firms). In GATT practice, over 90 percent of the disputes filed under Article XXIII have been violation complaints.[11]

An important distinction can be drawn between the procedures associated with "safeguard" exceptions as discussed above and those that are typically associated with nullification or impairment. The "safeguard" procedures contained in Articles XIX and XXVIII provide for the lawful suspension, modification, or withdrawal of previously negotiated concessions and spell out the permissible retaliatory responses of trading partners. Governments behave in a "GATT-legal" fashion when they act within the confines of these rules. By contrast, the dispute settlement procedures contained in Articles XXII and XXIII

---

11. The circumstances under which an action is interpreted to have nullified or impaired the expected benefits of another country are somewhat ambiguous, and the evolution of GATT practice has therefore led to the identification of three conditions for a prima facie finding of nullification or impairment: the breach of an obligation, the use of a domestic subsidy to inhibit imports in certain cases, and the use of quantitative restrictions. The burden of proof that no nullification or impairment occurred then falls on the country which breached or took such actions (Jackson 1997a, p. 115). The first condition corresponds to a violation complaint, but the other two conditions can arise without any explicit violation of GATT rules.

describe the procedures for retaliating against a country that takes a harmful action which its trading partners could not have anticipated under GATT rules. In the typical case, that of a violation complaint, the actions of the offending country have violated GATT rules, and retaliation here is more fundamentally concerned with the enforcement of rules.

The GATT procedure for settling disputes involves three stages: consultation between or among the parties in the dispute; investigation, ruling and recommendation by a GATT panel; and as a last resort, authorization for one or more countries to suspend GATT obligations against another (i.e., retaliation). In practice, the greatest emphasis has been placed on consultation and negotiation rather than on retaliation. Resolution is sometimes achieved in the first stage, and on other occasions it follows the GATT panel ruling. When the panel finds that nullification or impairment has occurred, it recommends that the offending country bring its illegal measures into conformity with GATT rules. If the offending country is unwilling to do so, then it may seek a negotiated resolution by offering the harmed country "compensation" through a reduction in its (MFN) tariff on some other goods. As Petersmann (1997, pp. 80–82) explains, compensation is voluntary under GATT, but it may be used as a means to forestall the last-resort response: an authorized (and discriminatory) suspension of tariff concessions by the harmed country.

In practice, retaliation has been authorized only in a few cases.[12] There have been several attempts to seek authorized retaliation, however, and at times GATT disputes have resulted in unauthorized retaliation. Furthermore other disputes between GATT members have occurred outside GATT procedures entirely (Kovenock and Thursby 1992). As Rhodes (1993, p. 109) argues, while the number of authorized retaliations is small, the threat of authorized retaliation is often the

---

12. Retaliation was authorized under GATT in only one case, concerning the use by the United States of import restraints on dairy products from the Netherlands. For seven years, the Netherlands was authorized to utilize import restraints on US grain, but it never acted on that authorization (Jackson 1997a, p. 116). More recently further cases have emerged under the WTO in which retaliation has been authorized (and used). As Mavroidis (2000) and WTO (2001, p. 28) detail, the United States and Ecuador were authorized to retaliate against the European Union in response to the EU's discriminatory tariffs on banana imports, and the United States and Canada were authorized to retaliate in response to the EU's prohibition of imports of hormone-treated beef. Additionally Canada was authorized to retaliate against Brazil as a consequence of Brazil's failure to remove illegal aircraft subsidies.

catalyst that ensures resolution in the consultation/negotiation stage. This reflects a theme that emerges from the drafting history of Article XXIII. The drafters of Article XXIII clearly understood the necessity of the retaliatory threat, but they sought as well to construct a rules-based system under which retaliation is limited in frequency and scope.[13]

With the WTO, the member governments significantly strengthened the dispute settlement procedures. While the GATT dispute settlement process evolved over time from an initial beginning of a few paragraphs in GATT 1947, the WTO dispute settlement process is elaborately defined so as to construct a unified procedure that permits application to both traditional and new trade-policy issues. In this context, one important innovation is that the ability of a single country to "block" a panel's ruling is now eliminated.[14] A second innovation is that the WTO has a Trade Policy Review Body, which conducts regular reviews of individual countries' trade policies. These trade policy reviews represent an explicit attempt on the part of the WTO members to monitor one another's trade policies and thereby enhance "transparency," so as to encourage governments to follow more closely WTO rules and to fulfill the obligations to which they have agreed under these rules.

3.3   Reciprocity, Nondiscrimination, and Enforcement under GATT

It should be apparent from the preceding discussion that the enforcement provisions are a central feature of GATT rules, as is the principle of nondiscrimination (MFN). The representation of the principle of reciprocity in these rules, however, is much less clear. Yet, along with the principle of nondiscrimination, the principle of reciprocity is widely recognized as a pillar of GATT. How is the principle of reciprocity represented in GATT?

---

13. We develop these points later in section 6.1.

14. Under the GATT dispute settlement process, the approval of the panel's ruling required consensus among member countries, and so it was possible for the country losing a case to block the adoption of the ruling. By contrast, under the new WTO dispute settlement process, the panel's ruling is "automatic," in the sense that it can be blocked only if there is consensus among the member countries that the ruling should be rejected. The panel finding may be appealed, however, in which case an Appellate Body of three experts evaluates the dispute and the panel ruling. The appellate report is also adopted in "automatic" fashion. As well, under the WTO approach all stages of the dispute settlement process are subject to fixed timetables, ensuring a timely resolution.

Broadly speaking, the principle of reciprocity in GATT refers to the "ideal" of mutual changes in trade policy that bring about changes in the volume of each country's imports that are of equal value to changes in the volume of its exports. Upon closer examination, the preceding discussion contains two important instances in which a reference to reciprocity arises. First, when governments negotiate in GATT rounds as allowed under Article XXVIII bis, they do so with the presumed goal of securing a mutually advantageous arrangement through a reciprocal reduction in tariff bindings. In particular, governments seek a "balance of concessions" in their negotiations. In this case reciprocity refers broadly to the philosophy with which governments approach negotiations.[15] Second, when a government seeks to modify or withdraw a previous concession as an original action, Article XXVIII requires moderation in the retaliatory response of the substantially affected trading partners, who are allowed to reciprocate by withdrawing "substantially equivalent concessions."[16] Thus, both when tariffs are being lowered in negotiation rounds and when tariffs are being raised as part of a renegotiation process, the principle of reciprocity implies a "balance" in the commercial treatment between GATT members.

This completes our general discussion of the history and design of GATT and the WTO. At this point we are prepared to return to the theoretical framework developed in chapter 2 and summarized in figure 2.3. Within this setting we investigate whether the rules of GATT assist governments as they attempt to navigate their way from the inefficient Nash point to the contract curve. At various points in our discussion some further clarification of GATT rules is required. We present these additional remarks in the company of the corresponding theoretical analysis. This serves both to promote a broad perspective of GATT in the present chapter and also to make the subsequent chapters somewhat more self-contained. We begin in the next chapter with a theoretical analysis of the principle of reciprocity.

15. For a discussion of the concept of reciprocity in GATT negotiations, as well as the various manners in which reciprocity has been measured in practice, see Dam (1970, pp. 58–61, 87–91), Enders (1997), and Hoekman and Kostecki (1995, pp. 68–76). See also notes 1 and 4 to chapter 4.

16. This second application of reciprocity comes up also in GATT's Article XIX, which provides for the temporary suspension of tariff commitments in response to injurious import increases, and as we discuss later in section 6.1 it can arise as well under Article XXIII. The application to Article XIX has been altered with the creation of the WTO, however, as we discuss further in section 6.2.1.

4   Reciprocity

Our purpose in this chapter is to offer an assessment of reciprocity as a principle that assists governments as they attempt to escape from a terms-of-trade-driven Prisoners' Dilemma. Building on the general discussion of reciprocity presented in the previous chapter, we develop below a detailed description of the role of reciprocity in GATT. We distinguish between the two ways in which reciprocity appears in GATT practice, and we then evaluate the economic logic of reciprocity. Finally, we return to the theme of rules-based versus power-based negotiations discussed above, and we discuss a broader interpretation of reciprocity as a means to bring "weaker" countries into the multilateral trading system.

4.1   Reciprocity in GATT

As mentioned earlier, the term "reciprocity" refers broadly to the ideal of mutual changes in trade policy which bring about changes in the volume of each country's imports that are of equal value to changes in the volume of its exports.[1] We begin by noting that the concept of reciprocity can be given a very simple formal representation. Utilizing

---

1. Nowhere in GATT is the term reciprocity specifically defined. Perhaps the clearest statement was given by the Legal Advisor to GATT's Director-General (GATT document C/M/220, pp. 35–36), as quoted in the context of Article XXVIII renegotiations in WTO (1995a). In describing the "fairly well established criteria" that were considered in determining what would constitute the withdrawal of substantially equivalent concessions, it was noted that: "The first criterion was the development of the imports during, normally, the three years before the renegotiations started. What was taken into account was not just a statistical average, but also the trend in the development of trade during that period. Furthermore, account was taken of the size of the tariff increase being negotiated. Moreover, an estimate was made of the price elasticity of the product concerned." (WTO 1995a, p. 949). See also Enders (1997).

the two-country model of trade presented in chapter 2 and following Bagwell and Staiger (1999a), we may define reciprocity more formally as follows: a set of tariff changes $\Delta\tau \equiv (\tau^1 - \tau^0)$ and $\Delta\tau^* \equiv (\tau^{*1} - \tau^{*0})$ conforms to *the principle of reciprocity* provided that

$$\tilde{p}^{w0}[M(p^1, \tilde{p}^{w1}) - M(p^0, \tilde{p}^{w0})] = [E(p^1, \tilde{p}^{w1}) - E(p^0, \tilde{p}^{w0})],$$

where $\tilde{p}^{w0} \equiv \tilde{p}^w(\tau^0, \tau^{*0})$, $\tilde{p}^{w1} \equiv \tilde{p}^w(\tau^1, \tau^{*1})$, $p^0 \equiv p(\tau^0, \tilde{p}^{w0})$, $p^1 \equiv p(\tau^1, \tilde{p}^{w1})$ and changes in trade volumes are valued at the existing world price.[2] We may now use the trade balance condition (2.1) in order to rewrite this expression as

$$[\tilde{p}^{w1} - \tilde{p}^{w0}]M(p^1, \tilde{p}^{w1}) = 0. \tag{4.1}$$

Thus, as (4.1) makes clear, mutual changes in trade policy that conform to the principle of reciprocity leave the world price unchanged. The potential importance of this property becomes apparent, when it is recalled from our previous review of the traditional economic and political-economy theories of trade agreements that a government sets its tariffs in an inefficient manner if and only if it is motivated by the *change* in the world price that its tariff choice implies.[3]

With a formal definition of the principle of reciprocity now in hand, we consider the application of this principle within GATT practice. As suggested in section 3.3, reciprocity arises in GATT practice in two ways. First, the principle of reciprocity is often associated with the manner in which government negotiators approach trade negotiations. A common perception is that governments enter into negotiations seeking a "balance of concessions," whereby the tariff reduction offered by one government is balanced against an "equivalent" concession from its trading partner.[4] The emphasis that governments place upon

---

2. In deriving (4.1), it is immaterial whether $\tilde{p}^{w0}$ or $\tilde{p}^{w1}$ is used to value changes in trade volumes.

3. While we have derived this property of reciprocity within the two-good two-country framework presented in chapter 2, it also extends naturally to a many-good many-country setting (see Bagwell and Staiger 1999a).

4. For example, Preeg (1970, pp. 130–34) remarks that in the GATT Kennedy Round, negotiators sought to achieve a balance in value between the forecasted increases in the volume of imports and the estimated increase in the volume of exports that would accompany a proposed set of tariff concessions. This observed practice of reciprocity in negotiation fits squarely with the formal definition of reciprocity presented above. Bhagwati (1988, 1991) also notes that reciprocity in tariff negotiations is defined with reference to a balance in the value of changes in trade volume, referring to this process as "first-difference reciprocity."

reciprocity in this sense has attracted the interest of many economists, as it stands in sharp contrast to standard economic arguments in favor of unilateral liberalization. A second application of the principle of reciprocity can be found within the actual articles of GATT itself. This application concerns the manner in which governments may renegotiate agreements. While economists have traditionally placed less emphasis on this application of reciprocity, GATT legal scholars routinely point out its potential significance as well (e.g., see Dam 1970, pp. 79–99; Jackson 1997a, p. 143). We argue that each of the two applications of reciprocity admits a natural economic interpretation. We consider the applications in turn.

4.2 Reciprocity and Trade Negotiations

The first application of reciprocity in GATT practice reflects the balance of concessions that governments seek through a negotiated agreement. This practice is described by Dam (1970, p. 59), who explains that under the language of Article XXVIII bis, which outlines the manner in which GATT tariff negotiations are to occur, negotiations are voluntary and are to be conducted on a "reciprocal and mutually advantageous basis." Dam (1970, p. 59) explains further that:

This permissive approach to the content of tariff agreements is often referred to under the heading of reciprocity. From the legal principle that a country need make concessions only when other contracting parties offer reciprocal concessions considered to be "mutually advantageous" has been derived the informal principle that exchanges of concessions must entail reciprocity.

This informal principle of reciprocity stands in contrast to standard economic logic, which implies that the optimal unilateral policy for a country is free trade. From this perspective it is perplexing to consider why a government would require a "concession" from its trading partner in order to do what is in any event best for its country. Appealing to this apparent violation of economic logic, many economists interpret the observation that governments seek reciprocity in negotiated agreements as direct evidence that government negotiators adopt a mercantilist perspective that is incompatible with basic economic reasoning and that therefore derives from underlying political forces. For example, Krugman (1991a, p. 25) observes:

To make sense of international trade negotiations, one needs to remember three simple rules about the objectives of negotiating countries:

1. Exports are good.
2. Imports are bad.
3. Other things equal, an equal increase in imports and exports is good.

In other words, GATT-think is enlightened mercantilism.

Against this backdrop, it can now be argued that the mercantilist approach to trade negotiations that seems to drive actual negotiations admits a simple economic interpretation.[5]

To see this, suppose that governments begin at the Nash equilibrium point. Appealing to (2.4), (2.7), and (2.8), at the Nash equilibrium it is true that $W_p < 0 < W_{p^*}^*$. This means that if governments could agree to liberalize tariffs in a reciprocal manner that preserved the world price, then the domestic local price p would fall (since $\partial p/\partial\tau = \tilde{p}^w > 0$) and the foreign local price p^* would rise (since $\partial p^*/\partial\tau^* = -(\tilde{p}^w)/(\tau^*)^2 < 0$), and as a consequence the domestic-government welfare would rise (since $W_p < 0$) and the foreign-government welfare would also rise (since $W_{p^*}^* > 0$). The simple point is that at the Nash equilibrium both governments would prefer more trade, if the increase in trade volume could be obtained without a deterioration in the terms of trade. A unilateral liberalization effort would indeed result in a decline in the terms of trade, and so neither government would seek unilateral liberalization. On the other hand, if the liberalization occurs under the principle of reciprocity, with one country's tariff reduction balanced against that of the other, then the terms of trade are held constant and each government can gain from an expansion in trade volume without experiencing a consequent decline in the terms of trade.

Reciprocal liberalization of this nature is sure to increase the welfare of both governments if they start at the Nash equilibrium. In fact, beginning at the Nash equilibrium, reciprocal trade liberalization that leaves the world price unchanged increases each government's welfare monotonically until this liberalization has proceeded to the point where one government has achieved its preferred local price (given the Nash world price).[6] If the domestic government achieves its preferred

5. The main argument is developed more fully in Bagwell and Staiger (1999a). The view that GATT negotiations are incompatible with economic reasoning and instead reflect mercantilist logic is further developed in Krugman (1997). Some of the advantages of reciprocity described by Bhagwati (1991, pp. 50–51), Gilligan (1997), and McMillan (1986, 1989) are more in line with the results we report here.

6. This proposition is first proved in Bagwell and Staiger (1996), and it is published in Bagwell and Staiger (1999a). See Bhagwati (2002) for a nice illustration of this point using offer curves.

local price first, then mutually beneficial liberalization proceeds until $W_p = 0$, and similarly this liberalization continues until $W_{p^*}^* = 0$ if the foreign government first achieves its preferred local price. A case of particular interest arises when the domestic and foreign countries are symmetric. In this case liberalization that preserves world prices raises the welfare of both governments monotonically until the single tariff pair is reached at which $W_p = 0 = W_{p^*}^*$. That is to say, when countries are symmetric and liberalize according to the principle of reciprocity, the liberalization process leads to the politically optimal tariffs.

The main intuition is illustrated in figures 4.1a and 4.1b. In figure 4.1a we assume that the countries are symmetric, in which case the iso-world-price locus that emanates from the Nash point N also runs through the politically optimal point PO. In this case, as governments liberalize in a manner that conforms to the principle of reciprocity, they traverse down the associated iso-world-price locus that runs through the initial Nash point, and each experiences gains in welfare along the way until the political optimum is hit. At this point they no longer have incentive for further negotiations as they are on the efficiency locus, having eliminated the inefficient restrictions in trade volume that arose under unilateral behavior as a consequence of the ability to manipulate the terms of trade. Figure 4.1b depicts the case of asymmetric countries. In this situation the iso-world-price locus that emanates from the initial Nash point N need not run through the politically optimal point PO. Liberalization that conforms to reciprocity and begins at the Nash point still raises the welfare of each government, but the mutual benefits from further liberalization terminate at point Z where (without loss of generality) the home government has achieved its preferred local price. In this case, if liberalization conforms rigidly to the principle of reciprocity, then the mutual benefits from further liberalization terminate before governments are able to achieve a set of tariffs that are efficient.

Drawing from the perspective of the (politically augmented) terms-of-trade theory, in which governments seek an escape from a terms-of-trade-driven Prisoners' Dilemma, it is therefore possible to offer a formal economic interpretation of the apparent mercantilist behavior that seems to characterize actual trade negotiations. Just as Krugman's (1991a) three rules of "enlightened mercantilism" would suggest, this perspective implies that governments have every reason to believe that "exports are good," since a reduction in the import tariff levied by the trading partner serves to improve the terms of trade. In addition

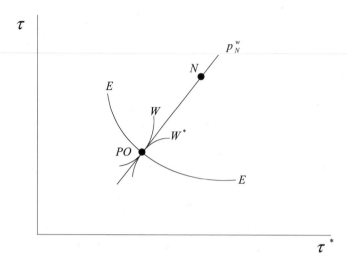

Figure 4.1a

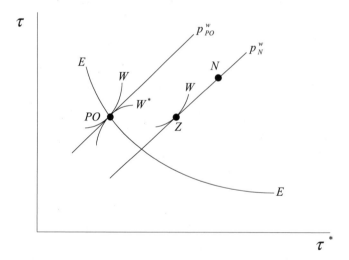

Figure 4.1b

governments naturally regard import liberalization as a concession, with the broader implication that "imports are bad," because unilateral liberalization entails reducing the import tariff below the best-response value and suffering a terms-of-trade decline. Finally, each government benefits from a concession at home that is balanced under reciprocity against an "equivalent" concession abroad, so that "other things equal, an equal increase in imports and exports is good," since the balance of concessions so achieved serves to neutralize the terms-of-trade decline that would have made unilateral liberalization undesirable.

Recalling now the discussion of the origin of GATT presented in chapter 3, we note that the interpretation of reciprocity developed here is in some respects a formal confirmation of the economic benefits associated with reciprocity that Hull suggested. It is also interesting to contrast this explanation of reciprocity with a seemingly separate political argument. As Hull recognized, a practical benefit of reciprocal (as opposed to unilateral) liberalization is that the reduction in the foreign import tariff mobilizes political support among domestic exporters that acts as a counterweight against the objections to liberalization that arise from domestic import-competing firms. It is clear, however, that the proposed export-sector support for reciprocity ultimately must derive from the anticipated economic benefit that is associated with a reduction in the foreign tariff. This benefit moreover travels through the improved world price that domestic exporters can expect to receive. Consequently the foreign tariff reduction benefits domestic exporters by contributing to an improvement in the domestic terms of trade. Evidently this "political" explanation of reciprocity can in fact be offered within the (politically augmented) terms-of-trade theory; furthermore, it then becomes apparent that the ability of reciprocity to neutralize the adverse terms-of-trade implications of unilateral liberalization is the essence of this explanation as well.[7]

At the same time it should be noted that a more sophisticated political argument for reciprocity also exists. This argument is developed in some detail by Gilligan (1997), who notes that the benefit to domestic exporters of a foreign tariff reduction is transmitted through an improved world price.[8] He then goes further and offers an interpretation of the political aspects of reciprocity, highlighting a dynamic process through which government preferences change over time. As Gilligan (1997, p. 35) puts it, "Reciprocity really created a 'friendly cycle' of liberalization: each round of trade agreements encouraged more exporter lobbying, and, as more exporters became politically active, legislatures became willing to allow deeper reductions in protection."

Krishna and Mitra (1999) explore a formal version of this process. In their model the domestic country first sets its import tariff, and this

7. Recall from chapter 2 that the model developed here can include a political-support constraint.
8. Bhagwati (1991, pp. 50–51) also discusses some of the political advantages of reciprocity.

selection alters the world price and thereby affects the incentives of private actors in the foreign country, who must decide whether to incur the fixed costs that are associated with forming a lobby. Lobbies can be formed in the import-competing sector or the exporting sector. Once the lobby structure is determined, the game within the foreign country proceeds as in the Grossman-Helpman (1994) model: the schedule of lobby contributions is presented to the government, who then selects its import tariff to maximize its welfare function.[9] There is an interesting analogy here to the commitment approach described in section 2.1.4. In the Krishna-Mitra (1999) model, the private-sector "investment" corresponds to the fixed costs that are associated with the endogenous formation of lobbies. The novel wrinkle, though, is that the government of the domestic country may offer a low tariff, in order to *influence* the commitment game between the foreign government and its private sector. In particular, the government of the domestic country seeks to steer lobby formation in the foreign country away from the import sector and toward the export sector, since this in turn induces the foreign government to offer a low tariff.

This suggests that unilateral trade liberalization may be desirable, because of the *subsequent* reciprocal tariff liberalization that it induces. As such, this argument offers an interesting interpretation of important historic episodes of unilateral liberalization (e.g., the unilateral repeal of England's Corn Laws in the 1840s). The argument may also contribute toward an improved understanding of the gradual process through which tariff liberalization has occurred (as discussed further in section 6.2.2). But the argument succeeds less well in directly accounting for the rules described by Krugman, which pertain to negotiations between trading partners who seek *simultaneous* reciprocal tariff liberalization.[10]

4.3   Reciprocity and Renegotiation

While the application of reciprocity considered above reflects the broad manner in which governments appear to approach trade negotiations,

---

9. Krishna and Mitra (1999) build upon Mitra (1999), who introduces to the Grossman-Helpman (1994) model a fixed cost for lobby formation and endogenizes the structure of lobbies.

10. An alternative attempt to explain the appeal of reciprocity in trade negotiations is provided by Ethier (2000). In Ethier's framework, which we discussed in section 2.1.3, governments seek reciprocity at a general level in order to compensate for (1) their assumed inability to directly help their exporters with targeted export-enhancement programs and (2) the assumed inability of their exporters to understand the general equilibrium effects of trade-policy intervention.

there is in fact no requirement in GATT that negotiations proceed in this manner. There is, however, a second application of the principle of reciprocity in GATT, and in this application GATT rules do require reciprocity. This second application concerns the manner in which trade agreements may be renegotiated. Under GATT Article XXVIII, a country may propose to modify or withdraw a concession agreed upon in a previous round of negotiation. In this case, if the country and its trading partner are unable to reach agreement regarding a renegotiated tariff structure, then the country is free to carry out the proposed changes anyway. The notion of reciprocity is then used to moderate the response of the country's trading partner, who is permitted to withdraw substantially equivalent concessions of its own.[11]

This suggests that GATT negotiations may be understood as a multistage game, in which governments first agree to an initial set of tariffs in a round of negotiations under Article XXVIII bis. Then each government considers whether it would prefer to raise its tariff with the understanding that the outcome of any Article XXVIII renegotiation that follows will, under GATT's reciprocity rule, preserve the world price implied by the original negotiation. Viewed from this perspective, it is clear that governments must evaluate the future incentives for renegotiation that might accompany a proposed initial agreement. A figure can capture some of the key ideas.

Consider then figure 4.2. This figure depicts three possible tariff pairs that might represent an initial agreement. These tariff pairs are represented as points A, B, and PO and, to make the argument as clear as possible, we suppose that each of the tariff pairs is on the efficiency locus. Figure 4.2 also depicts the iso-world-price loci that run through each of the candidate tariff pairs. Finally, the loci for which $W_p = 0$ and $W_{p^*}^* = 0$, respectively, are also represented. These loci are assumed to be downward sloping, although the argument developed here is not limited to this assumption. According to (2.10), each locus intersects the efficiency frontier at the politically optimal point PO and nowhere else.[12]

Consider first an initial agreement that corresponds to point A. Observe in this case that the foreign government would prefer to move

---

11. For further discussion of Article XXVIII and the GATT rules that govern renegotiation, see Dam (1970, pp. 79–99), Enders (1997), and Jackson (1997a, p. 143). Bagwell and Staiger (1999a) provide a formal analysis of reciprocity and renegotiation along the lines discussed here.

12. As (2.10) indicates, efficiency is possible if and only if both $W_p = 0$ and $W_{p^*}^* = 0$ (corresponding to the politically optimal point) or both $W_p \neq 0$ and $W_{p^*}^* \neq 0$.

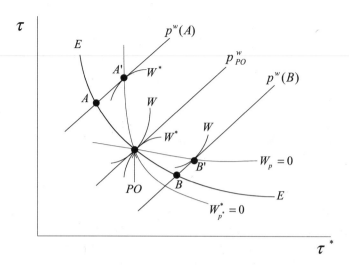

Figure 4.2

up the associated iso-world-price locus to the point A', where it achieves its preferred local price (given the world price determined at point A). Thus, while the tariff pair at point A is efficient, it is not robust to the type of renegotiation that GATT allows through Article XXVIII. The foreign government would request a renegotiation to raise its tariff to the value corresponding to point A', knowing that the domestic government would then be permitted under Article XXVIII to withdraw a substantially equivalent concession that would preserve the world price and therefore deliver the tariff pair at point A'. A similar argument applies for the efficient tariff pair associated with point B, except in this case it is the domestic government that first withdraws its original concession in order to induce the point B'. Reasoning in this fashion, it is now direct to see that there is only one efficient tariff pair which, if agreed to originally, would not be lost in the renegotiation process. This tariff pair is the politically optimal tariff pair, since this is the only point on the efficiency locus at which both governments achieve their preferred local prices given the associated world price.[13]

13. Recall that the iso-welfare curves of each government are tangent to the iso-world-price locus at the politically optimal tariffs. In the special case of national-welfare-maximizing governments associated with the traditional economic approach depicted in figure 2.1, the political optimum corresponds to reciprocal free trade and the locus at which the domestic (foreign) government achieves its preferred local price is horizontal (vertical) out of the reciprocal free-trade point. The efficiency locus passes through this

The logic embodied in figure 4.2 suggests that the principle of reciprocity as it applies to renegotiations of GATT agreements can allow governments to reach the efficiency locus. On the other hand, not every set of tariffs on the efficiency locus is compatible with the ability to renegotiate as allowed under the principle of reciprocity. In fact, as figure 4.2 implies, the politically optimal tariffs are the only efficient tariffs that are "renegotiation-proof" in this sense. From the perspective of the (politically augmented) terms-of-trade theory, there is a certain appeal to this finding, since the politically optimal tariffs are also those tariffs that arise when the source of inefficiency—governments' motivations to influence the terms of trade—is directly eliminated.

Recalling now the thought experiment described in section 2.1.3 which led to the definition of politically optimal tariffs, it can also be seen that this thought experiment bears a resemblance to what governments achieve with reciprocity. Under our thought experiment, governments were assumed to not value the movements in the terms of trade caused by their tariff choices, and in this hypothetical environment they were led to select politically optimal tariffs. We may think of reciprocity as corresponding to a related experiment in which governments ignore the terms-of-trade movements associated with their tariff increases, not because such movements are without value but because the mutual changes in tariffs implied by reciprocity guarantee that the terms of trade are in fact fixed. In this way reciprocity induces governments to act *as if* they did not value the terms-of-trade movements caused by their tariff selections, and reciprocity can therefore lead governments to select efficient politically optimal tariffs.[14]

As the political optimum represents the only efficient outcome that survives renegotiation under GATT's reciprocity rule, the set of outcomes that are renegotiation-proof in this environment rests inside the

---

point as well, but it otherwise lies below the loci associated with the preferred local prices. Thus, when governments maximize national welfare, the point of reciprocal free trade is the only point on the efficiency locus that can survive renegotiation under GATT's reciprocity rules.

14. This observation may be made more precise with reference to (2.7). As (2.7) implies, the domestic government's preferred tariff satisfies $W_p = 0$ when the term λW_{pw} is zero. This term would in fact be zero, either if the government were hypothesized not to value a change in the terms of trade (i.e., if $W_{pw} \equiv 0$) or if it were to expect a reciprocal tariff adjustment from its trading partner that would result in no change in the terms of trade (i.e., if $\lambda = 0$). See also note 11 to chapter 2.

efficiency frontier except at the political optimum. An implication is that governments are "penalized" under GATT's reciprocity rule if they seek to negotiate an outcome on the efficiency frontier other than the political optimum. For example, at point A in figure 4.2, notice that the home government achieves higher welfare than it would obtain at the political optimum. However, a portion of the gains that the home government might achieve in pushing the negotiations away from the political optimum and toward point A would be lost under GATT's reciprocity rule in the subsequent renegotiation to the point A', and the home government may therefore be less effective at pushing the negotiations in this direction. A similar observation applies to the foreign government with reference to the point B. In this way GATT's reciprocity rule can be viewed as helping to mitigate the power asymmetries that governments might otherwise wield at the bargaining table, as this rule serves to direct them toward the political optimum, an outcome that is defined without reference to countries' relative power status.[15] This observation is in line with the observations of Jackson (1997a) discussed in section 2.2 above regarding the nature of rules-based approaches to negotiations, but it does raise an important new question: Why would powerful countries agree to participate in GATT under the rule of reciprocity? We consider this question next.

4.4   Reciprocity and Participation: Rules versus Power

In section 2.2 we illustrated how a power-based approach to trade negotiations could allow governments to move to a point on the contract curve. Any difference between the negotiated outcome and the political optimum would then reflect "power asymmetries" across negotiating partners. In section 4.3 we argued that GATT's reciprocity rule serves to mitigate the influence of power asymmetries on negotiated outcomes. The reciprocity rule thereby guides governments back toward the political optimum. Why, then, would powerful countries support a multilateral system built on the pillar of reciprocity, when evidently this pillar serves to undercut their bargaining advantage?

---

15. Bagwell and Staiger (1999a) define a "bilateral negotiation game" and show for this game that reciprocity guides negotiations toward the politically optimal outcome, unless sufficient asymmetries are present.

At a broad level, the question of why powerful governments submit to a rules-based system is a fundamental question of international relations, and we do not presume to provide a complete answer here. We do, however, offer a partial answer: by serving to moderate the lawful response of powerful countries in case of disagreement, GATT's rule of reciprocity may encourage weaker countries to overcome their fear of exploitation by stronger trading partners and participate in GATT negotiations.[16]

The general idea draws from the commitment approach described in section 2.1.4, and McLaren's (1997) model suggests an especially interesting version. Let us suppose that the government of a smaller country were to contemplate entering into tariff negotiations with a large trading partner. As news of the negotiations spread, a process might naturally begin in which producers in the smaller country raced to make investments to position themselves so as to serve the large foreign market once trade barriers had been reduced. Such investments, however, once sunk, would tend to undercut the position of the smaller country's government at the bargaining table as a breakdown in negotiations would now be quite costly for the smaller country. As a result the government of the smaller country might well be "held up" at the bargaining table, and pushed by its larger trading partner into accepting terms that make it worse off than if negotiations had never begun. Anticipating this possibility, the government of the smaller country may be especially cautious about engaging in any trade negotiations with its larger trading partners, and potential efficiency gains from negotiations may remain unexploited.

It is in such a situation that prior commitments to a set of rules by which subsequent negotiations must abide could provide efficiency gains, as a commitment to rules could solve the "hold up" problem, and thereby serve the objectives of all governments by encouraging smaller countries to participate in negotiations with their more

---

16. The notion that a rules-based institution can assist small countries is advanced on the WTO Web site *http://www.wto.org/wto/about/devel5.htm*, where the importance of trade rules for small- and medium-sized countries is explained as follows: "The WTO provides a rules-based multilateral trading system. All members have both rights and obligations. The alternative is bilateral commercial relations based on economic and political power—small countries are then at the mercy of the large trading powers. Differences in influence between individual countries remain, of course, but even the smallest WTO member has a wide range of rights which are enforceable under the WTO's impartial dispute settlement procedures."

powerful trading partners. In particular, GATT's reciprocity rule can help to serve this purpose, as it can insure weaker countries against the possibility of exploitation by guiding negotiations toward the political optimum.[17]

---

17. See Bagwell and Staiger (1999a) for a full treatment of reciprocity as a means to induce participation along the lines outlined above. A similar holdup problem can be generated using the political-economy model of Fernandez and Rodrik (1991), which allows that voter preferences may change through time. It is also of interest to consider the extreme case of a country that is in fact truly "small" (i.e., unable to affect the world price with its tariff). In this case, GATT's reciprocity rule would effectively prevent the country from accepting meaningful tariff bindings, since it would be able to escape from these bindings "unilaterally" under the renegotiation rules of GATT (i.e., there would be no world-price effects for its trading partners to reciprocate against, as it raises its tariff to achieve its preferred local price for the given world price). That truly small countries are thus consigned in GATT to their unilateral tariff choices is, of course, consistent with efficiency—by definition, a small country cannot engage in inefficient cost-shifting—provided that the governments of all "large" countries negotiate to their politically optimal tariffs. See chapter 11, and especially note 2 to chapter 11, for further discussion concerning the existence of small countries and their treatment in GATT.

5   MFN

Does the MFN rule assist governments as they attempt to escape from a terms-of-trade-driven Prisoners' Dilemma? In this chapter we consider this question. We begin with a general discussion of MFN in GATT, and in particular of the difficulty in providing a formal rationale for MFN in bargaining environments. We then extend our general equilibrium modeling framework to allow for multiple countries, and we argue that the case for MFN in GATT can be seen most clearly when it is viewed in the company of GATT's principle of reciprocity.

5.1   MFN in GATT

As the discussion in chapter 3 indicates, MFN is a pillar of the multilateral trading system under GATT, and yet an account of the central benefits of MFN has largely eluded formal analysis. The difficulty in providing a formal rationale for MFN arises from several sources.

On the one hand, the MFN rule carries with it potential costs associated with "free riding" on the bargaining outcomes of others, and these costs have been emphasized since the work of Viner (1924, 1931, 1936). The free-rider effects associated with MFN are formalized in a bargaining framework by Caplin and Krishna (1988), who highlight the externality that MFN creates across bargaining pairs and argue that this ability to free ride can prevent governments from reaching the efficiency frontier. Ludema (1991) extends the analysis to allow each country the subsequent ability to approve or disapprove any agreement negotiated by its government before the agreement can come into force. This ratification process reduces the ability of any government to free ride on the agreements of others via the MFN clause, and so can be seen as a way to minimize the free-rider costs associated with MFN.

Nevertheless, the free-rider issues associated with MFN raise a potentially important cost associated with the adoption of this rule.

On the other hand, the potential benefits of MFN are less easily identified. As we discussed in chapter 3, Hull regarded MFN as beneficial, since it offered a way to "multilateralize" the reciprocal tariff reductions that governments might negotiate bilaterally. The formal validity of Hull's assessment, however, is not obvious. More generally, there is a basic impediment to formalizing the benefits associated with MFN. As Caplin and Krishna (1988, pp. 281–82) note:

> There is a simple observation which illustrates the difficulties in providing a general bargaining-theoretic rationale for MFN. There is a grand utility possibility frontier available to countries using all the commercial trading instruments at their disposal, such as tariffs. If we view the bargaining process as yielding efficient outcomes, as for example with the Nash bargaining solution, then MFN simply limits the tools available to different countries, shifting in the utility possibility frontier. Hence the most positive aspects of MFN can only be illustrated when the bargaining process absent-MFN yields inefficient outcomes.

This observation suggests that any potential benefits of MFN that can serve to counterbalance its free-riding costs can only become apparent in an environment where bargaining inefficiencies already exist in the absence of MFN.

What, then, is the source of the bargaining inefficiency which the MFN rule could correct? There are a number of possible sources which might be considered.[1] We identify in this chapter two institutional

---

1. The economics literature has recently considered several sources of inefficiency which MFN may help to correct. We mention here three possibilities. First, McCalman (2002) explores the possible efficiency-enhancing role of MFN in a bargaining setting where private information prevents countries from reaching efficient outcomes in the absence of MFN. Second, Choi (1995) considers the role that MFN may play as a commitment device that promotes greater investment, in a strategic trade-policy game between an importing government and foreign exporting firms who make investment decisions. Third, in Bagwell and Staiger (1999b), we examine the implications of MFN when governments have heterogeneous discount factors and enforcement considerations prevent them from reaching the efficiency frontier. We consider this model further in section 7.3. We note finally that Maggi (1999) identifies an efficiency gain associated with multilateral bargaining, as compared to a collection of bilateral bargains, in a setting where each bilateral trade relationship is separable from every other so that there are no externalities across different trading pairs. This inefficiency can arise if bilateral trades are imbalanced and governments have limited trade-policy instruments, but it reflects an inefficiency that derives from the absence of multilateral bargaining rather than the absence of MFN. We consider Maggi's results later in the context of our discussion of enforcement in section 6.3. Horn and Mavroidis (2001) offer an excellent survey of the economics literature that addresses the broader implications of MFN.

sources of bargaining inefficiency that arise under multicountry negotiations when MFN is not imposed. A first source emerges when trade negotiations occur through time and between the governments of many countries, so that there is a possibility of "bilateral opportunism" through discriminatory agreements. We describe how MFN can by itself offer only a partial solution to the bilateral opportunism problem, but we show that MFN in combination with reciprocity eliminates this problem. A second source of bargaining inefficiency arises when governments are permitted to renegotiate their agreements under reciprocity, and discriminatory tariffs are allowed. In this case it is the reciprocity rule itself that is the source of the bargaining inefficiency in discriminatory environments, and we describe how this inefficiency may be eliminated with the addition of the MFN rule. With each of these cases we thus establish that MFN can eliminate a problem when reciprocity is also present, and in this way provide an institutional rationale for MFN in the company of reciprocity. To develop this rationale, we first describe the multicountry general equilibrium model that underlies our discussion. We then proceed as in the previous chapter, considering first trade negotiations under reciprocity and second renegotiation under reciprocity.

5.2   The Multicountry Model

The basic insights can be communicated with the development of a three-country model, in which the home country imports good x from foreign countries *1 and *2 and exports good y to these same countries. To simplify the discussion, we suppose further that the two foreign countries do not trade with one another.[2] The home government is thus the only government that has the opportunity to set discriminatory tariffs across its partners. After developing this model, we define government preferences for the multicountry setting and consider the externalities that arise between governments.

5.2.1   The General Equilibrium Model

We begin with the direct extension of our two-country notation to the multicountry setting. As before, the home local relative price is denoted

2. This is a simple way to ensure that the home government can set discriminatory tariffs against its two foreign trading partners without prohibiting trade with the less-favored partner. A nonzero transport cost for trade between the two foreign countries would achieve the same purpose, but at the expense of complicating somewhat our exposition.

as $p = p_x/p_y$, and similarly we now represent the local relative price in foreign country i as $p^{*i} = p_x^{*i}/p_y^{*i}$ for $i = 1, 2$. The ad valorem tariff that the home government places on imports of x from foreign country i is denoted as t^i, and t^{*i} is likewise the ad valorem tariff levied by the government of foreign country i on imports of y from the home country. The world price for trade between the home country and foreign country i is defined as $p^{wi} \equiv p_x^{*i}/p_y$. This is the ratio of exporter prices for trade between the home country and foreign country i. Next, letting $\tau^i \equiv (1 + t^i)$ and $\tau^{*i} \equiv (1 + t^{*i})$, we may represent local prices in terms of world prices and tariffs by $p = \tau^i p^{wi} \equiv p(\tau^i, p^{wi})$ and $p^{*i} = p^{wi}/\tau^{*i} \equiv p^{*i}(\tau^{*i}, p^{wi})$. Thus, as in the two-country model, local prices are determined once tariffs and the world prices are given. Henceforth we use p to denote the function $p(\tau^i, p^{wi})$ and p^{*i} to denote the function $p^{*i}(\tau^{*i}, p^{wi})$.

Consider now the possibility that the home government selects discriminatory tariffs, in which case the home tariff on imports from foreign country 1 differs from that on imports from foreign country 2, or $\tau^1 \neq \tau^2$. Under discriminatory tariffs there exist two distinct world prices, but the world prices are linked by the requirement of a single home local price:

$$p = \tau^1 p^{w1} = \tau^2 p^{w2}. \tag{5.1}$$

By contrast, the MFN rule requires that the home country levy the same tariff on good x, whether the good emanates from foreign country 1 or 2, meaning that $\tau^1 = \tau^2$. Under MFN tariffs a single world price therefore arises: $p^{w1} = p^{w2} \equiv p^w$. Whether or not tariffs are discriminatory, the world price p^{wi} represents foreign country i's terms of trade. Likewise we may understand $1/p^{wi}$ as the home country's *bilateral* terms of trade with foreign partner i. The home country, however, has multiple trading partners, and the representation of its overall *multilateral* terms of trade is more complex, as we discuss below.

As in the two-country model, when the local and world prices are given, the various economic quantities (production, consumption, tariff revenue, imports, exports) are all determined. In fact, for each foreign country i, the derivation of these quantities proceeds precisely as in the two-country model, with each quantity ultimately being a function of the local price p^{*i} and the terms of trade p^{wi}. The home country, however, may experience different bilateral terms of trade with its different partners, and this complicates somewhat the expression of domestic quantities. This complication does not affect the determination of domestic production (which remains a function of the home local price p), and it likewise does not alter the expression of domestic consumption (which remains a function of the home local price p and domestic tariff revenue R). Rather, the additional complexity is associated with the representation of domestic tariff revenue R itself. In light of the possibility of discriminatory tariffs, domestic tariff revenue depends on both the total volume of x imported by the domestic country and the *composition* of this given volume across the foreign trading partners.

Domestic tariff revenue again can be expressed as a function of the local home price and the domestic country's (multilateral) terms of trade, once the latter has been appropriately defined for the multicountry setting. As might be expected, the domestic country's multilateral terms of trade can be defined as a function of the trade-weighted average of the bilateral terms of trade. To see this, we first define bilateral trade shares by

$$s^{*i}\left(p^{*1}, p^{*2}, p^{w1}, p^{w2}\right) \equiv \frac{E^{*i}\left(p^{*i}, p^{wi}\right)}{\sum_{j=1,2} E^{*j}\left(p^{*j}, p^{wj}\right)}, \tag{5.2}$$

where $E^{*i}(p^{*i}, p^{wi})$ is the export supply function for foreign country i. With this, we next define the domestic country's *multilateral terms of trade* by the trade-weighted average of the bilateral world prices:[3]

$$T(p^{*1}, p^{*2}, p^{w1}, p^{w2}) \equiv \sum_{i=1,2} s^{*i}\left(p^{*1}, p^{*2}, p^{w1}, p^{w2}\right) \cdot p^{wi}. \tag{5.3}$$

As we establish in Bagwell and Staiger (1999a, 2000a) and confirm in appendix B.1, using this definition, domestic tariff revenue can be represented as $R(p, T)$, and correspondingly each domestic quantity can be expressed ultimately as a function of the local price p and the multilateral terms of trade T. Thus the derivation of domestic quantities follows as in the two-country model, once the domestic terms of trade is appropriately defined for the multicountry setting (i.e., once we replace p^w with T).

Using (5.1) and (5.3), we already may identify an important relationship between the MFN rule and the multilateral terms of trade. In particular, if the home government adopts an MFN-tariff policy, then it follows that $T = p^{wi} \equiv p^w$. The multilateral terms of trade under

---

3. In fact T is a measure of the reciprocal of domestic terms of trade: an improvement in the domestic terms of trade corresponds to a lower value for T.

MFN is thus given by the single world price that then prevails. On the other hand, under a discriminatory tariff policy, there are two world prices, and so $T \neq p^{wi}$ for all i. As we discuss further below, this means that the multilateral terms-of-trade externality then fundamentally derives from the bilateral terms of trade *and* the respective export shares.

We are now prepared to define the trade balance and market-clearing conditions. With the natural modifications in notation, it can be verified that, for any world prices, home and foreign budget constraints imply that trade is balanced, so that[4]

$$T(p^{*1}, p^{*2}, p^{w1}, p^{w2}) \cdot M(p, T(p^{*1}, p^{*2}, p^{w1}, p^{w2}))$$
$$= E(p, T(p^{*1}, p^{*2}, p^{w1}, p^{w2})) \tag{5.4}$$

and

$$M^{*i}(p^{*i}, p^{wi}) = p^{wi} E^{*i}(p^{*i}, p^{wi}), \quad i = 1, 2. \tag{5.5}$$

Finally, for given domestic and foreign tariffs, $\tau \equiv \{\tau^1, \tau^2, \tau^{*1}, \tau^{*2}\}$, the market-clearing world prices, $\tilde{p}^{w1}(\tau)$ and $\tilde{p}^{w2}(\tau)$, are determined by the linkage condition (5.1) in combination with the market-clearing requirement for good x:

$$M(p, T(p^{*1}, p^{*2}, \tilde{p}^{w1}, \tilde{p}^{w2})) = \sum_{i=1,2} E^{*i}(p^{*i}, \tilde{p}^{wi}). \tag{5.6}$$

Market clearing in good y is then assured by (5.4), (5.5), and (5.6). Summarizing, with their selections of tariffs, governments determine the equilibrium world prices, and the tariffs and world prices together then imply equilibrium values for all local prices and quantities.

We assume that the prices so determined depend on tariffs in the "standard" manner. As in the two-country model, we assume that if foreign country i confronts a higher tariff on its exports (i.e., if τ^i increases) or if it lowers its own tariff (i.e., if τ^{*i} decreases), then it experiences a reduction in its terms of trade (i.e., $\tilde{p}^{wi}$ decreases). We assume as well that foreign country i experiences a terms-of-trade gain (i.e., $\tilde{p}^{wi}$ increases) whenever the other two countries raise tariffs on one another (i.e., whenever τ^j increases or τ^{*j} increases). Intuitively, if the home government taxes more heavily the exports of foreign country j, then the

---

4. To derive the home-country balanced trade condition (5.4), we adopt the convention when defining tariff revenue for any world prices that the share of multilateral imports M coming from foreign country i is given by s^{*i}.

home demand for exports from foreign country i is increased, resulting in a terms-of-trade gain for foreign country i. Likewise, if foreign country j were to raise its import tariff on exports from the home country, then those exports would be diverted to foreign country i, which would enjoy a lower price on the home export and thus a terms-of-trade gain. Finally, if the home government selects among MFN tariffs, then an increase in the home tariff amounts to a simultaneous increase in the tariff applied to the exports of both foreign countries. In this case, we assume that the direct effect of a higher tariff applied to one's own exports dominates, which is to say that each foreign country experiences a terms-of-trade loss.

5.2.2 Government Preferences

We next extend the representation of government preferences to the multicountry setting. As before, we allow for a general representation. The objectives of the home and foreign governments are respectively given as $W(p, T)$ and $W^{*i}(p^{*i}, \tilde{p}^{wi})$, where all prices and terms of trade are evaluated at their market-clearing levels. The key assumption is again that, with local prices held fixed, each government strictly prefers an improvement in its terms of trade:

$$W_T(p, T) < 0 \quad \text{and} \quad W^{*i}_{\tilde{p}^{wi}}(p^{*i}, \tilde{p}^{wi}) > 0. \tag{5.7}$$

In other words, each government prefers an international redistribution in income from other countries to its own country.[5]

The multicountry model admits an interesting pattern of externalities. Consider first the government of foreign country i. This government is affected by the tariffs of the home country and foreign country j, but, as in the two-country model, in each case the tariff externality travels through the associated world price $\tilde{p}^{wi}$. The home government's situation is more novel. As a general matter, the effect of foreign tariffs

---

5. This assumption ensures a welfare gain when the terms of trade are improved and the local price is held fixed. Later in our discussion we rely on a slightly stronger assumption: the initial tariffs from which negotiated adjustments are made are positioned so that government welfare rises (falls) whenever a single tariff is changed that induces for this government a terms-of-trade gain (loss). A formal statement of this assumption is provided in appendix B.2. This assumption simplifies the exposition, and it ensures that the welfare effect of a change in any particular tariff is always consistent with the terms-of-trade implications of this change. We thereby eliminate the possibility that a government would be so desirous of a local-price change that it would gain even if this change came about from a single policy adjustment (e.g., an increase in a trading partner's tariff) that resulted in a terms-of-trade loss.

on home-government welfare travels through the multilateral terms of trade T. But, as we have seen, this multilateral measure may be further decomposed into world-price and foreign-local-price (i.e., export share) influences, suggesting a potentially more complicated underlying pattern of externalities.

In particular, if the home government adopts discriminatory tariffs, then the externalities that are associated with foreign tariff choices travel through world prices *and* foreign local prices (and thereby through T). Intuitively, imagine that the government of the home country selects a tariff that is higher on imports from foreign country 1. Then the government of the home country is affected by the composition of the trade volume across its foreign trading partners: all else equal, the government of the home country would prefer that more of a fixed total trade volume come from foreign country 1, on which it places the highest tariff. But the respective export shares from foreign countries 1 and 2 are determined (in part) by the local prices in these countries, and so under discriminatory tariffs both world- and foreign-local-price externalities arise. On the other hand, if the government of the home country selects among MFN tariffs, then $T = p^{wi} \equiv p^w$, and so the foreign-local-price externality is removed. Intuitively, under nondiscriminatory tariffs the home government no longer has a direct interest in the composition of trade volume, and so the welfare of this government is no longer separately affected by foreign local prices. Therefore the principle of nondiscrimination ensures that the *only* externality that arises between governments is the world-price externality.

At a broad level, a benefit of the MFN rule within the GATT system now may be anticipated, when it is recalled that the principle of reciprocity works to neutralize the world-price externality. The two principles therefore may be generally interpreted to embody efficiency-enhancing properties.[6] In the remainder of this chapter we discuss the specific representations of this general interpretation that arise when governments negotiate and renegotiate trade agreements, respectively.

---

6. This rationale for the principle of nondiscrimination appears to be distinct from the "multilateralization" benefits that Hull associated with this principle. As Culbert (1987) discusses, Hull also attached to the principle of nondiscrimination wider benefits, including a reduction in the risk of war. Similar sentiments can be found as well in the League of Nations (1942) report. See also Pomfret (1997).

5.3   MFN, Reciprocity, and Trade Negotiations

With the multicountry model now in place, we return to consider the potential benefits of MFN treatment in multicountry negotiations. As the discussion above indicates, MFN restricts the instruments that governments may use in the negotiation of trade agreements, and so the potential benefits of MFN are most apparent if some bargaining inefficiency arises in its absence. Here we illustrate a multicountry bargaining inefficiency: two governments may conduct a bilateral negotiation in which they gain by appropriating welfare from the nonparticipating third government. We argue that this "bilateral opportunism" problem is potentially significant, we show that the problem is only partially addressed when bilateral negotiations must respect the MFN rule, and we observe as well that the principle of reciprocity cannot by itself address the problem. We show, however, that together the principles of nondiscrimination and reciprocity provide a valuable first line of defense against such "opportunistic" bilateral trade agreements. We also discuss the additional second line of defense that is provided under GATT's Article XXIII by the potential to bring a nonviolation nullification-or-impairment complaint. Finally, we return briefly to consider the free-rider problem associated with MFN in this setting.

Our discussion begins with the observation that GATT negotiations occur through time and between the governments of various countries. Horn and Mavroidis (2001, p. 271) describe the GATT/WTO bargaining process in this way:[7]

In the WTO, negotiations mainly take place between subsets of Member countries. Sometimes, this is "officially sanctioned," as in the case of Principal Supplier negotiations. However, also in seemingly multilateral negotiations, "actual" negotiations occur between a very limited number of countries.

This negotiation process raises a natural concern: a government may worry that the value of concessions that it wins today may be eroded in a future bilateral negotiation to which it is not party. This worry, in turn, may feed back to affect current negotiations. For example, if governments suspect that current market-access relations may be vulnerable to opportunistic bilateral agreements in the future, then they may well exchange concessions today with trepidation. As a general matter, then, the potential for opportunistic bilateral agreements suggests a

---

7. See also Hoekman and Kostecki (1995, pp. 56–83).

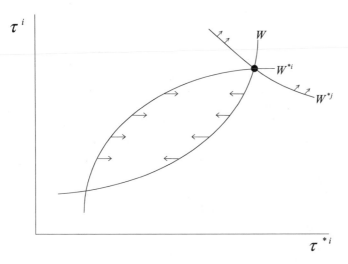

Figure 5.1

bargaining inefficiency that negotiation rules such as MFN might remedy.

Two questions are suggested. First, how significant is the potential for bilateral opportunism, anyway? Second, if there is indeed significant potential, can the key GATT rules in fact play an efficiency-enhancing role by protecting the welfare of nonparticipating governments?

5.3.1 Significance

To get a feel for the potential significance of the problem, let us suppose that the three governments have reached an efficient trade agreement, and let us consider whether the home government and the government of foreign country i can then negotiate a bilateral trade agreement in which they each gain. Given that the initial arrangement is efficient, the two negotiating governments can gain only if they reach a bilateral agreement that is opportunistic (i.e., that extracts welfare from the nonparticipating foreign government j). With the assumption of an initial efficient agreement, we are thus able to gain easily a rough sense of the general potential for bilateral opportunism.

As we show in Bagwell and Staiger (2000a) and confirm in appendix B.2, any point on the efficiency frontier must take the form that is illustrated in figure 5.1. This figure depicts the iso-welfare curves of the three governments, where the axes represent the negotiated tariffs τ^i and τ^{*i} that the home government and the government of foreign country i respectively apply to each other's exports. Notice that the iso-welfare curve for the (nonparticipating) government of foreign country j is downward sloping, since this government gains when either of the two negotiating governments raises the tariff that it applies to the exports of the other.[8] The iso-welfare curve for each negotiating government, however, is upward sloping, indicating that each negotiating government can maintain indifference only if the benefit of its own tariff increase is balanced against the cost of a tariff increase from its partner.

The most important lesson from the figure concerns the location of the lens within which the negotiating governments can both gain. The lens lies below the iso-welfare curve of the government of foreign country j.[9] The negotiating governments thus enter this lens by *reducing* the tariffs that they apply to one another, and the welfare gains that they enjoy reflect directly the welfare that they extract from the non-participating government of foreign country j, whose country then experiences a terms-of-trade loss. In fact, as every efficient tariff vector must generate a lens such as that depicted in figure 5.1, *every* efficient tariff vector is vulnerable to bilateral opportunism through "concession erosion" in this sense. While a complete analysis would fully describe the dynamic process through which governments pick negotiation partners (form coalitions), the discussion presented here strongly suggests an answer to our first question: the potential for bilateral opportunism appears quite significant.

5.3.2 MFN and Reciprocity
We turn now to our second question and consider whether the key GATT rules can play an efficiency-enhancing role. Such a role would

---

8. In figure 5.1 the iso-welfare curve for the government of foreign country j can also be described as an iso-$\tilde{p}^{wj}$ curve. This is because, with its own tariff held fixed, the government of foreign country j is affected by changes in τ^i and τ^{*i} only in so far as these changes affect its terms of trade, $\tilde{p}^{wj}$.

9. To understand the location of the lens, it is instructive to consider the opposite possibility, in which the lens lies above the iso-welfare curve of the government of foreign country j. The negotiating governments could then gain by *raising* their tariffs, but this would generate a terms-of-trade improvement for foreign country j, resulting in a welfare gain for all three governments, in contradiction to the assumption that the initial tariff configuration is efficient. A more subtle possibility is that there is no lens: the iso-welfare curves of the negotiating governments are tangent at the point at which they intersect the iso-welfare curve of the government of foreign country j. As we establish in Bagwell and Staiger (2000a) and confirm in appendix B.2, this arrangement also fails to be efficient, but a more involved alteration of tariffs is now required to produce gains to all three governments.

arise if these rules served to protect the welfare of non-participating governments, so that the value of concessions previously received could not be later eroded through an opportunistic bilateral agreement. It seems intuitive that MFN might play this role. Indeed, after considering the various costs and benefits of the MFN rule, Schwartz and Sykes (1997, p. 62) argue that the main benefit is that it prevents the concession erosion that opportunistic bilateral agreements imply:

> More important, the MFN obligation protects the value of concessions against future erosion through discrimination. If country A receives a concession from country B and is not entitled to MFN treatment from B, then the value of the concession can be undermined if country B later makes an even better concession to country C on the same goods (or close substitutes). Faced with this uncertainty, country A would offer less for the concession in the first place (as would country B for the reciprocal concession), and fewer valuable deals would be struck.

While it is clear that MFN provides some protection in this regard, we argue next that MFN on its own does not fully eliminate the potential for opportunistic bilateral agreements.

To establish this point, we imagine that the three governments have previously negotiated to some initial tariff configuration. The home tariffs satisfy the MFN rule, but we do not assume that this tariff configuration is necessarily efficient (even within the MFN class). We then consider whether the home government and the government of foreign country i can subsequently liberalize tariffs through a bilateral agreement, in a manner that *reduces* the welfare of the government of foreign country j, even though this government receives the home-country tariff reduction on an MFN basis and does not alter its own tariff. To see that this is possible, observe that the government of foreign country j is affected as a nonparticipant by the bilateral agreement only through any consequent change in its terms of trade. On the one hand, the government of foreign country j is pleased to experience a reduction in the MFN tariff of the home government, since this benefits its exporters and correspondingly improves its terms of trade. On the other hand, though, the government of foreign country j is distressed by the reduction in the tariff of foreign country i, since this diverts home-country exports away from foreign country j, harming foreign country j's consumers and diminishing its terms of trade. Clearly, if the reduction in foreign country i's tariff is large in comparison to the MFN tariff reduction of the home country, then the government of foreign country j

experiences an overall terms-of-trade loss and thus a reduction in welfare.[10]

As this discussion clarifies, the bilateral opportunism problem remains, so long as the rules of negotiation allow that the governments of the home country and foreign country i may enter into a bilateral agreement in which they alter foreign country j's terms of trade, $\tilde{p}^{wj}$. Taking this general perspective, MFN fails to protect nonparticipant welfare for a simple reason: while MFN ensures a single world price, $\tilde{p}^w \equiv \tilde{p}^{wi} = \tilde{p}^{wj}$, it does not *fix* that world price. In a similar manner, it can be demonstrated that reciprocity alone also fails to protect nonparticipant welfare. If the rules of negotiation restrain the home government and the government of foreign country i to consider only bilateral agreements that satisfy the principle of reciprocity, then, as in the two-country model of chapter 4, we may derive that such an agreement preserves the terms of trade between the negotiating partners, $\tilde{p}^{wi}$.[11] This, however, is not the same thing as fixing the nonparticipant's terms of trade, $\tilde{p}^{wj}$.

Suppose, though, that MFN and reciprocity are *both* required. In this case MFN ensures a single world price, while reciprocity guarantees that this world price is fixed. Together, MFN and reciprocity therefore ensure that the nonparticipant's terms of trade cannot be altered. It follows that the welfare of the nonparticipant government is not affected—for better or worse—by any bilateral agreement that strictly respects the principles of MFN and reciprocity.

In summary, this discussion illustrates a potential benefit to the MFN rule. In the absence of this rule, the bargaining inefficiency that is associated with bilateral opportunism is potentially significant in scope.

---

10. It may be wondered if the government of foreign country i would be willing to participate in such a bilateral agreement. Under the MFN rule the two foreign countries share the same terms of trade, and so a bilateral agreement can extract welfare from foreign country j only if it also reduces the terms of trade for foreign country i. In Bagwell and Staiger (2000a) we examine this issue, showing that the negotiating partners can find a bilateral agreement that reduces tariffs under which they both gain at the expense of the nonparticipating government, while still respecting the MFN rule, if the government of foreign country i would prefer a greater trade volume at the initial world price. In this case the bilateral agreement results in a change in tariffs that compensates the government of foreign country i for its terms-of-trade loss with a less trade-restrictive local price. (Note that this finding is consistent with the assumption presented in note 5 to chapter 5, since the bilateral agreement results in a change in two tariffs.)

11. This can be seen directly with reference to (5.5), from which it is clear that any agreement that results in an equal increase in the value of imports and exports for foreign country i preserves this country's terms of trade.

Further this problem is only partially addressed when bilateral negotiations must respect the MFN rule, and neither can the principle of
reciprocity by itself fully address the problem. But when the rules of
negotiation are strengthened to require that bilateral agreements honor
both MFN and reciprocity, the bilateral opportunism problem is eliminated. Under these rules governments can then negotiate without
fear of future bilateral opportunism and the consequent erosion in
concession value.

5.3.3   Nonviolation Nullification-or-Impairment Complaints

Before proceeding, we pause and consider further the treatment of
bilateral opportunism concerns within GATT. Our focus here is on the
potential role for nonviolation nullification-or-impairment complaints,
as allowed under GATT Article XXIII, in limiting the scope for opportunism. More generally, we interpret MFN, reciprocity, and Article
XXIII as offering multiple levels of defense in GATT practice against
opportunistic actions.

As we discussed in chapter 3, when a government takes an action
that nullifies or impairs a previous concession made to some trading
partner, that partner has a potentially legitimate basis from which
to file a complaint, even if no violation of GATT rules is alleged.
The logical foundation for such a "nonviolation" nullification-or-
impairment complaint is well articulated in a general statement
offered by a GATT panel (constituted for the oilseeds case, and as quoted
in Trebilcock and Howse, 1999, p. 80):

The idea underlying [nonviolation nullification or impairment] is that the
improved competitive opportunities that can legitimately be expected from a
tariff concession can be frustrated not only by measures proscribed by the
General Agreement but also by measures consistent with that Agreement. In
order to encourage contracting parties to make tariff concessions they must
therefore be given a right of redress when a reciprocal concession is impaired
by another contracting party as a result of the application of any measure,
whether or not it conflicts with the General Agreement.

As Petersmann (1997) details, in practice, the three conditions established under GATT Article XXIII for a successful nonviolation complaint are that (1) a reciprocal concession was negotiated between two
partners; (2) a subsequent action was taken by one government, which,
though consistent with GATT articles, adversely affected the market
access afforded to its partner; and (3) this action could not have been
reasonably anticipated by the partner at the time of the negotiation of

the original tariff concession. There are a variety of actions that have instigated complaints, including domestic subsidies, product re-classifications, and bilateral trade negotiations with other partners.[12]

In this context, the discussion here suggests that the principles of nondiscrimination and reciprocity together offer a valuable first line of defense against the potential for opportunistic bilateral agreements. These principles protect a government from a terms-of-trade loss that might otherwise be implied by a bilateral agreement between other governments. Given the relationship (see section 2.1.3) between a country's terms of trade and its access to a trading partner's market, we may similarly conclude that nondiscrimination and reciprocity together serve to protect a nonparticipant's previously negotiated market-access commitments. Accordingly the considerable reliance that GATT places upon these principles may serve to reduce the number of valid nonviolation complaints and ease the judicial burden of the dispute settlement procedures. At the same time, while these principles are prominent in GATT practice, they are not always applied with rigid precision. The ability of governments to bring nonviolation nullification-or-impairment complaints can thus serve an important role as a second line of defense against the bilateral opportunism problem.[13] It is even possible that the ability to bring nonviolation nullification-or-impairment complaints *induces* governments to negotiate in accordance with reciprocity in order to avoid being the target of such complaints.[14]

At a broader level, the notion that explicit GATT rules serve as a primary defense against the erosion of concessions, and that recourse to nonviolation complaints provides a secondary backup procedure, is well reflected in the writings of GATT legal scholars. For example, Petersmann (1997, p. 136) observes that ". . . the function of most GATT rules (such as Articles I–III and XI) is to establish conditions of competition and to protect trading opportunities . . . ," and then concludes

---

12. Examples of bilateral agreements that have led to nonviolation nullification-or-impairment complaints are (1) the US complaint regarding tariff preferences negotiated by the EC on citrus products from certain Mediterranean countries, and (2) the EC complaint regarding aspects of the bilateral agreement between the United States and Japan concerning trade in semiconductor products.

13. Furthermore, as we establish in Bagwell and Staiger (2000a) and confirm in appendix B.3, with multiple goods, there can arise a limited potential for opportunistic bilateral agreements, even when MFN and reciprocity are rigidly applied. This provides a further basis from which to view nonviolation nullification-or-impairment complaints as a valuable second line of defense.

14. This possibility is established formally in Bagwell and Staiger (2000b).

his review of the 14 dispute settlement reports examining nonviolation complaints as follows: ". . . These panel reports illustrated that the nonviolation complaints can strengthen the function of GATT, as well as of the WTO, as a negotiating forum by offering additional safeguards against the impairment of . . . market access commitments through unforeseen subsequent policy measures that are not prohibited by GATT/WTO law." (Petersmann 1997, p. 171).

We note in particular that preferential trading agreements, which are allowed as an exception to MFN under Article XXIV, represent a possible route to opportunistic bilateral agreements. This suggests the possibility of an enhanced role for nonviolation complaints following preferential trading agreements. We return to this suggestion in chapter 7.

5.3.4   The Free-Rider Problem

Thus far we have put aside any discussion of the "free-riding" costs often associated with MFN, emphasizing instead the potentially beneficial role played by MFN in helping to solve the bilateral opportunism problem. We have observed that the benefits accruing to MFN as a potential solution to the bilateral opportunism problem are enhanced—and that this problem is in fact only fully eliminated—when MFN is joined with the principle of reciprocity. We now make a related observation: the potential for third countries to free-ride on the MFN tariff cuts negotiated by others is in fact eliminated when those negotiations proceed in accordance with the principle of reciprocity.[15] This is because, as we have observed above, the nonparticipating government is unaffected when a bilateral agreement occurs that respects both MFN and reciprocity.

This observation reflects a broader point. Under MFN the balance of tariff concessions negotiated between countries is the key factor in determining how these negotiations affect nonparticipants. In this environment "free-riders" are simply third countries that stand to gain from the outcome of negotiations between others when the negotiated balance of tariff concessions moves in their favor, and reciprocity simply reflects a balance of tariff concessions that leaves third countries unaffected. But when viewed from this perspective, it is apparent that negotiating parties would have no reason to actually choose a

---

15. In section 7.3, we consider a further potential free-rider cost of MFN that may appear when the enforcement of trade agreements is considered.

om a grant to future negotiating partners of additional market
"for free"—why should these early negotiating partners stop
Vhy not configure the balance of negotiated tariff concessions
ɔ *diminish* the market access that future negotiating partners
tically enjoy, and thereby use early negotiations as a tool for
ening future bargaining power? Unlike the case of bilateral
ınism, nonviolation claims by third countries do not apply in
:umstance, since these third countries have not yet negotiated
ement, and so the general right to bring such claims cannot stop
:gotiating partners from manipulating the balance of negotiated
ɔncessions in this way.

:t the incentive of early negotiating partners to manipulate the
: of tariff concessions in this way represents a potential cost of
ıing under MFN. In particular, this incentive can give rise to
:nt "foot-dragging," whereby a government offers little in the
trade liberalization to early negotiating partners, in order to
e its bargaining position with later negotiating partners.[16] In
through this maneuver a government can commit to tariff-
agreements with its early negotiating partners that reduce the
access available to nonparticipants, making these nonpartici-
specially eager to reach agreement when they later become parts. The government thereby strengthens its bargaining position
re negotiations, at the cost of precluding bargaining outcomes
: efficient on a multilateral scale.

illustrates an important point: it is not necessarily the potential
-riders per se that leads to bargaining inefficiencies under MFN.
the potential for free riders simply indicates that there exist
ticipants that can be affected by the balance of tariff concessions
to in a given negotiation. The source of the inefficiency can then
ed to the efforts of early negotiators to structure the balance of
ɔncessions in their early agreements so as to position themselves
ıre negotiations with nonparticipants that are affected by this
:.

n viewed in this way, a possible solution to the inefficiency asso-
with the potential for free-riders under MFN is suggested:

---

point is shown formally in Bagwell and Staiger (2000b). Limao (2001) explores
idea. He shows that foot-dragging may occur under MFN when a government
enhance its bargaining position with regard to the nontrade policies of a subse-
gotiating partner.

balance of tariff concessions that left third p
could themselves benefit by instead choosin
(and presumably hurt) third parties. So it :
further whether there are reasons that gover
negotiate according to reciprocity. In this re{
tunism problem and the free-rider problem
differences.

As described above, the bilateral opportu
situation in which the home government joi
of foreign country i to "steal backward" fre
reached with the government of foreign cc
element is reflected, for example, in the quot
and Sykes (1997). We have observed that the a
of foreign country j to bring a nonviolation nul
complaint against the home government, sh
ment subsequently engage in bilateral opport
ment of foreign country i, can in principle
negotiations between the home government
foreign country i to conform to reciprocity. H
bilateral opportunism, the nonviolation nul
provisions of GATT may provide the ultime
problem.

But the free-rider problem, as it is usually d
looking" problem wherein, as the result of tai
tions between two governments, a third count
the additional market access extended to it und
third country some market access "for free," i
to extract concessions from the government o:
negotiations with it. For example, in describin
US Reciprocal Trade Agreements Program,
observes:

A serious problem is encountered in a program
favored-nation treatment with a bilateral tariff barg
example, we should grant, in agreements with a few
concessions upon our leading imports from them a
cessions to other nations, our bargaining power for
be greatly reduced.

While early negotiations could proceed accordi
thereby avoid the reduction in future bargaini

result
access
there?
so as
autom
*streng
oppor
this ci
an agr
early i
tariff i

In f
balan
barga
ineffic
way c
enhar
effect,
cuttin
mark
pants
ticipa
in fut
that a

Thi
for fro
Rathe
nonpe
agree
be tre
tariff
for fu
balan

Wh
ciatec

16. Th
a relat
seeks
quent

provide ample opportunities for renegotiation. More specifically, if
early negotiating partners have the ability to renegotiate their tariffs in
the event that later negotiations with other partners fail to reach agreement, then the credible impact of early negotiations on bargaining
power for future negotiations is diminished, and could in principle
even be eliminated. In this case early negotiating partners have no
reason to manipulate the balance of their tariff concessions to position
themselves for future negotiations with other partners, and this source
of bargaining inefficiency can be eliminated. To some extent the opportunities for renegotiation provided in GATT, and described in chapter
3, may help to play this role.[17]

5.4 MFN, Reciprocity and Renegotiation

In chapter 4, using a two-country model, we argued that the potential
to renegotiate subject to reciprocity directs the negotiation outcome
toward the particular point on the efficiency frontier at which governments select their politically optimal tariffs. We now reconsider the
implications of renegotiation under reciprocity in the context of our
multicountry model. We argue that a bargaining inefficiency is assured
when GATT's reciprocity rule is followed and discriminatory tariffs are
used. But we argue that this inefficiency can be prevented if the home
government's tariffs are nondiscriminatory. In this way GATT's pillars
of reciprocity and MFN again may be seen as complementary principles that permit governments to achieve efficient outcomes in a multicountry setting.

We begin by considering the properties of politically optimal tariffs
in the presence of multiple countries. For the multicountry model a
configuration of tariffs $\{\tau^1, \tau^2, \tau^{*1}, \tau^{*2}\}$ is *politically optimal* if $W_p = W_{p^{*i}}^{*i}$
$= 0$ for $i = 1, 2$. In other words, the tariff configuration is politically
optimal if each government achieves its preferred local price, when its
terms of trade are fixed. If the home government is allowed to choose
discriminatory tariffs ($\tau^1 \neq \tau^2$), then the property of political optimality
amounts to three requirements (one for each country) that are placed

---

17. More formally, early negotiating partners may reach an agreement among themselves that is in part motivated by the effect of that agreement on the "disagreement"
welfare (i.e., the threat point) for a later negotiator. This strategic effect can introduce a
bargaining inefficiency, but this effect is eliminated if the initial agreement can be renegotiated in the event that later negotiations fail. For a model in which renegotiation provisions can play this role, see Bagwell and Staiger (2000b).

on four tariffs.[18] In the multicountry model there are thus many politically optimal tariffs. But, if the tariffs of the home government must satisfy the MFN rule ($\tau^1 = \tau^2$), then there are only three tariffs to consider, and the model thus admits a unique configuration of *politically optimal MFN tariffs*.

We now recall that there are two fundamental channels through which foreign government i's tariff policy (τ^{*i}) may alter the home country's multilateral terms of trade (T) and thereby impose an externality upon the welfare of the home government. First, the foreign tariff selection affects the home government through the induced change in the bilateral terms of trade ($\tilde{p}^{wi}$). Second, when the home government uses a discriminatory tariff policy, it cares as well about the composition of its trade volume across its foreign trading partners. Under discriminatory home tariffs the tariff policy selected by the government of foreign country i can therefore also affect home-government welfare by altering the foreign local price (p^{*i}) and thus changing the export share that emanates from this country.

As we establish in Bagwell and Staiger (1999a) and confirm in appendix B.2, politically optimal tariffs are efficient if and only if the MFN rule is also satisfied. Drawing on the arguments developed in chapter 2, it is readily argued that politically optimal MFN tariffs are efficient in the multicountry setting. The underlying idea is now familiar. Under MFN the only externality between governments arises through the (single) world price, and governments are not motivated by world-price movements when they select politically optimal tariffs. A more surprising finding concerns the necessity of MFN tariffs: politically optimal tariffs are efficient *only if* they also conform to MFN. The bottom line then is that the politically optimal MFN tariffs are efficient and all other politically optimal tariffs are not.

Why are politically optimal tariffs efficient only if they satisfy MFN? Suppose that the governments adopt politically optimal tariffs and that the home-country tariffs violate MFN, with the home government placing a higher tariff on exports from foreign country 1. The home government could then suggest that, if the government of foreign country 1 would slightly lower its tariff, then the home government would in return adjust both of its tariffs downward slightly, in a

---

18. More generally, if the home country government trades with N foreign countries and can set discriminatory tariffs, then the property of political optimality amounts to $N + 1$ requirements that are placed on $2N$ tariffs.

manner that would leave both world prices unchanged. The government of foreign country 2 would be indifferent to these adjustments, since it does not change its own tariff and the combination of tariff adjustments maintains its original terms of trade. The government of foreign country 1 also experiences no change in its terms of trade; however, since this government adjusts its own tariff downward, it experiences a change in its local price. This local-price change does not result in a (first-order) welfare loss for the government of foreign country 1, though, since under political optimality this government begins with its preferred local price ($W_{p^{*1}}^{*1} = 0$). The suggested tariff adjustments thus leave unaltered the welfares of both foreign governments.[19]

The remaining step is to establish that the suggested tariff adjustments generate a first-order welfare gain for the home government. Such a gain cannot derive from a consequent change in the home local price, since under political optimality the home government begins with its preferred local price ($W_p = 0$). A first-order welfare gain for the home government therefore occurs if and only if the suggested tariff adjustments improve the home country's multilateral terms of trade. How could this happen? By construction, neither world price changes. Remember, though, that the tariff adjustments cause a local-price change in foreign country 1 that induces this country to trade a greater volume. The home government's multilateral terms of trade (T) are thus improved, since a greater share of trade now emanates from the partner on whom it places a higher tariff. As a consequence, when the home country uses discriminatory tariffs, politically optimal tariffs can be improved upon and are thus inefficient.

At an intuitive level it can now be understood that an efficient trade agreement in which the home government uses discriminatory tariffs cannot be implemented when governments are allowed to renegotiate under reciprocity.[20] Building on the intuition developed in the two-country model of section 4.3, it may be shown that when governments can renegotiate under reciprocity, at least one government obtains its

---

19. These suggested tariff adjustments would, in fact, cause a second-order welfare loss for the government of foreign country 1. As we show in appendix B.2, such losses can be eliminated under a modified set of tariff adjustments.

20. The argument that we present here is intuitive in nature, as the formal analysis is somewhat involved. The interested reader is referred to Bagwell and Staiger (1999a), where we consider a multilateral negotiation game and formalize this point (as well as those that follow).

preferred local price. If we require as well that the eventual outcome is efficient, then the fact that one government achieves its preferred local price implies that the other governments must as well.[21] Therefore, if an efficient outcome is to emerge when governments have the ability to renegotiate under reciprocity, then the outcome must be politically optimal. But, as the preceding discussion establishes, a politically optimal outcome is *not* efficient when home tariffs are discriminatory. When governments can renegotiate under reciprocity, a bargaining inefficiency is therefore implied, unless the home government selects MFN tariffs.

At the same time there does exist an efficient trade agreement in which the home government uses MFN tariffs that can be implemented when governments are allowed to renegotiate under reciprocity. Intuitively, when home tariffs conform to MFN, the multicountry model behaves like the two-country model, with all externalities channeled through the world price. Recalling the two-country discussion of reciprocity and renegotiation of section 4.3, it is thus not surprising that an efficient and nondiscriminatory trade outcome—namely the politically optimal MFN tariffs—can be implemented under reciprocity.

5.5   MFN and the Terms-of-Trade Theory: A Summary

We may summarize our discussion of MFN to this point as follows. In a multicountry setting the MFN rule ensures that the world-price externality is the only trade-policy externality that arises between trading partners. The potential benefit of the nondiscrimination principle within the GATT system is then apparent when it is recalled that the principle of reciprocity works to neutralize the world-price externality. Together, the two principles thus may be interpreted to embody efficiency-enhancing properties. In this chapter we developed two specific representations of this general interpretation. Our discussion indicated that the (politically augmented) terms-of-trade theory offers an interpretation both of the central problem that GATT is designed to solve and of the manner in which the pillars of the GATT framework assist governments in achieving a solution to this problem.

---

21. For the two-country confirmation of this point, see note 12 to chapter 4. We show in Bagwell and Staiger (2000a) that this point requires some slight modification when the home government's tariffs are restricted to satisfy the MFN rule and when efficiency is evaluated with respect to this restrictive class of instruments.

Before continuing, we pause briefly to speculate on the broader importance of MFN as a rule that guides governments toward a particular set of efficient tariffs: the politically optimal MFN tariffs. As we discussed in section 4.4, in a two-country setting, GATT's rule of reciprocity in renegotiations guides governments toward the politically optimal outcome. We showed there that this property of reciprocity has an additional benefit when power asymmetries across governments are allowed: since the politically optimal outcome is independent of such asymmetries, GATT's rule of reciprocity in renegotiations can enable a weak country to overcome its fear of exploitation by a strong country so that the weak country is willing to participate in trade-policy negotiations. In a multicountry setting, when the reciprocity rule is joined with MFN, it is again true that GATT's rules guide negotiating governments toward the politically optimal (and MFN) tariffs, and so an analogous participation benefit may be identified. But the potential significance of this benefit is perhaps even more vivid in the multicountry setting, as there are then a host of strategic issues that naturally arise in a power-based system and that can be restrained with a commitment to a rules-based system such as that created by the principles of reciprocity and nondiscrimination.

An example that has special practical importance is when new supplying countries arise, as in the case of new accessions to the GATT/WTO or the case of shifting comparative advantage among existing GATT/WTO members. In the former case, the timing of a country's accession—in light of its own level of economic development, or in light of the anticipated timing of the accession of competing supplying countries—could have strategic consequences for its negotiation payoff in a power-based system. In the latter case, a power-based system might provide governments with incentives to strategically manipulate their comparative advantage, perhaps by restraining their suppliers until others had negotiated reduced trade barriers in their potential export markets, or by assisting their suppliers to become dominant in a particular market in anticipation of future negotiations to which they would be party. In both cases the strategic concerns that would accompany power-based negotiations could lead to government policy choices that were inefficient from a global perspective, and these inefficiencies could be reduced or eliminated with the adoption of a rules-based approach.[22]

---

22. For further discussion of these points, see Bagwell and Staiger (2000b).

5.6   MFN and Political Externalities

As we discussed in section 2.1.3, Ethier (2000) develops an alternative model of trade agreements in which "political externalities" figure prominently. Here we consider one implication that follows from this approach: MFN may create a need for multilateral—as opposed to bilateral—negotiations when political externalities are the problem that a trade agreement can solve.

Like Bagwell and Staiger (2000a, b), Ethier (2000) highlights the possible role that MFN may play in providing assurances against "concession erosion" as described above by Schwartz and Sykes (1997, p. 62). As we explain in section 2.1.3, however, Ethier's approach assumes that (1) exporters are not cognizant of the general equilibrium effects of trade-policy intervention (i.e., they cannot be made to understand Lerner's symmetry theorem) and (2) governments are unable to overcome this limitation by offering their exporters direct export enhancement policies. These assumptions have an important consequence: in this environment, reciprocity does not solve the "free-rider" problem under MFN, because (1) exporters (about whom governments care) don't understand that the general equilibrium effect of their own government's (reciprocal) liberalization allows them to capture all the additional market access from a trading partner's MFN liberalization (i.e., it eliminates the possibility of free-riders, as we explain in section 5.3.2) and (2) governments cannot repackage this general equilibrium effect in a form that exporters could understand (i.e., as a direct export enhancement program). As a result Ethier argues that bilateral negotiations under MFN, even when these negotiations conform to reciprocity, must ultimately give way to multilateral negotiations (so as to eliminate free-riders).

6

Enforcement

In the previous two chapters we focused on a literature that assumes that a trade agreement once negotiated can be enforced. While this focus serves to highlight the efficiency properties that may be associated with the principles of reciprocity and nondiscrimination, the manner in which a trade agreement is enforced is also of fundamental importance. As we discussed in section 3.2.3, an international agreement must be self-enforcing if it is to be credible, and an agreement to open markets is in turn self-enforcing only if it also specifies credible retaliatory measures against any country that deviates from the agreement and places additional restrictions on trade. In the present chapter we return to the topic of enforcement and develop more fully some of the themes from this literature. We begin with a careful consideration of the various roles for retaliation within GATT. We next draw relationships between these roles and the theory of repeated games, on which we rely in offering a formal representation of the requirement of a self-enforcing trade agreement. We then discuss a pair of predictions that emerge, once enforcement considerations are featured. Finally, we discuss the possibility that a multilateral institution such as the GATT/WTO can better enable governments to enforce trade agreements.

6.1 GATT Enforcement and the Theory of Repeated Games

The basic enforcement problem may be understood with reference to figure 2.3. As this figure illustrates, each government could gain if both agreed to adhere to a rule that binds tariffs at a tariff pair on the contract curve corresponding, say, to the political optimum. It is also true, however, that each government has an immediate incentive to cheat on such an agreement, by deviating to a tariff on its tariff reaction curve (not pictured) and exploiting its ability to shift the costs of intervention onto its trading partner. This raises a central issue that confronts governments as they design a trade agreement: By what mechanism is the tariff binding to be enforced?

Since countries trade repeatedly over time, the natural possibility is that a trade agreement is made self-enforcing through the prospect of retaliation. By this logic, each government balances its short-term incentive to cheat against the long-term cost that such behavior implies, once the other governments retaliate by raising their own tariffs. Governments can thus push tariffs down and achieve a more efficient arrangement, until the incentive to cheat becomes so large that it matches the long-term welfare loss that would be associated with the retaliatory consequences. An interesting implication of this repeated-game perspective is that the tariffs specified by a trade agreement ultimately may be determined by the enforcement incentive constraints.

As we discussed in sections 2.3 and 3.2.3, the GATT dispute settlement procedures may be generally understood from this perspective. In broad terms, the creation of GATT and its Articles XXII and XXIII nullification-or-impairment procedures may be interpreted as an attempt to move from a noncooperative to a cooperative equilibrium outcome, by limiting the use of retaliation along the equilibrium path and repositioning retaliation as an off-equilibrium-path threat that enforces cooperative equilibrium-path rules. This perspective is consistent, for example, with the following statement of one of the drafters of Article XXIII (as found in Petersmann 1997, p. 83):

We have asked the nations of the world to confer upon an international organization the right to limit their power to retaliate. We have sought to tame retaliation, to discipline it, to keep it within bounds. By subjecting it to the restraints of international control, we have endeavored to check its spread and growth, to convert it from a weapon of economic warfare to an instrument of international order.[1]

At the same time, it should be stressed that a limited role for retaliation indeed *does* arise along the equilibrium path, and this role for on-equilibrium-path retaliation is spread across a number of GATT

---

1. Similarly a drafter of Article XXIII remarks (as quoted in Jackson, 1969, pp. 170–71): "What we have really provided, in the last analysis, is not that retaliation shall be invited or sanctions invoked, but that a balance of interests once established, shall be maintained." Further support for this perspective is offered by Dam (1970, pp. 80–81), as quoted in section 3.2.3.

articles.[2] For instance, retaliation along the equilibrium path arises when a government seeks a retaliatory exception to obtain compensation for an original tariff adjustment by its trading partner, where the original adjustment is justified as a GATT-permissible exception, as allowed under Article XIX (safeguards) or Article XXVIII (renegotiation). A role for retaliation along the equilibrium path can arise as well when a government uses the nonviolation provisions of Article XXIII to seek redress for nullification or impairment that was caused by an original action taken by its trading partner that was not itself proscribed by GATT rules. As we discuss further below, it even may be argued that a role for retaliation arises along the equilibrium path if a trading partner takes an action that nullifies or impairs a government's market-access rights and this action is subsequently determined in an Article XXIII ruling to be in violation of GATT rules. This all suggests that the role of retaliation as it is found within the various GATT articles is more subtle than a standard application of repeated-game theory might suggest.

The distinct roles for retaliation within GATT are recognized by legal scholars. For example, Jackson (1969, pp. 169–71) points to a potential conflict between the goals for retaliation that are found within Article XXIII itself. On the one hand, the drafters sought to use the prospect of retaliation within Article XXIII to "play an important role in obtaining compliance with the GATT obligations." This goal resonates with the off-equilibrium-path role for retaliation in the standard repeated-game formulation, as here the role of retaliation is to generate a balance between the short-term incentive to cheat on the agreement and the long-term costs of retaliation. On the other hand, the drafters sought as well to use retaliation in Article XXIII "as a means for ensuring continued reciprocity and balance of concessions in the face of possibly changing circumstances." The role of retaliation here may be best interpreted as an on-equilibrium-path means of obtaining compensation, so that "unilateral" actions can be converted to "reciprocal" actions as in this way it is possible to allow for tariff adjustments to changing circumstances without upsetting the balance of concessions.

---

2. Jackson (1969, p. 165) lists seven different GATT articles within which provisions for the compensatory withdrawal or suspension of concessions may be found. As Petersmann (1997, pp. 177–78) explains, the integrated dispute settlement system of the WTO attempts to unify to some extent the settlement of disputes, and thereby provides less scope for "rule shopping" than did the "legally fragmented" GATT procedures, but many of the agreements within the WTO still contain their own special dispute settlement rules and procedures.

The distinction between the on- and off-equilibrium-path roles of retaliation within GATT may be further clarified with the consideration of three situations. Suppose first that a foreign government raises its tariff above its bound rate and justifies its behavior as a GATT-permissible exception. The home government may then seek compensation. If, however, the parties are unable to reach an agreement on the appropriate compensation, then the home government may take its own retaliatory exception, with a tariff hike that is of a "substantially equivalent" nature.[3] Retaliation here is best interpreted as an on-equilibrium-path event whose purpose is to discipline the use of GATT-permissible exceptions so that their application reflects a legitimate purpose and not a desire to shift the costs of intervention onto a trading partner.

As a second possibility, suppose that the foreign government raises its tariff but argues that the circumstances are such that its tariff hike does not warrant compensation or retaliation. The home government disputes this interpretation of GATT rules and takes the case to a GATT panel. Suppose further that the panel rules in favor of the home government and authorizes the home government to impose retaliatory tariffs.[4] This second possibility is different from the first only in that a panel decision is required to resolve the legality of the protectionist measure. Given the wide range of issues that may be raised between trading partners, it is to be expected that honest disputes of interpretation will arise from time to time. Arguably, in such a case, the authorized retaliation that follows a panel's resolution of a dispute may again be viewed as an on-equilibrium-path retaliation, whose purpose is effectively to ensure that the unilateral action of the foreign government is converted to a reciprocal action by it and its domestic trading partner, so that the foreign government does not shift the costs of its intervention onto home-country exporters.[5]

---

3. See, however, section 6.2.1 for a discussion of the extent to which retaliation under Article XIX is allowed following the formation of the WTO.

4. As an example of such a possibility, the EU has argued that it is entitled under GATT Article XX to prohibit the importation of hormone-treated beef because of the possible associated health risks and its intepretation of the WTO Sanitary and Phytosanitary Agreement, which provides for governments to impose product standards on imports when scientific evidence indicates a health risk. The United States, by contrast, has argued that scientific studies do not support the EU view and that the ensuing protection requires compensation or retaliation. The WTO panel ruled in favor of the United States position and authorized the United States to pursue retaliatory tariffs.

5. The distinction between on- and off-equilibrium-path retaliation is not as clear in this second possibility, because technically the foreign government stands in violation of the

Finally, consider a third possibility. Suppose that the home government complains that a change in the foreign trade-policy has nullified
or impaired the access to the foreign market that it initially expected.
The two governments again disagree as to the legality of the foreign-
government action, and the case is brought before a dispute panel.
Now allow for either of two scenarios: the panel finds in favor of the
foreign government, and yet the home government proceeds anyway
to set (unauthorized) retaliatory tariffs, or the panel finds in favor of
the home government, but after the home government sets its (authorized) retaliatory tariffs the foreign government counter-retaliates with
its own (unauthorized) tariff increases. These two scenarios describe
episodes of unauthorized retaliatory tariffs that are set in contradiction
to the then-known ruling of the dispute panel. The line is not perfectly
clear, but it seems reasonable to interpret such defiant behavior as an
off-equilibrium-path deviation. The fundamental deterrent to such
behavior, and the deterrent that therefore rests at the foundation of all
others, is the fear of initiating a breakdown in the entire cooperative
arrangement and thereby causing a "trade war." Simply, if a government plows over the final backstop (the panel ruling) in the GATT
dispute settlement process, other governments may naturally question
the relevance of this process.[6] This view is in line with Dunkel's

---

agreement if it does not bring its policy into conformity with GATT rules once the panel
ruling (subject to possible appeal) is issued. But as Petersmann (1997, p. 77) observes,
"... the illegality of a trade measure may be removed not only by the withdrawal of
the measure concerned but also by its justification through invocation of one of GATT's
safeguard clauses." Such an invocation would have the effect of converting the (illegal)
unilateral act of the foreign government into a (legal) reciprocal act between it and the
domestic government. Hence we interpret this second possibility as an on-equilibrium-
path retaliation, since as a result of the "rebalancing" brought about by this retaliation
the market-access outcome associated with the foreign government's illegal action is converted effectively to what it would be under a legal action.

6. One implication of this reasoning is that governments may exhibit care in deciding
which disputes to submit to the GATT dispute panel. Suppose, for example, that a government is known to have violated a certain GATT rule but that it is also known that
domestic political constraints might prevent this government from complying with a
GATT dispute-panel ruling against it (even to the point of accepting authorized retaliation). In this case, rather than submit the violation to the GATT Dispute Panel and possibly threaten the integrity of the GATT system, an injured trading partner might seek
some less confrontational means of gaining compensation.

Such concerns are reflected in current trade-policy practice. For example, with regard
to the US Helms-Burton Law, the EU has shown willingness to pursue negotiations
outside of the WTO. On the other hand, the EU has taken to the WTO a politically sensitive dispute with the United States concerning the US Foreign Sales Corporation Law.
The *Financial Times* (2000, editorial) has argued that the EU and the United States are

perception of a "balance of terror," which we discussed in section 2.3.

With this institutional description in place, we turn now to a formal representation of a repeated game of tariff formation. We begin with a standard infinitely repeated tariff game between two governments. The two governments interact in each of an infinite number of periods, where the environment is stationary over time and the static tariff game of the (politically augmented) terms-of-trade theory serves as the associated stage game. Thus in each period the two governments observe all previous import tariff selections and simultaneously make their respective current import tariff selections. In order to feature the key issues that are associated with the enforcement of trade agreements, we assume further that the two countries are symmetric. We consider stationary and symmetric subgame perfect equilibria in which the two governments select the same tariff in each period. If a deviation from this common tariff occurs, then we assume that a retaliatory trade war erupts, in the spirit of the third example above, whereby in the next and all future periods governments revert to the Nash equilibrium tariffs of the static game, given by τ^N.[7] The discount factor between periods is denoted as $\delta \in (0, 1)$.

In this repeated tariff game, governments may enforce a cooperative tariff τ^C, with $\tau^C < \tau^N$, since the short-term benefit that any government enjoys from raising the current-period tariff above the agreed-upon level is balanced against the long-term loss that this (and the other) government experiences as future cooperation is lost and a retaliatory war is initiated. Intuitively, an agreement to bind tariffs at τ^C can be enforced if the short-term incentive to cheat is sufficiently small relative to the discounted future value of avoiding the trade war that would be triggered as a consequence. We assume, however, that governments are unable to enforce the politically optimal tariff, τ^{PO}. This assumption ensures that the level of cooperation that governments may

---

thereby "playing with fire" and "risk mortally wounding the organization that they were largely responsible for creating." Such concerns may arise more often in the future, as it can be expected that many disputes will occur that relate to politically sensitive policies (e.g., GM foods).

Finally, while we develop our discussion here in terms of the GATT dispute settlement process, we note that the WTO dispute settlement process includes as well an Appellate Body that rules on appeals to the panel ruling. See also note 14 to chapter 3.

7. The formal points that we wish to emphasize here are not particularly sensitive to the exact specification of the retaliatory process. Thus we may also view the Nash reversion threat as a simple means of representing the qualitative idea that a deviation today results in diminished cooperation and a corresponding loss in welfare tomorrow.

achieve is indeed determined by the enforcement constraint. This will be the case if each government anticipates a significant short-term gain in defecting from τ^{PO}, and discounts sufficiently the cost of future retaliation.

We now formally characterize the short-term incentive that a government has to cheat. Given the assumed symmetry across countries, there is no loss of generality in considering only the incentives of the domestic government. For a fixed cooperative tariff $\tau^C < \tau^N$, and given the class of subgame perfect equilibria upon which we focus, if the domestic government deviates and selects $\tau \neq \tau^C$, then it will deviate to its best-response tariff, $\tau^R(\tau^C)$, as defined implicitly by (2.7). The domestic government's incentive to cheat is thus given by

$$\Omega(\tau^C) \equiv \int_{\tau^C}^{\tau^R(\tau^C)} \frac{dW(p, \tilde{p}^w)}{d\tau} d\tau$$

$$= \int_{\tau^C}^{\tau^R(\tau^C)} W_p(p, \tilde{p}^w) \frac{dp}{d\tau} d\tau + \int_{\tau^C}^{\tau^R(\tau^C)} W_{\tilde{p}^w}(p, \tilde{p}^w) \frac{\partial \tilde{p}^w}{\partial \tau} d\tau$$

where $\tilde{p}^w \equiv \tilde{p}^w(\tau, \tau^C)$ in the integrands.

We separate the short-term benefit from cheating into two components. The first represents the welfare impact of the deviation through the change in the local price and the second represents the welfare impact of the deviation through the change in the terms of trade. The first component is negative (since $W_p < 0$ over the entire range of integration), and it reflects the unfavorable trade-off between the benefits and costs of achieving the local price implied by the best-response tariff when the welfare impact of the associated terms-of-trade improvement is not included. The second component is positive, as it reflects the welfare gain to the government from the transfer of income to itself from its trading partner that occurs through the change in the terms of trade (i.e., from shifting costs onto its trading partner). The sum of these two terms is positive for $\tau^C < \tau^R(\tau^C)$ and is zero at $\tau^C = \tau^R(\tau^C)$, by the definition of the domestic tariff reaction function in (2.7). It follows that $\Omega(\tau^C)$ is strictly positive for $\tau^C < \tau^N$, and the domestic government is faced with the temptation to cheat on the agreement by succumbing to cost-shifting motives.

When the domestic government cheats, however, it triggers a retaliatory phase, and the long-term cost of this retaliation also must be considered. We characterize first the one-period value to the domestic government of avoiding a trade war and sustaining the cooperative tariff. This value is given by

$$w(\tau^C) \equiv -\int_{\tau^C}^{\tau^N} \frac{dW(p, \tilde{p}^w)}{d\tau} d\tau = -\int_{\tau^C}^{\tau^N} W_p(p, \tilde{p}^w)\tilde{p}^w d\tau$$

where $\tilde{p}^w \equiv \tilde{p}^w(\tau, \tau)$ in the integrands.[8] With the world-price effects of a trade war neutralized under the assumed symmetry, the short-term value in avoiding a trade war and sustaining the cooperative tariff reflects the gains from the more efficient local prices that are associated with the greater trade volume that cooperation implies. Under our assumption that $\tau^C > \tau^{PO}$ we have that $W_p < 0$ for $\tau \in [\tau^C, \tau^N]$; therefore it follows that $\omega(\tau^C) > 0$ for $\tau^C < \tau^N$, while $\omega(\tau^C) = 0$ for $\tau^C = \tau^N$.

We are prepared now to define the total discounted value to cooperation that the domestic government forfeits when it cheats. This value is given as $V(\tau^C) \equiv [\delta/(1-\delta)]\omega(\tau^C)$, since once a government deviates and selects a higher tariff, the cooperative tariffs are thereafter replaced by the higher Nash tariffs. With this, it follows that the domestic government's incentive constraint can be written as

$$\Omega(\tau^C) \leq V(\tau^C). \tag{6.1}$$

Any cooperative tariff τ^C that satisfies this incentive constraint can be enforced as a subgame perfect equilibrium of the repeated tariff game.

Consider now the "most-cooperative" tariff, $\bar{\tau}^C$, defined as the smallest tariff that satisfies the incentive constraint given in (6.1). Under the assumption that the politically optimal tariff cannot be enforced (i.e., that τ^{PO} violates 6.1), we have $\bar{\tau}^C > \tau^{PO}$. The determination of the most-cooperative tariff is illustrated in figure 6.1. Observe there that $\Omega(\tau^C)$ is monotonically decreasing in τ^C for $\tau^C < \tau^N$, while $\Omega(\tau^C)$ is flat and equal to zero at $\tau^C = \tau^N$. Intuitively, a government gains less in deviating from a cooperative tariff τ^C the closer is that tariff to the Nash tariff τ^N, and the government gains nothing from cheating when the "cooperative" tariff is already at the Nash level. Observe also that $V(\tau^C)$ is zero at $\tau^C = \tau^N$, monotonically decreasing in τ^C for $\tau^C < \tau^{PO}$, and flat at $\tau^C = \tau^{PO}$. These properties arise because the gains from avoiding a trade war decline to zero as the tariffs stipulated in the agreement rise from τ^{PO} and approach the Nash level that would be selected in a trade war anyway; furthermore, at τ^{PO}, a small symmetric increase in cooperative tariffs has no impact on government welfare (by the first-order condition that defines τ^{PO}). The range of tariffs that can be enforced is thus

---

8. In deriving this expression, we use the fact that under symmetry $d\tilde{p}^w(\tau, \tau)/d\tau = 0$ and $dp(\tau, \tilde{p}^w(\tau, \tau))/d\tau = \tilde{p}^w$.

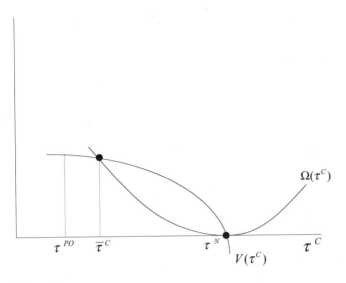

Figure 6.1

represented by the interval $[\bar{\tau}^C, \tau^N]$, and the most cooperative tariff $\bar{\tau}^C$ is the tariff at which the incentive constraint in (6.1) binds.[9]

This completes our description of the standard infinitely repeated tariff game. Retaliation plays an important role in this game, as it represents the off-equilibrium-path and long-term cost that would be experienced were a government to cheat in the present. This game, however, is stationary, and so it fails to offer a role for GATT-permissible exceptions and the associated on-equilibrium-path retaliation that we discuss in the first and second examples above. As well, this stationary framework fails to account for the gradual manner in which trade liberalization has proceeded under GATT. We turn to these possibilities next.

6.2 Predictions

When viewed from the perspective of figure 6.1, the task of enforcing a trade agreement amounts to first achieving and then maintaining a

---

9. In the formal model of section 2.1.3, the functions Ω and V possess the properties ascribed to them at and around τ^N and τ^{PO}. The functions may or may not be convex and concave, respectively, as depicted in figure 6.1, so it is possible that the functions intersect more than once. We assume here that the curvature properties are met, and simply note that the analysis can be generalized to handle the possibility of multiple intersections.

balance between (1) the short-term temptation to deviate unilaterally from an agreed-upon trade policy and enjoy the terms-of-trade benefits and (2) the long-term costs of a consequent future loss of cooperation. This balance is reflected in the determination of the most-cooperative tariff in figure 6.1. If the world were stationary as we represent it here, then the role of a dispute settlement mechanism simply might be to allow governments to coordinate on this most-cooperative tariff once and for all, and then monitor the agreement for violations.

The world, however, is not stationary, and a self-enforcing agreement must be responsive to this fact. In view of the balance between short- and long-term incentives that a self-enforcing trade agreement requires, it is evident that any event that alters the current incentive to cheat or the expected future value of cooperation can upset this balance. The enforceable level of cooperation may thus change with underlying market conditions. This suggests that countries cannot be held rigidly to tariff commitments in a self-enforcing agreement: if properly designed, GATT must provide its members with ample flexibility to adjust tariff levels up or down as underlying circumstances change. We describe next two predictions that emerge from this suggestion.

6.2.1   Rebalancing the Agreement: The GATT Escape Clause

In GATT Article XIX a government is allowed to temporarily suspend a concession agreed upon in a previous negotiation if its import-competing industry is injured as a consequence of a temporary surge in import volume. Following Bagwell and Staiger (1990), we argue here that this "escape clause" can provide the flexibility that promotes greater cooperation as part of a self-enforcing trade agreement for an economic environment characterized by trade-volume volatility. To make this point, we assume for simplicity that the politically optimal tariff is invariant in the presence of trade-volume fluctuations. This is the case, for example, if governments maximize national welfare, as in this event the politically optimal tariff corresponds to free trade.

The basic idea can be understood with reference to figure 6.1. If the import volume experiences a temporary surge, then the function Ω shifts up, reflecting the greater terms-of-trade gains that are possible in light of the larger trade volume. On the other hand, given that the import swing is temporary, the function V tends to remain stable, as the future value of cooperation is unaffected by temporary fluctuations. As figure 6.1 suggests, if governments were to prohibit an adjustment in the cooperative tariff, then the incentive constraint would be "out of balance," as the short-term incentive to cheat would be larger than the long-term cost of a breakdown in cooperation. If, however, governments were to include in the trade agreement an escape clause under which the import tariff could be temporarily increased in the event of an import-volume surge, then the higher tariff would diminish the incentive to cheat, thereby restoring intertemporal balance.[10] Continuing in this fashion, we may argue that GATT's Article XIX is an escape clause or "safeguard" that prevents a breakdown in cooperation that would otherwise occur were imports to surge.[11]

Taking this perspective, when a country experiences a surge in its import volume, it restores the intertemporal balance between its short- and long-term incentives by adopting a higher tariff. This exception, however, raises the prospect that a government may be motivated in part by a desire to shift the costs of its intervention onto its trading partner, thus upsetting a different balance: the balance of concessions. In its original formulation, GATT's Article XIX addresses this possibility by allowing that the trading partner can then take a retaliatory exception (on the equilibrium path) and withdraw its own substantially equivalent concession. In this way governments simultaneously maintain balance with respect to their intertemporal enforcement incentives and their concessions. Put differently, this approach enables governments to maintain the incentives for cooperation in the face of changing circumstances, without providing a means for one government to shift the costs of its intervention onto the other.[12]

---

10. This point is established in Bagwell and Staiger (1990), and it is related to an earlier contribution by Rotemberg and Saloner (1986), who consider self-enforcing collusion among firms that experience i.i.d. demand shocks. In Bagwell and Staiger (1995), we allow also for persistent (business-cycle) shocks to the trade-volume growth rate, and we find that protection is then countercyclical. This point is related to our earlier model (Bagwell and Staiger, 1997a), in which we consider self-enforcing collusion among firms that experience persistent shocks to the demand growth rate.

11. Further support for this interpretation is offered, for example, by Dixit (1996), Hoekman and Kostecki (1995, p. 167), and Ostry (1997, p. 68). Hoeckman and Kostecki (1995, p. 168) further observe that Article XIX safeguard actions were used 150 times from the inception of GATT through 1994.

12. A similar interpretation may be offered for episodes of (on-the-equilibrium-path) retaliation under Article XXIII.

Despite the theoretical virtue of this approach, however, the practical experience with GATT's Article XIX has been somewhat mixed. As Ostry (1997, pp. 77, 99–100, 178–79) and Grimwade (1996, pp. 89–92) explain, while GATT members used Article XIX to legitimize temporary protection with great frequency in the 1970s, they turned more toward instruments of managed trade (e.g., VERs) in the 1980s. The apparent reason was that managed-trade policies often fell outside of GATT rules and were in any case somewhat "nontransparent"; by contrast, when a government raised a tariff under GATT Article XIX, the affected countries required notification and consultation and were permitted to seek retaliatory exceptions that constituted compensation for the original action.

This disturbing trend toward managed trade motivated the member governments to adopt a number of changes as part of the formation of the WTO. Governments agreed to phase out managed-trade policies, make trade-policy actions more "transparent," and amend Article XIX so that retaliatory responses by affected partners were prohibited for a three-year period following the original action. These changes are designed to encourage governments to use Article XIX as opposed to managed-trade policies when temporary import surges result in injury. At the same time these changes limit the scope for retaliation and thus diminish the discipline that is applied to the safeguard exception, raising the possibility that governments may now be tempted to shift costs onto one another through this exception.

6.2.2   Gradualism: Rounds of Trade Liberalization

While the extent of liberalization achieved under GATT is certainly remarkable for the depth in the reduction of trade barriers, the process by which this liberalization has occurred through eight rounds of negotiation spread over a five-decade period is no less remarkable for its gradualism. This feature is not well-explained in the context of a stationary model of enforcement; for example, in the context of figure 6.1 there is no reason that the liberalization from the high Nash tariff to the lower most cooperative tariff couldn't be achieved in one great leap. What then accounts for the gradual manner in which tariffs have been reduced through GATT rounds?

We sketch here an argument that derives from the work of Devereux (1997). He emphasizes that production technologies may exhibit "learning by doing": as a firm produces more in the current period, it learns better how to produce its output, and its production costs in all future periods fall. Consider now the implications of learning by doing for the enforcement of trade agreements. Suppose that the two governments initially select some high tariff but then, through a GATT round, negotiate a lower cooperative tariff that reflects the current balance between the short-term benefits from protection and the long-term value of a cooperative relationship. The initial liberalization effort induces exporting firms to produce greater output, and as time passes, these firms experience the lower production costs that learning by doing implies. As a consequence the gains from trade for the two countries tend to grow as well, which is to say that the value of cooperation as represented by the function V in figure 6.1 tends to shift up as time passes. When governments enter the next GATT round, they may therefore find that they can enforce a lower most cooperative tariff than was possible in the previous round.[13]

This reasoning suggests that the gradual manner in which tariffs have been reduced through GATT rounds reflects a "virtuous cycle" that plays out through the incentive constraints associated with enforcement: an initial round of liberalization gives rise to changes in the economy (e.g., learning by doing), which in turn enhance the value of cooperation, thereby permitting a further round of liberalization, and so on.[14]

---

13. As the countries specialize further, the volume of trade grows, and the function Ω may also shift up, reflecting a heightened incentive to cheat. As Devereux (1997) finds, this means that the Nash tariffs are higher when more learning has occurred. The flip-side of this is that the gains to cooperation also rise with time, and Deveraux (1997) shows that the corresponding increase in the function V dominates, in that most-cooperative tariffs decline through time.

14. A related theory is presented by Staiger (1995b), who develops a model in which workers have skills that are specific to the import-competing industry but gradually depreciate when not in use. The relocation of these workers in response to trade liberalization plays a role analogous to learning by doing in Deveraux's (1997) model. See also Chisik (forthcoming) and Furusawa and Lai (1999). This approach is related to that of Bhagwati (1990), Gilligan (1997), and Krishna and Mitra (1999), in their analyses of reciprocity (as described above in section 4.2). In all of these cases gradualism reflects a changing government preference function, where the change may be explained by learning-by-doing technology, worker relocation, or growing political support from exporters. A distinct approach to modeling gradual trade liberalization is taken by Bond and Park (forthcoming), who show that a form of gradualism can also arise in stationary environments when countries are asymmetric.

6.3 The Exchange and Aggregation of Enforcement Power

Our discussion to this point describes in some detail the role of retaliation in GATT and a pair of predictions that emerge once enforcement constraints are considered. This suggests that GATT is an instrument through which governments coordinate and achieve a self-enforcing cooperative trade-policy relationship. In the real world such large-scale coordination is not a trivial accomplishment, and indeed, as we discussed in section 3.1, the first attempts at coordination failed. Putting aside the issue of coordination, however, there remains the further theoretical question of whether GATT's multilateral enforcement mechanism facilitates greater cooperation than would occur were instead cooperation achieved through a web of bilateral agreements. The question is addressed by Maggi (1999), whose work we now describe.

Maggi (1999) identifies two broad categories of gains from a multilateral enforcement mechanism over a collection of bilateral agreements. The first gain arises in the presence of local "imbalances of power," defined as a situation where different governments stand to lose different amounts from a trade war, with the more "powerful" governments standing to lose less. In such a circumstance the exchange of enforcement power that can be affected under a multilateral dispute settlement procedure can serve to support lower tariffs than would be possible under purely bilateral procedures. Specifically, in a multilateral enforcement mechanism, each country can serve as a third-party enforcer of low tariffs in bilateral relationships where it is "strong" in exchange for receiving third-party enforcement from others in bilateral relationships where it is "weak." Purely bilateral enforcement mechanisms cannot affect this exchange of enforcement power.

An extreme example illustrates the underlying idea. Suppose that there are three countries, A, B, and C, and think of the three countries as being positioned at the vertices of a triangle. Suppose further that the preferences and endowments in the three countries are such that any given country imports a good from the country to its right and exports a good to the country to its left. Thus country A might export a good to country B while having as its only import a good from country C. Can the governments of these countries use the threat of retaliation to achieve cooperative (i.e., below-Nash) tariffs? If the government of country B were to cheat and raise its tariff on the good it imports from country A, then country B's government would experience a short-term welfare gain. Notice, though, that the country A's government is unable, on its own, to retaliate: there is no good that country A imports from country B (and export taxes are ruled out by assumption). The governments can thus cooperate and achieve greater-than-Nash welfare only if a multilateral agreement is in place, in which country C's government stands ready to retaliate with a Nash tariff on the good it imports from country B, if the government of country B cheats the government of country A in the described manner.

A second kind of gain from multilateral enforcement mechanisms identified by Maggi (1999) is associated with the aggregation of enforcement power. The key idea is that tariffs levied by different governments on the same imported good tend to be strategic complements (see Bagwell and Staiger 1997b for an initial statement of this property). Intuitively, when two countries import the same good, if the government of one country raises its import tariff, then a greater volume of the good is diverted to the other country, whose government thus has an increased incentive to increase its own import tariff and enjoy the associated terms-of-trade gains. As a consequence of this property, a multilateral enforcement mechanism which has many governments joining in the punishments can lead to proportionately more severe punishments than would be forthcoming under bilateral enforcement procedures.

When either local imbalances of power or strategic tariff complementarity effects are present, Maggi's (1999) results suggest that a multilateral dispute settlement procedure may be necessary to achieve the gains from exchange and aggregation of enforcement power.[15] This perspective of GATT suggests that the monitoring and information dissemination effects of the dispute settlement procedure represent a key ingredient in facilitating greater cooperation from multilateral trade agreements. This suggestion is directly consistent with the creation through the WTO of a Trade Policy Review Mechanism. As we discussed in section 3.2.3, this represents a process through which the WTO gathers and disseminates information concerning the trade policies of its member governments. The "transparency" so implied enables governments to monitor each other's compliance with

---

15. The essential institutional role played by multilateral dispute settlement procedures in Maggi (1999) is the dissemination of information about violations of agreements. An alternative institutional role for WTO dispute settlement procedures is identified in a recent paper by Klimenko, Ramey, and Watson (2000). These authors highlight the cooperation-enhancing role that can be played by delays in WTO dispute procedures.

previous agreements, permitting in turn a level of cooperation that may exceed that which would occur in the absence of such a multilateral institution.[16]

---

16. Renato Ruggiero (1995), then director-general of the WTO, explains further: "For all countries, new and detailed obligations have been created to notify policies and measures, so that trading partners can be confident that they have full knowledge of each other's policies. Transparency is an essential ingredient for fostering mutual trust and encouraging respect for the rules. Indeed, one of the results of the Uruguay Round was the creation of a trade policy review mechanism, whereby the trade policies of individual WTO members are examined multilaterally by turn, and in depth. These examinations provide an opportunity for countries to hold frank and nonlitigious exchanges of views about each other's policies. They are a valuable contribution to transparency, and help to raise awareness among trading partners of policy issues." Transparency also may facilitate greater cooperation even when third-party enforcement possibilities are not relevant. The collusion model of Green and Porter (1984) illustrates that nontransparency has negative consequences for the level of self-enforcing cooperation among, say, two firms. In related work Riezman (1991) explores the implications of nontransparency for self-enforcing trade-policy agreements.

7   Preferential Trading Agreements

In the previous three chapters we interpreted GATT's central design features from the perspective of the (politically augmented) terms-of-trade theory. We described how GATT's pillars of reciprocity and nondiscrimination can provide governments with an escape from a terms-of-trade-driven Prisoners' Dilemma, and we described how GATT's enforcement procedures can be evaluated from this perspective as well. In the present chapter we consider an important exception to nondiscrimination that is allowed under GATT Article XXIV, whereby under certain conditions countries are allowed to form preferential trading agreements (PTAs). An extensive economics literature exists that addresses the welfare benefits and costs of preferential trading agreements, and these contributions are comprehensively reviewed in Panagariya's (2000) recent survey.[1] Our focus here is more narrow: we consider the impact of Article XXIV for the functioning of the multilateral trading system, paying particular attention to the interplay between this exception and the GATT rules that pertain to reciprocity, non-discrimination and enforcement.

7.1   Preferential Trading Agreements in GATT

Under Article XXIV, a subset of GATT members may form a PTA provided that they set a tariff of zero between themselves on substantially all goods that they trade. The PTA members may simultaneously tax imports from nonmember countries at a positive rate. PTAs are thus inherently discriminatory, and they may take two forms. In a *free-trade*

---

1. For further perspectives on the broader literature on PTAs, see Anderson and Blackhurst (1993), Bagwell and Staiger (1998), Baldwin and Venables (1995), Bhagwati, Greenaway and Panagariya (1998), Bhagwati and Panagariya (1996), Ethier (1998b), Fernandez and Portes (1998), Pomfret (1997), and Winters (1996).

area, each member country of the PTA independently selects its own external tariffs. By contrast, in a *customs union*, a common external tariff policy is adopted by all members in the union. The exception to non-discrimination for PTAs was controversial in its inception and has met with renewed controversy recently as many GATT members have increasingly exercised their rights under Article XXIV to negotiate PTAs.

We divide our discussion of PTAs and GATT as follows. We first consider how PTAs may affect the performance of GATT in light of its pillars of reciprocity and nondiscrimination. Then, we turn to consider how PTAs may affect the enforcement of multilateral obligations in GATT. We conclude with a discussion of recent work that explores alternative modeling frameworks within which to consider PTAs and GATT.

7.2 Preferential Trading Agreements and Reciprocity

We focus here on a simple but important question: Will PTAs interfere with the functioning of a multilateral trading system that is built upon the pillars of reciprocity and nondiscrimination? To frame the discussion, we consider an immediate extension of the multicountry modeling framework presented above. Suppose that the home country imports good x from three foreign countries, denoted as 1, 2, and 3, and in turn exports good y to these same three countries. Suppose further that the home country forms a PTA with one of the foreign countries. After the PTA is formed, the home government may set a non-discriminatory tariff that applies to each of the remaining two foreign countries, or it may choose to discriminate between these countries. Since this scenario involves three foreign countries, we are able to consider both possibilities. Given the complexity of the issues involved, however, we emphasize here the intuition that underlies the main points.[2]

In accordance with Article XXIV, we consider two forms of PTAs. The home country forms a free-trade area with foreign country i if $\tau^i = 1 = \tau^{*i}$ and $\tau^j > 1$ for some $j \neq i$. A customs union is the same as a free-trade area, except that the members of a customs union also adopt a common external tariff policy. As the external tariff decisions of the customs union are centralized, the objectives of the tariff authorities in the

---

2. Formal analysis can be found in Bagwell and Staiger (1999a, 2001b).

customs union must be defined. If the home country forms a customs union with foreign country i, we represent the objectives of the customs union by the function $U(W, W^{*i})$, where U is increasing in both arguments.[3]

Consistent with our discussion in chapter 5, we consider first the extent to which PTAs may achieve bilaterally opportunistic welfare gains, in a trade-negotiation framework that is otherwise governed by MFN and reciprocity. Second, we consider the potential impact of PTAs for the efficiency properties of Article XXVIII, under which governments may renegotiate under reciprocity.

7.2.1 PTAs and Trade Negotiations

In chapter 5 we argued that any bilateral agreement that honors both MFN and reciprocity leaves the welfare of any nonparticipating government unaltered. Thus, when these principles are rigidly imposed, the scope for bilaterally opportunistic trade agreements is removed. Each government can then conduct its current trade negotiations without the fear that the value of a concession received will be subsequently eroded, as a consequence of some future bilateral agreement to which it is not party. On the other hand, when it is possible to negotiate a future bilateral agreement that is discriminatory, the welfare of nonparticipating governments can be appropriated. Bilateral opportunism and the associated fear of concession erosion are then potentially significant concerns for negotiating governments. Following this reasoning, it is clear that PTAs represent a possible route to opportunistic bilateral agreements. This suggests in turn the exception to nondiscrimination allowed in GATT for PTAs may promote inefficient bargaining outcomes.

Following on the discussion in chapter 5, we now describe in more detail the manner in which PTAs can achieve bilaterally opportunistic welfare gains. Suppose that the home country and foreign country 1 form a PTA and thus set $\tau^1 = 1 = \tau^{*1}$. To isolate the significance of this event, let us suppose further that no other tariffs are altered from their initial values. Consider now the welfare of foreign country 2. The

---

3. Note that in this setting, the foreign custom union partner has no "external tariff" to set in common with the home country, as it has no other trading partner. But what is important for our discussion here is not the harmonization of the external tariff per se, but rather that unlike a free-trade area, in a customs union the external tariffs are set in accordance with the welfare of both member governments (as represented by the function U).

exporters in this country are harmed, since they are at a disadvantage compared to the competing exporters from foreign country 1. Likewise the consumers in foreign country 2 suffer, since the supply of the home country's export good is diverted to foreign country 1, and as a consequence this good becomes more scarce in foreign country 2. For both reasons foreign country 2 experiences a terms-of-trade loss. In the absence of any change in its own tariff, the government of foreign country 2 must therefore experience a welfare loss. In turn, if the formation of a PTA is appealing to the governments of the home country and foreign country 1, then some (or even all) of the appeal may correspond to welfare that these governments appropriate from nonparticipating governments. In this regard it is interesting to mention the empirical analysis of Winters and Chang (2000), who find that PTAs can significantly diminish the terms of trade for nonparticipating countries.

At the same time, it should be noted that provisions do exist within GATT that can reduce the potential for bilaterally opportunistic PTAs if they are actively applied. In particular, the theory that we describe suggests that PTAs present a natural and appropriate target for nonviolation nullification-or-impairment complaints, as allowed through Article XXIII. Such complaints are not often directed toward bilateral agreements, but possibly complaints of this kind should be further encouraged within the GATT/WTO, as such complaints could in turn play an important role in diminishing the attractiveness of PTAs as a route to bilateral opportunism.[4]

7.2.2 PTAs and Renegotiation

We consider now the interaction between PTAs and GATT's renegotiation provisions. Suppose first that the home country forms a free-trade area with foreign country i. In line with our discussion in chapter 5 regarding the principle of nondiscrimination, it then can be shown that externalities travel between the home government and foreign governments through both foreign local prices and world prices. As a consequence the efficiency properties of a multilateral trade agreement that is founded on the principle of reciprocity are undermined. The key

---

4. As we discussed in note 12 to chapter 5, nonviolation complaints have been raised against bilateral agreements in the past, but certainly it would be possible to further encourage this option.

point is that when the foreign countries regard the world prices as fixed (as under reciprocity) and set tariffs that induce their preferred local prices, these choices nevertheless impart an externality to the home country, which would prefer, all else equal, to receive a greater proportion of trade volume from the foreign country j on whom it places a positive tariff. Arguing in this fashion, it can be shown that an efficient trade agreement cannot be implemented when the renegotiation of multilateral commitments is possible under the principle of reciprocity and the home country is engaged in a free-trade agreement with foreign country i.

As a second possibility, suppose that the home country forms a customs union with foreign country i. While there remains a presumption that the associated tariff discrimination will conflict with the effectiveness of the principle of reciprocity, there is now a special case that warrants emphasis. In particular, if the home country and foreign country i are sufficiently similar, then it becomes possible to think of the customs union as being like a single country that chooses import tariffs and whose government's welfare is given by the function U.[5] The situation is then directly analogous to the three-country model described in chapter 5, with the customs union playing the role of the home country in that model. Thus, if the customs union satisfies the principle of nondiscrimination when setting its external tariffs and if the customs union and the remaining foreign countries also set politically optimal tariffs, then the resulting tariffs will be efficient and robust to the possibility of renegotiation under the principle of reciprocity as provided by Article XXVIII.

In total, the arguments presented here suggest a quite limited set of circumstances under which PTAs can coexist in harmony with a multilateral system such as GATT that is founded on the principle of reciprocity. We next consider whether a more favorable view of PTAs arises when the multilateral enforcement implications of their existence is recognized.

7.3   Preferential Trading Agreements and Multilateral Enforcement

In chapter 6 we noted that the enforcement of a multilateral trade agreement involves a balance between the short-term incentive for each

---

5. Similarity between the domestic country and foreign country i is important, as it ensures that the internal tariff of zero required under Article XXIV is efficient.

government to cheat on the agreement and the long-term cost of the retaliation that would then ensue. When the associated enforcement incentive constraint binds, governments may be unable to enforce fully efficient trade-policy outcomes; furthermore changes in the underlying economic environment that alter this balance by affecting the short-term incentive to protect and/or the long-term cost of retaliation can in turn influence the "most-cooperative" tariff that can be enforced. Here we note that the creation of a PTA can be a source of "imbalance" at the multilateral level, and we examine the manner in which such agreements might affect the level of multilateral cooperation that can be enforced.[6]

An important feature of PTAs is that they are typically formed over a lengthy transition period during which the trade-policy changes associated with the agreement are phased in. It is thus of some particular interest to ask how emerging PTAs may affect the ability to enforce multilateral cooperation during the transition period.[7] Historical and current experiences motivate this question further. Beginning in 1957, the EC customs union was formed over a 12-year phase-in period, and it underwent a period of major expansion to include Great Britain, Denmark, and Ireland beginning in 1972. These episodes of customs union formation and enlargement corresponded with periods of enhanced multilateral tariff cooperation and, as a WTO report (WTO 1995b, pp. 53–54) concludes, were factors behind the launching of the GATT Dillon Round (1960–62), Kennedy Round (1964–67), and Tokyo Round (1973–79) of multilateral negotiations.[8] More recently important PTAs include the 1988 US–Canada Free-Trade Agreement and its

---

6. The various implications of PTAs for the ability to enforce multilateral tariff co-operation have been explored in a number of papers, including Bagwell and Staiger (1997b,c, 1999b), Bond and Syropoulos (1996a) and Bond, Syropoulos, and Winters (1996). Putting enforcement issues to the side, Krishna (1998) and Levy (1997) consider the implications of PTAs for the political support that is associated with multilateral free trade. Finally, while we emphasize here the consequences of PTAs for multilateral liberalization, a separate issue concerns the consequences of a PTA for the likelihood of additional PTAs in the future. Baldwin (1995) develops a "domino" theory of regionalism whereby the formation of one regional agreement raises the value of a regional agreement to non-members, and thereby leads to a possible spate of regional agreements in the future. Further work that emphasizes endogenous regionalism is developed by Ethier (1998a), Freund (2000a,b), Grossman and Helpman (1995b), Krishna (1998), and Yi (1996).

7. GATT's Article XXIV acknowledges the practical need for "interim agreements" to facilitate the process of preferential integration, and requires only that the transition to a completed free-trade area or customs union be accomplished "within a reasonable length of time."

8. Hoekman and Kostecki (1995, p. 229) reach the same conclusion.

expansion to include Mexico in NAFTA. As Bhagwati (1991) explains, the implementation of these agreements, by contrast, appears to have taken place against a backdrop of strained multilateral relations in which preferential initiatives are viewed as a potential threat to the GATT system.[9]

We begin with two effects of PTAs that are important in determining the consequence of these agreements for enforcement at the multilateral level. According to the *trade diversion effect*, when a PTA is formed, trade volumes among member countries increase at the expense of trade between member and nonmember countries.[10] The second effect is the *market power effect*, which occurs if member countries form a customs union and adopt a common external tariff policy that (as a consequence of the strategic-tariff-complementarity effect mentioned in chapter 6) enables them to impose higher credible tariffs on their multilateral trading partners should such a punitive tariff action be desired. We consider each in turn.[11]

Consider first the implications of the trade-diversion effect for multilateral tariff cooperation between a member country and a nonmember country. We may think of their relationship as passing through three phases. In the first phase, before the PTA is proposed, the countries are able to sustain a most-cooperative tariff, such as depicted in figure 6.1. Then, in the second phase, the agreement is announced and the transition begins. The countries then still have a high current volume of trade, but they recognize that their trade volume will decline in the future, once the PTA is fully implemented. Thus, in this second

---

9. As the WTO report (WTO 1995b, p. 54) states, existing PTAs were a less significant factor in the 1986 launching of the Uruguay Round of GATT negotiations, since ". . . at the time, regional integration was still confined mainly to Western Europe, with the United States maintaining its traditional multilateralism." Nevertheless, while the failure of these negotiations to conclude at the Brussels Ministerial in December 1990 reflected the strained multilateral tensions of the time, this failure together with the subsequent increase in new preferential initiatives after 1990 were ". . . major factors in eliciting the concessions needed to conclude the Uruguay Round" in 1994, as they raised the specter that a failed Uruguay Round would lead to a world in which future trade and economic relations would be based primarily on preferential agreements.

10. The concept of trade diversion is typically associated with the impact of PTAs on world welfare, as in Viner's (1950) classic analysis. See also Kemp and Wan (1976). Recent empirical evidence on the trade-diverting impact of NAFTA is provided by Romalis (2001).

11. These effects also play a role in the static models of regionalism and trade policy put forth by Krugman (1991b) and Bond and Syropoulos (1996b). Offering a generalization of Krugman's (1991b) model, Bond and Syropoulos (1996b) show that the relationship between the (absolute) size of blocs and the level of external tariffs is ambiguous.

phase, Ω remains relatively constant, but V shifts downward, and as a consequence the multilateral tariff rises during the period of transition. Finally, in the third phase, the PTA is fully implemented, and the full trade-diversion effect takes force. In this third phase, therefore, the current trading volume is low, which implies that the function Ω then shifts downward as well. This implies in turn that the multilateral tariff falls back toward its initial (first-phase) level once the PTA is fully implemented. Overall, this discussion suggests that the transition to trade-diverting PTAs is likely to bring about a period of temporarily heightened multilateral trade tensions in which trade disputes pro-liferate and further efforts to reduce multilateral tariffs become temporarily stalled.[12]

While trade diversion is one important consequence of the formation of PTAs, in the case of customs unions there is an additional market power effect that must be considered. To understand the implications of this effect, we again examine the multilateral relationship between a member and nonmember country as they pass through three phases. In the first phase, the customs union has yet to be proposed, and a multilateral tariff is determined (as in figure 6.1). In the second phase, the customs-union agreement is announced and the transition begins. The recognition of an eventual customs union raises the cost of a trade war, at least as viewed by the nonmember country, since the market power effect implies that the Nash tariff of the eventual customs union would be high. Thus, in terms of figure 6.1, as countries pass from the first to the second phase, the function V shifts up for the nonmember country, and this country is thus willing to cooperate with a lower multilateral tariff. Finally, in the third phase, the customs union is fully implemented. At this point the external tariffs of member countries are harmonized, and so the market power effect becomes real. This implies in turn that the temptation to cheat for the member country (i.e., the customs union) increases, corresponding to an upward shift in Ω for this country. Multilateral tariffs may thus rise once the agreement is fully implemented. Overall, this discussion suggests that the transition to a market-power-enhancing customs union is likely to bring about a "honeymoon" period of temporary tranquility in multilateral trade relations in which low multilateral tariffs can be negotiated and, for a while, sustained.[13]

---

12. See Bagwell and Staiger (1997c) for a formal treatment of these ideas.
13. See Bagwell and Staiger (1997b) for a formal treatment of these ideas.

The theories presented here suggest a novel interpretation of the historical experiences mentioned above. As discussed, over the transition phase corresponding to the formation and extension of the EC, multilateral tariff cooperation under GATT was enhanced. If it is accepted that the EC customs union offered its member countries greater market power than they would have otherwise possessed, then it can be argued that the enhanced multilateral cooperation was spurred in part by the growing awareness of the United States and others that a breakdown in multilateral cooperation might have especially dire consequences in the presence of a united group of European countries.[14] More recent PTAs, by contrast, have largely taken the form of free-trade areas. In this case the market-power effect is absent, and so the trade-diversion effect warrants emphasis. To the extent that an apparent tension has arisen between the formation of PTAs and the performance of GATT/WTO, it can be argued that these tensions will diminish as the transition process progresses.

We consider finally a third effect of PTAs that emerges when member and nonmember countries are asymmetric. We refer to this effect as a *free-rider enforcement effect*, since it highlights a potential free-riding cost to MFN that is associated with the enforcement of multilateral tariff cooperation. To see the general point, imagine a "competing exporters" model, with three countries and three goods, where consumers in each country consume all goods and each country imports exactly one good from each of its two trading partners. Thus country A imports good α from countries B and C, country B imports good β from countries A and C, and country C imports good γ from countries A and B. In line with the two-country model of chapter 6, if the respective countries and governments were symmetric, then the governments would each balance the short-term incentive to cheat against the long-term cost of a consequent trade war, and some most-cooperative tariff would be implied. Suppose now, though, that the governments of countries A

---

14. For example, appearing before the Joint Economic Committee to speak on the Trade Expansion Act of 1962 (which provided US negotiating authority for the Kennedy Round), former Secretary of State Christian Herter summarized the challenge posed by the newly forming EC customs union and the US response to that challenge as follows: "... if we are to go in one direction and Europe go in the other, inevitably, you will find trade barriers growing as between two large free trade areas. With these trade barriers growing, you would find ... the slowing down of trade, both imports and exports ... So what is the alternative to this picture? The alternative, to my mind, is to reconcile our policies with those of Europe, with a view to increasing trade on both sides ..." (Herter 1961, p. 12).

and B are more patient than is the government of country C. Then, as the cooperative tariff is lowered, eventually a critical tariff is hit at which the incentive constraint binds for the government of country C. At this critical tariff, the incentive constraint for the governments of countries A and B is slack: these more patient governments are able to enforce greater cooperation (a lower tariff).

Suppose first that the MFN rule is rigidly applied, so that PTAs are forbidden. In this case the governments of countries A and B can enjoy bilateral liberalization between themselves only if they extend tariff reductions multilaterally to country C as well. In the most-cooperative equilibrium the three governments enforce tariffs that lie below the critical symmetric level just described. The interesting point is that the two patient governments offer tariff reductions in excess of that which they require from the impatient government. This is because the government of country C is not sufficiently patient to support further symmetric tariff liberalization. Under the MFN rule the patient governments therefore provide hegemonic leadership, and the impatient government free rides on this leadership. Consider now a second case where countries A and B are joined through a PTA. If the governments of these countries are sufficiently patient, then they are able to enforce free trade between themselves, so that the PTA conforms with Article XXIV. The free-rider benefits enjoyed by the impatient government now may be lost, however: the governments of countries A and B no longer need to extend a multilateral tariff reduction in order to liberalize with one another. Consequently the free-rider enforcement effect suggests that the formation of a PTA may be associated with higher multilateral tariffs between member and nonmember governments.

In view of this third effect, does world welfare rise with the formation of a PTA? The answer to this question hinges on the extent to which governments are able to enforce low MFN tariffs. If under the MFN rule governments are able to enforce sufficiently low tariffs, then the further bilateral liberalization that a PTA offers is small, and a PTA thus may harm world welfare. By contrast, if under the MFN rule the most-cooperative tariffs remain high, then a PTA may enhance world welfare, since the gains from further bilateral liberalization may overwhelm the cost of any diminishment in the extent of multilateral tariff cooperation. In very broad terms we conclude then that PTAs may enhance (diminish) efficiency when the level of multilateral tariff cooperation under the MFN rule is modest (significant).[15]

We conclude the discussion to this point with some brief remarks concerning the implications of PTAs for the multilateral trading system. On net, the (politically augmented) terms-of-trade approach suggests that PTAs may pose a threat to the existing multilateral trading system. Ignoring the enforcement implications of PTAs, we argued here that such agreements may compromise the effectiveness with which the principles of reciprocity and nondiscrimination can deliver efficient outcomes. Moreover the consequence of PTAs for the enforcement of multilateral trade agreements is ambiguous, as it is sensitive to the time period of analysis, the relative significance of the trade diversion and market-power effects and the extent to which governments can achieve multilateral cooperation under the MFN rule.

7.4   Other Approaches

Before proceeding to our next topic, we pause to discuss recent work that considers PTAs and the multilateral trading system using alternative modeling approaches. We describe first work by McLaren (2002), who adopts the commitment approach to trade agreements and argues that this approach, too, suggests that PTAs are potentially threatening for the multilateral trading system. Second, we discuss Ethier's (1998a,b) approach, wherein the value of a trade agreement derives from an international scale economy and the consequences of multilateral liberalization for PTAs are featured.

McLaren (2002) emphasizes the investments that private-sector agents may make in anticipation of a regional trade agreement (a PTA with a neighboring country). If agents anticipate the regional agreement, then they make investments that are appropriate for that outcome. Then, when it comes time for the governments to choose

---

15. See Bagwell and Staiger (1999b) for a formal development of this conclusion. As we argue there, this conclusion receives further support from a tariff-complementarity effect that the competing-exporter model implies. Namely, when countries A and B form a PTA in order to lower their bilateral tariffs, they each import less from country C, so the optimal tariff that each would apply to country C's exports falls as well. According to this effect a PTA may enhance multilateral tariff cooperation if the initial level of cooperation is modest, as then the divergence between cooperative and optimal tariffs is small. Otherwise, the reduction in the optimal tariff that a PTA implies may diminish the level of multilateral tariff cooperation, since the Nash punishment threat is then less severe.

whether to liberalize regionally or multilaterally, these investments, being most valuable in the context of the regional trading pattern, ensure that the governments indeed follow through and liberalize regionally. As McLaren (2002) notes, regionalism may thus obey a kind of Say's Law, with the anticipated supply of regionalism inducing investments that result in an ex post demand for regionalism.[16] While the regional agreement is sensible ex post, the regional equilibrium can be Pareto inferior from an ex ante perspective: it would have been better if agents had anticipated a multilateral agreement and invested accordingly. Thus the negative effects of regionalism are somewhat "insidious," operating under the surface through the investments; correspondingly a case can be made that governments may benefit from committing to a multilateral trade institution under which regional agreements are not allowed (in contrast to GATT's Article XXIV).

At the same time it is important to note that the commitment approach also may be utilized to suggest that governments may benefit from committing to a multilateral trade institution under which regional agreements *are* allowed. To make this point, we recall the discussion in section 2.1.4 of the work by Maggi and Rodriguez (1998), who argue that a government may sometimes choose to commit to a free-trade agreement, in order to deter socially inefficient investments that otherwise would be made by private-sector participants in the expectation of subsequent protection. The comparison of these two papers suggests that there may be a robust benefit to governments from using a trade agreement as a vehicle through which to make a commitment. The comparison also suggests, however, that the *form* of commitment that a government should make may well vary significantly with the fine details of the model.

Ethier (1998a,b) emphasizes international scale economies and advances a positive view of regional agreements. In Ethier's model a multilateral trade agreement among developed countries allows those countries to jointly set their tariffs in a way that internalizes the international externality associated with these scale economies. The resulting creation of a large, integrated market produces a direct welfare benefit for the developed countries, and it also increases the motivation for small developing countries to undertake policy reforms and join the multilateral system. Ethier assumes that the success of such

---

16. Freund and McLaren (1999) offer some empirical support for this general approach. Looking at various regional agreements, they argue that the data provide strong support for anticipatory sunk investments.

reform attempts is enhanced if the reforming country can attract foreign investment, and this is where a potentially important role can be played by regional agreements. Specifically, a regional agreement between a developed and a developing country can serve to bring foreign investment into the developing country, because foreign investors seek to take advantage of the preferential access to the markets of the developed country which the developing country enjoys as a result of this agreement. According to this argument, then, regional agreements can be used by reforming developing countries to attract foreign direct investment, and in this way to ensure that their reform efforts—and thereby their attempts to join the multilateral system— succeed. And the growth in regional agreements can be interpreted as indicative of the growing attractiveness of being part of the multilateral system, which is itself an indication of the success of multilateral trade liberalization.[17]

---

17. Freund (2000a) also considers the impact of multilateral liberalization on the formation of PTAs. A further issue is whether a regional or multilateral path to free trade is preferred. Under the assumption that free trade is eventually achieved, Freund (2000c) argues that world welfare during free trade is greater when it is achieved through expanding regional agreements. Working with a Cournot model, she shows that firms in a PTA have a strategic incentive to make sunk investments that reduce marginal costs, as they then fare better in the eventual free-trade outcome. Such investments increase output and thus world welfare.

8   Labor and Environmental Standards

We now turn to the issue of labor and environmental standards. Choices over traditionally "domestic" policies such as these raise difficult questions concerning GATT's ability to promote global efficiency while respecting national sovereignty. Existing GATT rules speak to this issue only to the extent that market-access concerns are directly involved, and the domestic labor and environmental standards that member governments choose to adopt have never been the subject of direct GATT/WTO negotiations. But there is mounting pressure for this to change. A number of industrialized countries have recently proposed the adoption of a "social clause," in which a set of minimum international standards would be negotiated and then enforced with the threat of trade sanctions. Such proposals appear to be responsive to growing fears of a "race to the bottom" fueled by rising imports from low-standards countries, but these proposals encroach on traditional limits of national sovereignty and challenge prevailing norms of international economic relations among sovereign states. Is the GATT/WTO's traditional preoccupation with market access misplaced when the issue of labor and environmental standards is raised? Should WTO member governments embark on negotiations within the WTO over their national labor and environmental standards? Should the WTO's limited enforcement ability be utilized to ensure that national labor and environmental standards are set in an appropriate fashion? In this chapter we summarize a literature that provides answers to these questions.

8.1   Labor and Environmental Standards in GATT

As our description in chapter 3 indicates, GATT's central concern is with the removal of trade barriers to market access. By contrast, its approach to labor and environmental standards is best characterized as somewhere between "neglect" and "benign neglect." There are really two dimensions of GATT's approach to this issue, and they correspond to (1) the freedom each country has to determine its own domestic standards (i.e., the range of domestic standards that are GATT-legal), and (2) the freedom with which each country may claim an exception for an "original" action so that it can respond with trade measures to the (GATT-legal) standards chosen by its trading partners.[1] To understand the implications of GATT rules along these two dimensions, it may be helpful at a broad level to distinguish further between domestic standards that relate to production (e.g., a country's child labor laws or its regulations regarding the disposal of industrial waste) and domestic standards that relate to consumption (e.g., a country's recycling laws or its regulations controlling the sale and distribution of the products of prison labor). In general, countries have broad freedom under GATT's rules to determine their own standards, though this freedom is somewhat greater with regard to production standards than it is with regard to consumption standards. On the other hand, as far as the ability to claim exceptions for an original action in order to respond to the (GATT-legal) standards choices of their trading partners, countries face fairly significant limitations under GATT rules.

Consider first the case of production standards. The determination of such standards is regarded by GATT to be the legitimate domain of each national government. In effect, then, each country is free under GATT rules to determine its own (nondiscriminatory) labor and environmental standards as these standards relate to production processes within its borders, and in particular, weak labor or environmental standards do not constitute a violation of GATT obligations. This is the first dimension of GATT's approach to production standards, and it has implications for the second dimension: as a general rule, GATT/WTO members are not granted exceptions from their market-access obligations (e.g., nondiscrimination, tariff bindings) to respond to the (weak) labor or environmental production standards of a trading partner.[2]

---

1. For a very useful discussion of the way standards are currently handled in the WTO, see Enders (1996).

2. Hence, in the high-profile 1991 GATT tuna–dolphin dispute between the United States and Mexico, it was not the right of the United States to set its own environmental (production) standards with respect to the protection and conservation of dolphins that was challenged. What was challenged as GATT-illegal was the decision by the United States

Consider next the case of consumption standards. As with production standards, the determination of consumption standards is also considered by GATT to be the legitimate domain of each national government, but there is an important difference: whereas the implementation of production standards typically does not involve direct measures to restrict market access, consumption standards frequently require interference with or outright bans on imports that do not meet those standards, and this in turn often requires a government to exercise an exception for an original action. More specifically, exceptions from GATT Article I (nondiscrimination), Article III (national treatment), Article XI (which prohibits the use of quantitative restrictions), and other articles are provided under GATT Article XX so that, for example, governments may restrict importation of the products of prison labor and impose trade restrictions as necessary to conserve exhaustible natural resources or to protect human, animal, or plant life or health. Evidently the implementation of a stringent consumption standard could, in principle, offer governments a fairly direct route to reimpose, in a "disguised" form under an Article XX exception, protection they had previously negotiated away. Recognizing this possibility, the chapeau of Article XX requires that these exceptions must not be ". . . applied in a manner which would constitute a means of arbitrary or unjustifiable discrimination between countries where the same conditions prevail, or a disguised restriction on international trade. . . ."

In effect, then, each country is free under GATT rules to determine its own (nondiscriminatory) labor and environmental standards as they relate to consumption within its borders, but unusually stringent consumption standards—and more specifically, the trade measures that are introduced to implement these standards—may constitute a violation of GATT obligations, if they are deemed to reflect protectionist

---

to impose a discriminatory trade embargo against Mexican tuna imports in response to the environmental standards of Mexico. Note also that erecting (nondiscriminatory) trade restrictions per se in response to the labor or environmental standards of a trading partner is not GATT-illegal: if the tariff in question is not bound in a GATT schedule, then a country is of course free to raise the tariff for this (or any other) reason, and needs no exception from its GATT obligations in order to do so. And even where the tariff in question is covered by a GATT binding, the country could still take an exception and raise its tariff through an Article XXVIII renegotiation, but as we have described in chapter 3 it would then be required to offer a compensatory adjustment or face a reciprocal tariff increase from its trading partner (see also note 9 to chapter 3).

motives and for this reason do not qualify as an exception under Article XX.[3]

With regard to the freedom that countries have to set their own standards, GATT's rules are thus somewhat less permissive for consumption than production standards. In terms of the freedom that countries have to respond to the (GATT-legal) standards of others, however, GATT rules do not draw a sharp distinction between consumption and production standards: as a general rule, GATT/WTO members are not granted exceptions from their market-access obligations (e.g., nondiscrimination, tariff bindings) to respond to the (strong) labor or environmental consumption standards of a trading partner.

We have described the specific GATT rules by which the domestic labor and environmental policies chosen by member governments are accommodated. But, as a means to ensure that the commercial opportunities (market access) implied by tariff commitments are not eroded subsequently by *changes* in domestic policy choices, these specific rules have shortcomings that have long been a source of concern. Hudec (1990, p. 24) describes the problem as it was perceived by the original GATT drafters:

. . . The standard trade policy rules could deal with the common types of trade policy measure governments usually employ to control trade. But trade can also be affected by other "domestic" measures, such as product safety standards, having nothing to do with trade policy. It would have been next to impossible to catalogue all such possibilities in advance. Moreover, governments would never have agreed to circumscribe their freedom in all these other areas for the sake of a mere tariff agreement.

The shortcomings of the standard legal commitments were recognized in a report by a group of trade experts at the London Monetary and Economic Conference of 1933. The group concluded that trade agreements should have another more general provision which would address itself to any other government action that produced an adverse effect on the balance of commercial opportunity. . . .

---

3. A recent prominent example of an Article XX action that was successfully challenged under Article XXIII was the (violation) complaint brought by the United States and Canada against EU prohibitions on the importation of hormone-treated beef. In this case the EU (consumption and production) standard was set above internationally recognized standards, and was deemed to lack a sufficient scientific basis to justify the unusual stringency. The rules for the application of Article XX were elaborated upon in the Agreement on the Application of Sanitary and Phytosanitary Measures (the SPS Agreement) that energed from the Uruguay Round. The Beef Hormones case resulted in the first decision by a WTO panel based on the SPS Agreement.

As Hudec documents, these concerns eventually led to the inclusion of provisions for nonviolation nullification-or-impairment complaints in GATT's Article XXIII.[4]

As we noted in chapter 3 and discussed further in chapter 5 (section 5.3.3), the ability to bring nonviolation Article XXIII complaints provides each GATT/WTO member government with a general right of redress whenever it can show that market-access commitments which it had previously negotiated are being systematically offset by an unanticipated change in the policies—any policies but including in principle the labor and environmental standards—of another GATT member, even if these policy changes broke no explicit GATT rules. As detailed in section 5.3.3, under a successful nonviolation complaint, the complaining country is entitled to a rebalancing of market-access commitments, wherein either its trading partner finds a way to offer compensation for the trade effects of its domestic policy change (typically in the form of other policy changes that restore the original market access) or the complaining country is permitted to withdraw an equivalent market-access concession of its own. In principle, nullification-or-impairment complaints can therefore secure the balance of negotiated market-access commitments against erosion as a result of future changes in labor or environmental standards, and in this way such complaints constitute a potentially important element of GATT's approach to these domestic policies.

Indeed, as it was originally conceived, the concept of nonviolation complaints was to have just this kind of broad applicability. For example, the possibility of bringing nullification-or-impairment claims in the context of labor standards was clearly envisioned. Article 7 of the Havana Charter for the ITO states that "The Members recognize that unfair labour conditions, particularly in production for export, create difficulties in international trade, and, accordingly, each Member shall take whatever action may be appropriate and feasible to eliminate such conditions within its territory," and then makes explicit reference to the use of the nullification-or-impairment clauses of the Havana Charter in "matters relating to labour standards." More generally, there was an expectation that nonviolation nullification-or-impairment complaints might arise in a very broad set of

---

4. In particular, as Hudec (1990 p. 24, n. 1) observes, the draft nullification-or-impairment clause contained in the conference report of the London Conference (League of Nations 1933, p. 30) is thought to be the origin of the "nullification-or-impairment" concept.

circumstances, but this expectation has in fact not been borne out in GATT practice (Petersmann 1997, p. 170).[5] Nevertheless, as we consider further below, the possible role that nonviolation complaints can play in preventing governments from distorting their labor and environmental policies for commercial advantage should not be overlooked.

In summary, and as the forgoing discussion indicates, GATT's approach to the issue of labor and environmental standards reflects the primacy of market-access concerns in GATT more broadly. In essence, GATT rules are designed to provide governments with a legal framework within which to make and secure market-access commitments, and provided that this is achieved, the rules also respect the sovereignty of domestic decisions over labor and environmental standards. Put differently, GATT rules allow each member government to choose its own domestic standards without GATT involvement, so long as the existing market-access commitments it has made are not undermined by those choices.

From the backdrop of this description of GATT's approach to labor and environmental standards, we now extend the basic model to incorporate the choice of standards policies so that we can interpret and evaluate this approach. We first describe the extended model. Next we consider the purpose of a trade agreement; that is, we identify the "problem" that an appropriately designed trade agreement may "solve" in this extended setting. With this identification we may then pose and answer the three questions raised at the beginning of this chapter: Is the GATT/WTO's traditional preoccupation with market access misplaced when the issue of labor and environmental standards

---

5. The limited use of nonviolation complaints in GATT practice is explained in the report of the WTO Appellate Body in the recent Asbestos case this way: "Like the panel in Japan—Measures Affecting Consumer Photographic Film and Paper ('Japan—Film'), we consider that the remedy in Article XXIII:1(b) 'should be approached with caution and should remain an exceptional remedy'. That panel stated: Although the non-violation remedy is an important and accepted tool of WTO/GATT dispute settlement and has been 'on the books' for almost 50 years, we note that there have only been eight cases in which panels or working parties have substantively considered Article XXIII:1(b) claims. This suggests that both the GATT contracting parties and WTO Members have approached this remedy with caution and, indeed, have treated it as an exceptional instrument of dispute settlement. . . . The reason for this caution is straightforward. Members negotiate the rules that they agree to follow and only exceptionally would expect to be challenged for actions not in contravention of those rules." (para 185). As observed in Bagwell, Mavroidis, and Staiger (2002), however, the Asbestos report goes on to state clearly that while nonviolation cases traditionally have been concerned with commercial policies (e.g., subsidies), nonviolation claims can in principle be made against "noncommercial," such as health, measures as well.

is raised? Should WTO member governments embark on negotiations within the WTO over their national labor and environmental standards? Should the WTO's limited enforcement ability be utilized to ensure that national labor and environmental standards are set in an appropriate fashion?

8.2   The Model with Domestic Standards

The essential features of the arguments can be highlighted by extending the basic two-country model developed in chapter 2 to allow each government the choice of a domestic standard, in addition to its choice of tariff policy. We restrict attention to cases in which the underlying motive for standards reflects national issues (e.g., a government's concern for the health and safety of its citizens, or the environmental quality within its borders) so that one country's standards become a concern to the government of another country only as a result of the implications of these standards for the trading relationship between the two countries. This restricted focus rules out cases (e.g., global warming) in which an international nonpecuniary externality is of central concern and allows us to focus instead on concerns (e.g., the "race to the bottom") that are tied inextricably to trade. Following Bagwell and Staiger (2001a), we first extend the basic two-country two-good general equilibrium model to incorporate the effects of domestic standards, and we then define government preferences in this extended setting.

8.2.1   The General Equilibrium Model

Beginning from the basic two-country two-good general equilibrium trade model described in section 2.1.1, in which the home (foreign) country imports x (y) in exchange for exports of y (x), we now introduce a standards policy for the domestic country, which we represent by the parameter s, and similarly a standards policy for the foreign country, which we represent by s^*. To fix ideas, we may think of each country as being endowed with supplies of a variety of productive factors, including workers of various ages, and of the domestic and foreign standards as corresponding to the minimum legal working age in the domestic and foreign import-competing sectors, respectively. We maintain this interpretation throughout our discussion, though many other kinds of (production or consumption) standards also fit within this general framework (see Bagwell and Staiger 2001a).

As before, each country's import demand and export supply can be expressed as functions of its local relative price and the terms of trade, but these functions now depend as well on the choice of standards.[6] In particular, the home country's import demand and export supply functions depend on the minimum legal working age in the import-competing sector of the home country, s, while the foreign country's import demand and export supply functions depend on the minimum legal working age in the foreign country's import-competing sector, s^*. Hence s and s^* act as "shift" parameters in the import demand and export supply functions of the home and foreign country respectively, and we assume that these functions are differentiable in their respective standard levels.

Incorporating the level of standards into each country's import demand and export supply functions, we may then write the home and foreign budget constraints, in analogy with (2.1) and (2.2), as

$$p^w M(s, p, p^w) = E(s, p, p^w), \tag{8.1}$$

$$M^*(s^*, p^*, p^w) = p^w E^*(s^*, p^*, p^w). \tag{8.2}$$

Making explicit the dependence of the local prices on the tariffs and the world price, we now determine the equilibrium world price, $\tilde{p}^w(\tau, s, \tau^*, s^*)$, by the requirement of market clearing for good y:

$$E(s, p(\tau, \tilde{p}^w), \tilde{p}^w) = M^*(s^*, p^*(\tau^*, \tilde{p}^w), \tilde{p}^w), \tag{8.3}$$

with market clearing for good x then implied by (8.1), (8.2), and (8.3). Thus, given national standards in each country and a pair of tariffs, the equilibrium world price is determined by (8.3), and the equilibrium world price and the given tariffs then determine in turn the local prices. In this way the national standards and tariffs imply local and world prices, and together with these the production, consumption, import, export, and tariff revenue levels are determined. Finally, we continue to assume that the Metzler and Lerner paradoxes are ruled out so that $dp/d\tau > 0 > dp^*/d\tau^*$ and $\partial \tilde{p}^w/\partial \tau < 0 < \partial \tilde{p}^w/\partial \tau^*$, and we impose the additional assumption that the Marshall-Lerner stability conditions are met so that an inward shift of the domestic (foreign) import demand curve leads to a lower (higher) equilibrium world price.

---

6. We may think of a country's labor standards as altering its production possibilities set and the distribution of income across its citizens, and in this way affecting its import demand and export supply functions.

8.2.2 Government Preferences

We next extend our representation of government preferences to include a country's standards. We represent the objectives of the home and foreign governments with the general functions $W(s, p, \tilde{p}^w)$ and $W^*(s^*, p^*, \tilde{p}^w)$ respectively. In analogy with our earlier representations of government preferences, we assume that, holding its local price and its national standards fixed, each government achieves higher welfare when its terms of trade improve,

$$W_{\tilde{p}^w}(s, p, \tilde{p}^w) < 0 \quad \text{and} \quad W^*_{\tilde{p}^w}(s^*, p^*, \tilde{p}^w) > 0, \tag{8.4}$$

but we leave government objective functions otherwise unrestricted.

Notice that each government cares about the policy choices—both tariffs and domestic standards—of its trading partner only indirectly, through the effects that these choices have (via trade) on equilibrium world prices. This important property derives from two features of our extended framework. First, we are, by assumption, ruling out global social concerns and international nonpecuniary externalities of any kind. Hence one government has no reason to care about the labor laws chosen by its trading partner unless those choices have consequences for trade between the two countries. With this assumption, we therefore restrict attention to the international economic interaction between countries. And second, the nature of international economic interaction itself ensures that the trade effects imposed on one government by the policy choices of the other travel through equilibrium world prices.

8.3 The Purpose of a Trade Agreement

As in section 2.1 we begin with the most basic question: What is the purpose of a trade agreement? In this extended setting, where governments choose domestic standards as well as trade policies, we wish to identify any new sources of inefficiency that might arise (and which an appropriately designed international agreement could then correct) when governments set their trade and domestic policies unilaterally.

We proceed in three steps. We first characterize efficient trade and domestic policy choices, and we interpret the conditions for efficiency. Next we characterize the noncooperative policy choices that governments would make if they set their trade and domestic policies unilaterally, and we interpret this characterization as well. Our final step is to compare the efficient and noncooperative policy choices so that we may identify and interpret the sources of inefficiency that an appropriately designed international agreement can correct.

8.3.1 Efficient Policies

An efficient set of trade and domestic policies for the home and foreign government must achieve the maximal level of home-government welfare for any given level of welfare for the foreign government. The (necessary) conditions that characterize the solutions to this optimization problem can be represented, after some manipulation, as

$$W_s\left(\frac{1}{\partial \tilde{p}^w/\partial s}\right) = W_p\left(\frac{\tilde{p}^w}{\partial \tilde{p}^w/\partial \tau}\right), \tag{8.5}$$

$$W_{s^*}^*\left(\frac{1}{\partial \tilde{p}^w/\partial s^*}\right) = W_{p^*}^*\left(\frac{-p^*/\tau^*}{\partial \tilde{p}^w/\partial \tau^*}\right), \tag{8.6}$$

$$(1 - AW_p) = \frac{1}{1 - A^* W_{p^*}^*} \tag{8.7}$$

where, as before,

$A \equiv (1 - \tau\lambda)/(W_p + \lambda W_{\tilde{p}^w})$

$A^* \equiv (1 - \lambda^*/\tau^*)/(W_{p^*}^* + \lambda^* W_{\tilde{p}^w}^*),$

$\lambda \equiv [\partial \tilde{p}^w/\partial \tau]/[dp/d\tau] < 0,$

$\lambda^* \equiv [\partial \tilde{p}^w/\partial \tau^*]/[dp^*/d\tau^*] < 0.$

These conditions may be given a useful interpretation. In particular, (8.5) and (8.6) may be interpreted as "national" efficiency conditions for the home and foreign government respectively, while (8.7) may be interpreted as the "international" efficiency condition.

To see this interpretation, consider first the home government national efficiency condition (8.5). This condition says that at an efficient policy combination, any small changes in τ and s that together leave the equilibrium world price unaltered must leave the welfare of the home government unchanged as well.[7] Intuitively, such policy changes have no effect on the welfare of the foreign government, as by construction they leave the equilibrium world price unaltered, and so efficiency requires that the home government is not able to improve its

---

7. Changes in τ and s which preserve $\tilde{p}^w$ must satisfy $d\tau/ds = [-\partial \tilde{p}^w/\partial s]/[\partial \tilde{p}^w/\partial \tau]$. The condition that home-government welfare cannot be altered by such changes is then $W_s + W_p[\tilde{p}^w(-\partial \tilde{p}^w/\partial s)/(\partial \tilde{p}^w/\partial \tau)] = 0$, which simplifies to (8.5).

own welfare with such changes. Next observe from the market-clearing condition (8.3) that changes in τ and s, which together leave the equilibrium world price unaltered, must leave equilibrium trade volumes unaltered as well. Recalling now the definition of market access given in section 2.1.3, we may interpret the home-government national efficiency condition (8.5) as saying that the domestic government should be allowed to adopt its preferred *policy mix* for delivering the given amount of market access at the given equilibrium world price. An analogous interpretation holds for the foreign-government national efficiency condition (8.6): the foreign government should be allowed to adopt its preferred policy mix for delivering the given amount of market access at the given equilibrium world price. Finally (8.7) now may be interpreted as the international efficiency condition, since it requires that policies are set so that the equilibrium trade volumes (market-access levels at the equilibrium world price) are indeed efficient.

8.3.2 Noncooperative Policies

We next consider the noncooperative Nash policy choices in this extended setting. In the Nash equilibrium, each government sets its trade and domestic policies to maximize its objective function taking as given the policy choices of its trading partner. These optimization problems generate a pair of home-government reaction functions, and a pair of foreign-government reaction functions, that can be written respectively as

$$W_s\left(\frac{1}{\partial \tilde{p}^w / \partial s}\right) = -\left(\tau W_p + W_{\tilde{p}^w}\right), \tag{8.8}$$

$$W_p + \lambda W_{\tilde{p}^w} = 0, \tag{8.9}$$

$$W_{s^*}^*\left(\frac{1}{\partial \tilde{p}^w / \partial s^*}\right) = -\left(\frac{1}{\tau^*} W_{p^*}^* + W_{\tilde{p}^w}^*\right), \tag{8.10}$$

$$W_{p^*}^* + \lambda^* W_{\tilde{p}^w}^* = 0. \tag{8.11}$$

The Nash equilibrium policy choices for the home and foreign governments require that each government be on its pair of reaction curves, and hence noncooperative policy choices simultaneously solve (8.8) through (8.11).

To interpret these conditions, consider the home government's reaction curves defined by (8.8) and (8.9). Condition (8.8) requires that the home government sets its national standard so that the direct effect on its welfare of a small change in this standard just offsets the indirect effect on its welfare that the induced world price movement implies.[8] Similarly (8.9) dictates that the home government sets its tariff so that the welfare effect of a small change in the local price induced by a change in its tariff is just offset by the indirect welfare effect that the world price movement induced by this tariff change implies.

We may also observe that with $\lambda < 0$ and $W_{\tilde{p}^w} < 0$, (8.9) implies that $W_p < 0$ in the Nash equilibrium as well. Hence, as in the basic model described in section 2.1.3, the home government is induced by the terms-of-trade effects of its policy choices to protect its import-competing sector (and therefore raise its local import-competing price) by a greater amount than it would choose based on the local-price effects of this protection alone. Moreover, with $W_p < 0$ now established, it also may be seen that (8.8) implies that $\text{sign}(W_s) = \text{sign}(\partial \tilde{p}^w / \partial s)$: the home government is induced by the terms-of-trade effects of its policy choices to adopt national standards that are more favorable to its terms of trade than it would choose to adopt based only on the direct impact of these standards on its welfare.

8.3.3 Identifying the Inefficiency

Conditions (8.5) through (8.11) and their interpretations allow a rather direct identification of the nature of the inefficiency that arises when governments set trade and domestic policies noncooperatively. When governments set their trade and domestic policies unilaterally in a non-cooperative fashion, they restrict market access below efficient levels. This is *the* inefficiency that an appropriately designed international agreement can correct.

Formally this can be seen by noting that (8.8) and (8.9) imply (8.5), while (8.10) and (8.11) imply (8.6), but (8.9) and (8.11) violate (8.7). Hence only the international condition for efficiency is violated by non-cooperative policy choices. This may be understood intuitively, once it is recalled that the national efficiency conditions simply require that no government can gain from changes in its policy mix that preserve the given amount of market access at the given equilibrium world price. But at the Nash equilibrium, this requirement must hold, since then no government can gain from a unilateral policy change of any kind.

---

8. This interpretation follows, once it is observed that $-[\tau W_p + W_{\tilde{p}^w}]$ gives the impact on home government welfare of a small decrease in $\tilde{p}^w$, when the home tariff is held fixed.

When governments set their trade and domestic policies unilaterally therefore, they get the policy mix right, but they get the level of market access wrong. In fact it can be shown (see Bagwell and Staiger 2001a) that conditions (8.5) through (8.11) imply that market-access levels are inefficiently low. At a broad level, these observations suggest a sort of "targeting approach" to the design of an appropriate international agreement in this setting: let governments negotiate over the levels of market access that they are willing to deliver, and then let each government decide unilaterally on the best policy mix with which to deliver the agreed-upon access to its markets. As we next confirm, this is effectively the logic behind GATT's approach to labor and environmental standards.

8.4 Trade Agreements and National Sovereignty

We are now ready to consider the first two questions raised at the beginning of this chapter: Is the GATT/WTO's traditional preoccupation with market access misplaced when the issue of labor and environmental standards is raised? Should WTO member governments embark on negotiations within the WTO over their national labor and environmental standards? The observations above can help provide answers to these questions.

Consider the first question posed above. At one level, the answer to this question follows as a direct corollary to the identification of the inefficiency that an appropriately designed international agreement can correct: the essential problem for an international agreement to solve is one of insufficient market access, and so aiding its member governments in their attempts to negotiate increased market access should be the overriding concern of the GATT/WTO, whether the particular issue before it involves the tariff policies of its member governments, their choice of labor or environmental standards, or any other policy decisions that have significant market-access implications. At this level the GATT/WTO's preoccupation with market access is then well suited to handle the issue of labor and environmental standards.

At another level, the answer to this first question is more subtle. While insufficient market access *is* the problem to solve, there is a risk that if the international agreement is not appropriately designed, the efforts of governments to achieve greater levels of market access can become the root *cause* of inefficient choices over labor and environmental policies. This risk can be seen clearly by returning to the model

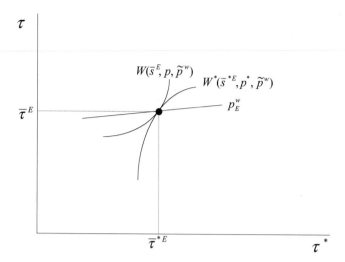

Figure 8.1a

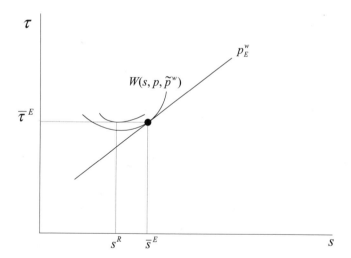

Figure 8.1b

described above, and considering the incentives to distort standards policies that are created when the home and foreign governments attempt to achieve efficient market-access levels through negotiated tariff reductions.

Figure 8.1 illustrates. With τ on the vertical axis and τ^* on the horizontal axis, figure 8.1a depicts the international efficiency condition (8.7) that must hold if the two governments do succeed in implement-

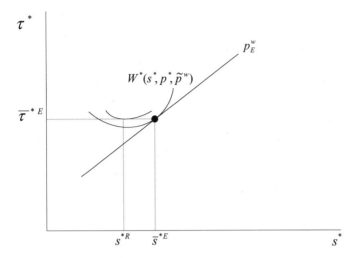

Figure 8.1c

ing an efficient combination of tariffs and domestic standards, ($\bar{\tau}^E$, $\bar{s}^E$, $\bar{\tau}^{*E}$, $\bar{s}^{*E}$). As this figure demonstrates, given their efficient standards choices, the efficient agreement will bind each country's tariff below its noncooperative level so as to achieve efficient levels of market access, and at this point no further adjustments in tariffs can benefit one government without hurting the other. To achieve this efficient policy combination, the two governments might agree to bind their tariffs at efficient levels, in the hope that each government would then follow through with the associated efficient national standard level that satisfies its respective national efficiency condition. But this hope would be in vain: having granted additional market access through its negotiated tariff concession, each government would now have an incentive to withdraw unilaterally a portion of this market access, by *distorting* its national standards choice.

These incentives are illustrated in figure 8.1b and c. Consider, for example, the incentive of the home government, illustrated in figure 8.1b. With the domestic tariff τ on the vertical axis and the domestic standard s on the horizontal axis, this figure illustrates the policy mix of the domestic government, and its depiction is consistent with our interpretation of the domestic standard as reflecting the minimum legal working age in the home-country import-competing sector. In particular, by raising the minimum legal working age in the import-competing sector, it is natural to assume that the home government causes an outward shift in the domestic import-demand curve, and hence an increase in $\tilde{p}^w$ (a deterioration in its terms of trade). This increase in $\tilde{p}^w$ can be offset by an appropriate increase in the domestic tariff τ, and the iso-$\tilde{p}^w$ loci in this figure are thus upward sloping. At the efficient policy combination, the domestic national efficiency condition (8.5) says that any small changes in τ and s that together leave the equilibrium world price unaltered must leave the welfare of the home government unchanged as well. This is also reflected in the figure, where the home-government indifference curve (which opens "up" because the efficient tariff binding is positioned below the domestic best-response tariff) is tangent to the iso-$\tilde{p}^w$ locus at the efficient policy choices.

As figure 8.1b makes clear, if the domestic government expected the foreign government to follow through with efficient foreign labor practices in light of the two governments' tariff commitments, the domestic government would then have an incentive to distort its labor standards away from the efficient level. In the particular case under consideration, the domestic government would benefit by *weakening* its labor standard and reducing the minimum legal working age in its import-competing sector from $\bar{s}^E$ to s^R, where in light of its bound tariff it achieves an optimal balance between the costs of further distorting its domestic labor standard and the benefits of the additional unilateral withdrawal of negotiated market access that this distortion implies. An analogous incentive for the foreign government to weaken its labor standard is reflected in figure 8.1c.

In this way figure 8.1 illustrates the potential for a kind of "race to the bottom" in national standards which is fueled by the efforts of governments to achieve greater market access through negotiated tariff commitments. At the same time it is clear that the race to the bottom is itself an indication of ineffective commitments to efficient levels of market access. But we may now draw an important lesson from this discussion. The race to the bottom, if it indeed exists, is *not* fueled by the weak standards of one's trading partners (notice that the preceding discussion of home-government incentives assumed that the foreign standard was set at its efficient level). Rather, it is caused by the shortcomings of the tariff binding as a means to secure commitments over market access.

Hence, in answer to our first question posed above, we may conclude that the GATT/WTO's preoccupation with market access is indeed well-suited to handle the issue of labor and environmental standards. But it is important that the market-access levels achieved through negotiated tariff commitments are secure under GATT/WTO rules.

Recalling now our discussion above of GATT's approach to labor and environmental standards, a potentially important role can be seen for GATT's provisions concerning non-violation nullification-or-impairment complaints. Specifically, the prospect of nonviolation complaints in GATT can enhance the security of market-access commitments, by mitigating the incentives—created by tariff liberalization— of governments to distort their standards policies for commercial advantage. In terms of figure 8.1b the prospect of a nonviolation complaint by the foreign government would prevent the domestic government from frustrating the foreign government's market-access expectations, by weakening the domestic labor standard subsequent to the conclusion of the tariff negotiations. This would in turn hold the domestic government to positions along the efficient iso-$\tilde{p}^w$ locus (labeled in the figure as p_E^w). From this vantage point, the domestic government no longer has an incentive to distort its labor standard away from the efficient level $\bar{s}^E$, and in this general manner the efficient combination of tariffs and domestic standards, ($\bar{\tau}^E$, $\bar{s}^E$, $\bar{\tau}^{*E}$, $\bar{s}^{*E}$), may be implemented with tariff negotiations alone.[9] With this observation, we have now provided an answer to the second question posed above as well: evidently, there is no need for governments to negotiate directly over their labor and environmental standards in order to achieve efficient tariff and domestic standards.

An alternative to addressing the "race to the bottom" identified above would be to incorporate labor standards directly into the negotiations so that governments would negotiate binding agreements over tariffs and standards policies. In some ways this alternative is reminiscent of the approach advocated by supporters of a WTO "social clause." But especially when compared to this alternative, it is clear that the approach taken by GATT bears a close resemblance to the logic of the "targeting approach" described above, which was in turn suggested by the identification of the inefficiency that an appropriately designed trade agreement can solve. In this sense GATT's approach to labor and environmental standards may be said to reflect rather tightly the logic of the underlying inefficiency that it exists to correct.[10]

---

9. For a formal demonstration of this point, see Bagwell and Staiger (2001a).

10. At a general level, Srinivasan (1996, p. 221) also observes that GATT's approach to labor and environmental standards can be viewed as reflecting a "targeting approach" logic as applied to international economic institutions. The reflection of this logic in GATT rules is not exact, however, and in Bagwell and Staiger (2001a) we identify where this reflection breaks down and consider ways to strenghten it. See also Bagwell and Staiger (2001d) and Bagwell, Mavroidis, and Staiger (2002).

8.5   Enforcement of Labor and Environmental Standards

We now turn to the third question raised at the beginning of this chapter: Should the WTO's limited enforcement ability be utilized to ensure that national labor and environmental standards are set in an appropriate fashion? This is a complex question with a number of distinct dimensions. To make progress in answering it, we first consider this question while maintaining our assumption that international nonpecuniary externalities are not the central concern when a standards issue arises. We then discuss the qualifications to our answers that must be added when important nonpecuniary externalities are present.

Where the underlying motives for standards reflect national issues, the preceding discussion applies. When this discussion is combined with the perspectives on enforcement contained in chapter 6, it suggests a simple answer to the question raised above: the WTO's limited enforcement power should be utilized to ensure that the policy mix of each government is always efficient and that market-access levels are set as close to their efficient levels as the enforcement incentive constraints permit. Intuitively, as described in section 6.1, the problem of enforcement boils down to keeping the market access that each country delivers to its trading partner at a manageable level. Shifts in the policy mix away from the choices that efficiently deliver a given level of market access serve only to reduce the value of maintaining the agreement, and so exacerbate the enforcement problem.

This is the point made in a recent paper by Ederington (2001). To make this point starkly, Ederington adopts a particular model in which the efficient domestic policy involves a Pigouvian tax to offset a domestic distortion, and this tax level continues to be efficient regardless of the level of the accompanying tariff chosen by the domestic government. Hence, in terms of our discussion above, in Ederington's model the efficient policy mix always involves setting the Pigouvian tax, for any given level of market access. In a repeated-game setting of the kind discussed in section 6.1, Ederington then shows that when two such countries attempt to cooperate over trade and domestic policies in a self-enforcing agreement, they agree to set their domestic taxes at the Pigouvian level, independently of the degree to which they discount the future, and then tailor their tariff bindings (and so adjust the level of market access) to satisfy the enforcement incentive constraint.

This answer is of special interest, in light of the government incentives discussed above. Evidently it is *never* a good idea to permit governments to distort their standards choices in order to obtain commercial advantage, regardless of how weak GATT/WTO enforcement mechanisms might be or how tempting these incentives may become with changing market conditions. This in turn provides a basis of support, from the perspective of limited enforcement power, for the broad efforts taken by the GATT/WTO (as discussed in section 3.2.1) to induce member governments to eliminate "disguised" protection and instead concentrate national protective measures in the form of tariffs.[11]

We now discuss several qualifications to the preceding discussion that must be added when important nonpecuniary international externalities (e.g., global warming) are present. Two new issues arise in the presence of such externalities. First, it is no longer possible in general to reach efficient policy outcomes with international negotiations over tariff bindings alone. This is because the inefficiency associated with unilateral policy choices can no longer be identified as simply an insufficient level of market access: the existence of nonpecuniary international externalities creates additional inefficiencies that have nothing to do with market access per se. This suggests that such inefficiencies might be best addressed through negotiations outside the GATT/WTO, such as those that led to the 1973 Convention on International Trade in Endangered Species (CITES) and the 1997 Kyoto Protocol to limit carbon emissions. But even then, there is still an important question about how such agreements are to be enforced, and especially whether trade sanctions should be part of the enforcement arsenal. This raises the second new issue: Should enforcement mechanisms be "linked" across agreements?

These issues are addressed in interesting recent work. Spagnolo (1999, 2000) considers a class of interdependent supergames and identifies general conditions under which issue linkage can create enforcement power and thus facilitate greater cooperation. In a subsequent effort Limao (2000) undertakes a similar analysis for a distinct class of interdependent supergames. Limao's analysis is of particular relevance for our purposes here, since he develops his arguments in the context of a fully specified political-economy model of trade and environmental policy. We thus discuss his paper in some detail.

Limao constructs a two-country, two-good model in which domestic production in the import-competing sector gives rise to a

---

11. This contrasts with the "transparency" justifications that are often given at an informal level for the GATT/WTO's preference for protection in the form of tariffs.

nonpecuniary (environmental) externality that is felt by domestic and (perhaps to an important degree) foreign residents. Each government has available two instruments: an import tariff and a domestic production tax. In the absence of any international agreement, each government would set its tariff at a higher-than-efficient level and its production tax at a lower-than-efficient level. Governments can thus gain from international agreements in which they cooperate by lowering tariffs and raising production taxes.

There are two approaches that might be considered. One approach is to construct *nonlinked agreements*, whereby a deviation by a government in any policy induces retaliation from the other government only in the same policy. Cooperation under nonlinked agreements is constrained by three incentive constraints: a government must be dissuaded from (1) cheating with a higher tariff and facing a retaliatory tariff hike, (2) cheating with a lower production tax and facing a retaliatory production tax decrease, and (3) cheating with a higher tariff and a lower production tax and then facing retaliation in both policies. The second approach is a *linked agreement*, whereby a deviation in any policy induces retaliation from the other government in both policies. In this case, if a government were to deviate, it would do so in both policies at once, and so only incentive constraint 3 is relevant. This reduction in constraints ensures that government welfare cannot be reduced by moving from nonlinked to linked agreements.[12]

A more subtle question, though, is: How does linkage affect the level of cooperation on a policy-by-policy basis? One possibility is that linkage results in a *reallocation* of cooperation across policies, for example, with linkage leading to greater cooperation in environmental policies (i.e., higher production taxes) and diminished cooperation in the trade policies (i.e., higher import tariffs). This possibility corresponds to a fear expressed by many economists that linkage may somehow work against trade-liberalization efforts. But another possibility is that a linked agreement may result in the *creation* of greater cooperation, with each policy moving under linkage in the desired direction (i.e., higher production taxes and lower import tariffs).

To explore the response of individual policies, Limao considers first the case in which all tariffs and policies enter as *independent* arguments in the governments' welfare functions. Here he finds that when linkage

---

12. In the context of collusion among firms, Bernheim and Whinston (1990) and Telser (1980) offer earlier statements of this general point.

leads to strictly higher government welfare, it does so by reallocating cooperation from one policy to another. Linkage in effect enables governments to allocate optimally enforcement power across policies. As margins are equated, the greater cooperation that is achieved in one policy is balanced against the diminished cooperation that occurs in the other policy. Limao turns next to the more realistic case, where the policies enter the welfare function in an *interdependent* fashion. In particular, he emphasizes the situation in which the various policies enter as strategic complements (positive cross partials) in the governments' welfare functions. The main point is that linkage may then create cooperation.

To gain some intuition, suppose that a government's import tariff and production tax enter its welfare function as strategic complements. The government's immediate gain from cheating in both policies is then less than its combined gain from cheating in its tariff alone and in its production tax alone. This is because cheating involves higher tariffs and lower production taxes, and under strategic complementarity a co-movement of this kind is less attractive than the combined gains from separate movements in the two policies. Building on this line of argument, Limao shows that when all policies are strategic complements, the incentive constraint 3 above is slack in the optimal nonlinked agreement. He thus concludes that a linked agreement can create additional cooperation in each variable when all policies are strategic complements.

The final question to ask is then: Under what circumstances are all policies strategic complements? Limao shows that strategic complementarities arise only if there are weak import-competing lobbies and substantial international nonpecuniary externalities that are given important welfare weight. These conditions are also sufficient for strategic complementarity, if as well the nonpecuniary externality loss function has appropriate curvature. Overall, the striking implication is that enforcement considerations suggest that linkage may give policy-by-policy gains in cooperation when international non-pecuniary externalities are substantial and important.

Competition Policy

In the previous chapter we argued that GATT tariff bindings are effective only if they imply secure market-access commitments, and we observed that the security of these implied commitments can be undermined if governments retain unlimited ability to alter "domestic" policies such as labor and environmental standards. As we explained, when these commitments are not secure, an attempt to reach a more efficient level of market access through a GATT tariff negotiation may itself contribute toward inefficient domestic policy choices. Potentially this could lead to a "race-to-the-bottom" -type problem with regard to labor and environmental standards, and the market access that is actually achieved through GATT negotiations also may be inefficient.

With these concerns in mind, we considered the constraints that GATT rules place on a government's ability to alter domestic standards, and we asked whether, in principle, these constraints are sufficient to enable governments to achieve efficient choices of both trade and domestic standards without the need to negotiate directly over the latter. At a broad level we concluded that there is an economic logic associated with a "targeting approach" to the design of an appropriate international agreement in that setting: let governments negotiate over the levels of market access that they are willing to deliver, and then let each government decide unilaterally on the best policy mix of tariffs and domestic standards with which to deliver the agreed-upon access to its markets. We argued further that this is effectively the logic behind GATT's approach to labor and environmental standards, with the right to bring "nonviolation" nullification-or-impairment complaints potentially playing a key role in this regard.

In this chapter we consider whether a similar logic might apply in the context of competition policy. At an informal level the notion that each government might be left alone to choose the design of its own domestic standards, so long as its choice does not undermine its market-access commitments, has an appeal in the context of competition policy that is perhaps more immediate than in the case of labor and environmental standards. For one thing, there is arguably less scope for important international nonpecuniary externalities when competition policy is chosen; as a consequence the position that direct international negotiations over domestic policies are needed to address international nonpecuniary externalities seems less compelling in the context of competition policy. For another, the potential to manipulate the choice of competition policy so as to alter the conditions of competition in the domestic market and restrict foreign access seems very real, and this potential suggests a fairly direct link between trade policy and competition policy.

At a formal level, however, the arguments discussed in the previous chapter do not apply in the context of competition policy. Those arguments are made within a perfectly competitive market structure, whereas a formal discussion of competition policy requires consideration of imperfectly competitive firms. Plausibly, the existence of such firms could complicate the nature of international externalities in a way that would make the GATT/WTO's traditional emphasis on market access inadequate for dealing with issues relating to competition policy. A possible implication is that the logic behind GATT's approach to labor and environmental standards is not well suited for competition policy. The purpose of this chapter is to extend the formal model to allow for imperfectly competitive firms so that the links between competition policy and the effectiveness of international agreements to liberalize trade can be formally explored. We argue that the logic developed above for labor and environmental standards applies also in the context of competition policy.

9.1 Competition Policy in GATT

The links between competition policy and the effectiveness of international agreements to liberalize trade have long been thought to be important. This thinking was evident in the original Charter of the ITO (Chapter V), in which extensive rules governing restrictive business practices were included. However, this comprehensive set of rules died with the ITO, and the GATT rules that apply specifically to restrictive business practices are far more limited. The primary rule governing restrictive business practices in GATT applies only to import monopolies, and is contained in Article II, paragraph 4, which says, in part,

If any contracting party establishes, maintains or authorizes, formally or in effect, a monopoly of the importation of any product described in the appropriate Schedule annexed to this Agreement, such monopoly shall not, except as provided for in that Schedule or as otherwise agreed between the parties which initially negotiated the concession, operate so as to afford protection on the average in excess of the amount of protection provided for in that Schedule. . . .

In effect the intended purpose of this rule is to secure the integrity of market-access commitments against the subsequent exploitation of (import) monopoly power. As Jackson (1969, p. 356 n. 5) observes,

The primary concern of the drafters of Article II, paragraph 4, was that after states had completed negotiations and bound themselves to a tariff Schedule they would then form new import monopolies in the hope that these monopolies would not be limited to the bound tariff in setting an import margin.

More recently the links between trade and competition policy have received renewed attention. For example, these links have been emphasized in discussions within the WTO, where a working group on the interaction between trade and competition policy has been given the task of evaluating them.

In a recent communication to the members of this WTO working group, the US government described the link between trade policy and competition policy in this way:

. . . In short, we can observe a gradual evolution in trade policy toward a broader understanding of the potential impediments to market access. This evolution looks beyond border barriers such as tariffs in order to secure other meaningful improvements in market access conditions, by turning attention to the range of barriers that affect conditions of competition in the market and that may restrict the ability of foreign firms to effectively operate in a given market. . . . (WTO 1998, p. 10).

According to this perspective a government's choice of competition policy can be used to alter the conditions of access to that country's markets in much the same way that tariffs can affect market access, and this defines a natural link between trade policy and competition policy: the effectiveness of international agreements to liberalize trade hinges on the presumption that governments will not set their national competition policies in a way that frustrates the enhanced trade flows implied by their negotiated trade policy commitments. Of course, this concern was precisely what motivated the drafters of Article II, paragraph 4. But as observed above, Article II addresses this concern in a very limited way (i.e., applying only to import monopolies). Indeed, as the US communication observes, ". . . the members of the multilateral trading system are just beginning to appreciate the full impact which anticompetitive practices can have on the flow and direction of global trade as well as the certainty of the concessions made and obligations undertaken by governments over the course of one half-century of trade liberalization" (WTO 1998, p. 1).

Perhaps surprisingly, in light of the inevitable market imperfections that must be acknowledged in any sensible discussion of competition policy, the perspective described above suggests that the key international externalities associated with the competition policy choices of individual nations nevertheless can be characterized in a remarkably succinct manner: one government cares about the competition policy choices of its trading partners for the same reason that it cares about their tariff choices, solely as a result of the market-access consequences of those choices. If this characterization is correct, then it implies a provocative conclusion: if the WTO can ensure the security of the market-access commitments that are agreed to by its member governments through their negotiated tariff bindings, then it can facilitate the attainment of choices over tariffs and the national competition policies of its member governments that are efficient from an international perspective. In effect, under this characterization, governments need only negotiate directly over their tariffs to achieve efficient levels of market access, since the security of negotiated market-access levels then ensures that each government sets its national competition policy in a globally efficient manner. Put differently, despite the imperfectly competitive market structure inherent in any discussion of competition policy, the characterization of the associated international externality as described above implies that the issue of competition policy, in principle, can be approached by the WTO in the same fashion as we argued in the previous chapter that the WTO could approach labor and environmental standards.

The main task of this chapter is to consider whether the simple characterization of international externalities associated with the national choice of competition policy, as described above, is indeed correct. Below we describe how, in at least one important area of competition policy (merger policy), this characterization admits formal support.[1] Whether this characterization extends to the wider range of issues that are raised by competition policy remains an open question. But the findings we describe below do suggest that a well-working nonviolation nullification-or-impairment right can, to some degree, substitute for direct WTO negotiations over competition policy.

We also note that, in the context of competition policy, the recent Kodak–Fuji dispute over Japanese imports of consumer photographic film and paper (see also note 5 in chapter 8) is highly relevant. This dispute was primarily an attempt by the United States to exercise its nonviolation rights in the context of Japanese competition policy, and the findings we describe suggest that the right to bring this kind of complaint may make it possible for governments to achieve efficient policy outcomes without the sacrifice of national sovereignty that would be implied by direct negotiations over competition policy in the WTO. This suggestion stands in contrast to the sometimes-expressed view that the forces of globalization demand direct international negotiation over competition (as well as other traditionally "domestic") policy choices. For example, in a recent Op-Ed, Laura Tyson, former chief economic adviser to President Clinton, wrote:

> . . . Like the Clinton administration, the Bush administration . . . opposes negotiating a WTO agreement on competition policy, fearing the loss of national sovereignty to international rules. This opposition is shortsighted and ill-advised. It is only a matter of time before there will be so many companies with global reach that developing a common international set of antitrust principles becomes a necessity.
>
> In this area, as in many others, globalization will continue to chip away at the power of the nation state. As the Europeans know from their experience over the last 50 years, surrendering some degree of national autonomy is a natural and inevitable concomitant of growing economic interdependence." (*New York Times*, Op-Ed, Saturday, July 14, 2001)

Before introducing direct negotiations, however, it is important to ask whether reliance on existing GATT/WTO rules might provide a route to efficient trade and domestic policies. Our findings raise the possibility that GATT's nonviolation nullification-or-impairment rights might play such a role.

To develop this conclusion, we begin in the next section with an extension of the two-country model to a world of noncompetitive

---

1. These arguments are developed more fully in Bagwell and Staiger (2001e).

firms where governments choose both trade and competition policies. After developing this extended model, we then consider in the remaining two sections of this chapter the purpose of a trade agreement in this setting and the extent to which national sovereignty must be sacrificed to achieve globally efficient choices of trade and competition policies.

9.2   The Model with Competition Policy

We illustrate the essential points by extending the basic two-country model developed in chapter 2 to allow for imperfectly competitive firms and an instrument of competition policy. In particular, we consider an imperfectly competitive production structure in which firms compete in a Cournot fashion and a nation's competition policy amounts to choosing the number of its firms. By modeling competition policy in this way, we follow most of the literature (e.g., see Horn and Levinsohn 2001, and the review of the literature therein). At the same time we acknowledge the many ways that this approach oversimplifies the complexity of actual competition policy. Following Bagwell and Staiger (2001e), we first extend the basic two-country, two-good general equilibrium model to incorporate the existence of imperfectly competitive firms, and we then define government preferences in this extended setting.

9.2.1   The General Equilibrium Model

Beginning from the basic two-country, two-good general equilibrium trade model described in section 2.1.1., in which the home (foreign) country imports x (y) in exchange for exports of y (x), we now introduce an imperfectly competitive production structure. For simplicity we allow only the import-competing producers of x in the domestic country to be imperfectly competitive, and we capture this by assuming that entry is not free in this sector and denoting the number of domestic import-competing firms by n_x. Domestic competition policy amounts to a choice of n_x, and given this choice and the choices of domestic and foreign tariffs, the n_x domestic import-competing firms are then assumed to compete in a Cournot fashion facing import competition from competitive producers abroad. We assume that all goods are produced with constant-returns-to-scale technologies so that the choice of n_x is immaterial from the point of view of technological efficiency. We denote the output of domestic import-competing producer

i by q_x^i, and the domestic import-competing industry output by Q_x, where

$$Q_x \equiv \sum_{i=1}^{n_x} q_x^i.$$

Let π^i denote the profit of the i'th domestic import-competing firm, measured (at domestic prices) in units of good y, and let Π denote industrywide profits. Regardless of the number of home-country import-competing producers, trade ensures that the two arbitrage conditions hold that link world prices to the prices in each local market: $p = \tau p^w \equiv p(\tau, p^w)$ and $p^* = p^w / \tau^* \equiv p^*(\tau^*, p^w)$. As before, we use p and p^* to denote these price functions. Hence, for a given (nonprohibitive) domestic tariff, the output decisions of the n_x domestic import-competing firms affect domestic goods prices p only through their impact on world prices p^w. Domestic factor prices, on the other hand, are determined as a function of Q_x, and hence each domestic import-competing firm faces the marginal cost function $mc(Q_x)$, where these marginal costs are measured (at domestic prices) in units of good y.[2] The profits of the i'th domestic import-competing firm thus may be written as $\pi^i = [p - mc(Q_x)]q_x^i$, and summing over i yields an expression for industry profits in the domestic import-competing sector:

$$\Pi(Q_x, p) \equiv [p - mc(Q_x)]Q_x.$$

Under the assumption that only the industry profit level (and not the profit levels of individual firms) matters for the determination of aggregate domestic demand, an assumption that holds, for example, if all actual and potential owners of production facilities in the x-sector have identical and homothetic preferences, domestic demand for good x is a function of Q_x, τ, and p^w: $D_x(Q_x, p, p^w)$. The level of Q_x affects domestic demand because it determines the level and distribution of factor income and also affects the level of profit income in the domestic economy. Domestic demand for x is also affected by p, as p affects the level of profit income and determines the trade-off faced by domestic consumers. Finally, for a given level of Q_x and p, the level of p^w determines the tariff revenue available to the domestic economy, and hence contributes to the determination of domestic demand as well. With domestic import demand defined by $M \equiv D_x - Q_x$, it follows that

---

2. See Feenstra (1980) for a detailed analysis of monopsony power in a general equilibrium open economy setting.

domestic import demand for good x is a function of Q_x, τ, and p^w as well: $M(Q_x, p, p^w)$. The domestic export supply function may be analogously defined.

As perfect competition continues to prevail by assumption in the foreign country, the foreign country import demand and export supply functions are expressed as in section 2.1.1. Hence, for a given level of Q_x and for tariff levels τ and τ^*, the market-clearing world price $\hat{p}^w(Q_x, \tau, \tau^*)$ is determined so as to equate domestic import demand of x with foreign export supply:

$$M(Q_x, p(\tau, \hat{p}^w), \hat{p}^w) = E^*(p^*(\tau^*, \hat{p}^w), \hat{p}^w), \tag{9.1}$$

where we have made explicit the dependence of the local price on the tariff and the world price. If Lerner- and Metzler-type paradoxes are ruled out, the following restrictions apply: $\partial \hat{p}^w(Q_x, \tau, \tau^*)/\partial \tau < 0$, $\partial \hat{p}^w(Q_x, \tau, \tau^*)/\partial \tau^* > 0$, and $dp(\tau, \hat{p}^w(Q_x, \tau, \tau^*))/d\tau > 0$.

Having determined the market-clearing world price as a function of the home and foreign tariffs and the output levels chosen by the home-country firms in sector x, we may now proceed to solve for the equilibrium home-country output choices. Writing the profits of the i'th domestic import-competing firm as $\pi^i = [p(\tau, \hat{p}^w(Q_x, \tau, \tau^*)) - mc(Q_x)]q_x^i$, and assuming that the income of the owner of the i'th firm comes only from profits, the indirect utility function of a representative owner is denoted by $v(p, \pi^i)$. Each domestic x-sector firm i chooses its output q_x^i to maximize $v(p, \pi^i)$ given the output choices of all other domestic x-sector firms. Using Roy's identity, and denoting by c_x^i the amount of good x consumed by the owner of the i'th firm, it is straightforward to derive that the symmetric Nash equilibrium is characterized by

$$
\begin{aligned}
&\frac{p(\tau, \hat{p}^w(Q_x^N, \tau, \tau^*)) - mc(Q_x^N)}{p(\tau, \hat{p}^w(Q_x^N, \tau, \tau^*))} \\
&= \frac{1}{n_x} \times \left[\left(\frac{q_x^N - c_x^N}{q_x^N} \right) \xi_{Q_x}^p + \frac{mc(Q_x^N)}{p(\tau, \hat{p}^w(Q_x^N, \tau, \tau^*))} \xi_{Q_x}^{mc} \right],
\end{aligned}
\tag{9.2}
$$

where ξ_w^u denotes the elasticity of the variable u with respect to the variable w (taken positively). Expression (9.2) determines the Nash equilibrium level of domestic output in the import-competing sector as a function of n_x, τ and τ^*, or $Q_x^N(n_x, \tau, \tau^*) \equiv n_x q_x^N(n_x, \tau, \tau^*)$.

Expression (9.2) says that in the symmetric Nash equilibrium the n_x domestic import-competing firms choose outputs so that the implied markup of price over marginal cost for each firm (the left-hand side of 9.2) is equal to that firm's "share" (i.e., $1/n_x$) of a weighted sum of the elasticities with respect to domestic import-competing output of (1) the local domestic price ξ^p_{Qx} and (2) marginal costs ξ^{mc}_{Qx}. The ability to raise domestic prices by restricting domestic import-competing output (the collective monopoly power of domestic import-competing firms) contributes toward a higher equilibrium markup to the extent that the domestic owners of import-competing firms are net sellers of good x (i.e., $q^N_x > c^N_x$). The ability to reduce marginal costs by restricting domestic import-competing output (the collective monopsony power of domestic import-competing firms) also contributes toward a higher equilibrium markup.

In light of (9.1) and (9.2) we may now write

$$\tilde{p}^w(n_x, \tau, \tau^*) \equiv \hat{p}^w(Q^N_x(n_x, \tau, \tau^*), \tau, \tau^*).$$

Under the assumption that Q^N_x is monotonically increasing in n_x, and that Lerner- and Metzler-type paradoxes are ruled out, we may impose the following restrictions: $\tilde{p}^w(n_x, \tau, \tau^*)$ is decreasing in n_x, decreasing in τ, and increasing in τ^*; $p(\tau, \tilde{p}^w(n_x, \tau, \tau^*))$ is decreasing in n_x, increasing (in total) in τ, and increasing in τ^*; $Q^N_x(n_x, \tau, \tau^*)$ is increasing in n_x, increasing in τ, and increasing in τ^*; and $p^*(\tau^*, \tilde{p}^w(n_x, \tau, \tau^*))$ is decreasing in n_x, decreasing in τ, and decreasing (in total) in τ^*.

9.2.2 Government Preferences

We next extend our representation of government preferences to allow for the presence of imperfectly competitive firms in the home country. In particular, we continue to represent the objectives of the foreign government by the general function $W^*(p^*, \tilde{p}^w)$, but we now represent the objectives of the home-country government by the function $W(Q^N_x, p, \tilde{p}^w)$. In analogy with our earlier representations of government preferences, we assume that all else equal, each government achieves higher welfare when its terms of trade improve,

$$W_{\tilde{p}^w}(Q^N_x, p, \tilde{p}^w) < 0 \quad \text{and} \quad W^*_{\tilde{p}^w}(p^*, \tilde{p}^w) > 0, \tag{9.3}$$

but we leave government objective functions otherwise unrestricted.

Before continuing, let us pause and discuss the meaning of the assumptions we have placed on government objective functions. We recall from the discussion in section 2.1.3 that our assumption about the foreign objective function (i.e, that $W^*_{\tilde{p}^w} > 0$) is not very restrictive, as it is satisfied in a wide variety of models that include the leading political-economy motives. We now observe that the assumption we place on the objectives of the domestic government (i.e., that $W_{\tilde{p}^w} < 0$)

remains no more restrictive than our assumption on foreign government objectives. In particular, notice that we only require the domestic government to benefit when its terms of trade improve, holding fixed Q_x^N and p. But with Q_x^N and p held fixed, the level and distribution of factor incomes and the level of profits in the domestic economy are held fixed, as is the price faced by domestic consumers, and so the terms-of-trade improvement is equivalent to a pure income transfer from abroad (just as in the case where perfect competition prevails).

The structure we place on the objectives of the domestic government may be further illustrated with the help of figure 9.1. In this figure we consider the effect of a change in τ from an initial level τ^0 to a new slightly higher level τ^1, holding fixed the levels of n_x and τ^* at n_x^0 and τ^{*0}, respectively. We may use figure 9.1 to decompose the effect of this change on W into its three component effects running through Q_x^N, p, and $\tilde{p}^w$ (an analogous decomposition could be illustrated for the effect of a change in n_x on W). Let us denote $Q_x^{N0} \equiv Q_x^N(n_x^0, \tau^0, \tau^{*0})$, $\tilde{p}^{w0} \equiv \tilde{p}^w(n_x^0, \tau^0, \tau^{*0})$, and $p^0 \equiv p(\tau^0, \tilde{p}^{w0})$, and analogously we denote $Q_x^{N1} \equiv Q_x^N(n_x^0, \tau^1, \tau^{*0})$, $\tilde{p}^{w1} \equiv \tilde{p}^w(n_x^0, \tau^1, \tau^{*0})$, and $p^1 \equiv p(\tau^1, \tilde{p}^{w1})$. Finally, let us define n_x' and τ' as the solution to the two equations $Q_x^N(n_x', \tau', \tau^{*0}) = Q_x^{N0}$ and $p(\tau', \tilde{p}^w(n_x', \tau', \tau^{*0})) = p^1$, and denote $\tilde{p}^{w'} \equiv \tilde{p}^w(n_x', \tau', \tau^{*0})$.

Figure 9.1a illustrates the determination of n_x' and τ'. As illustrated, the restrictions imposed above imply that $n_x' < n_x^0$ and $\tau^0 < \tau' < \tau^1$. In figure 9.1b, movements in τ and τ^* are depicted, with n_x adjusting to fix

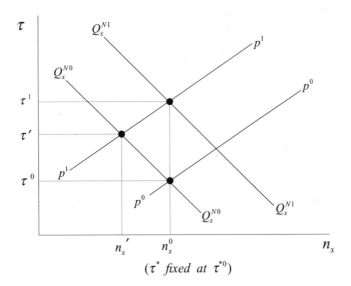

$(\tau^* \text{ fixed at } \tau^{*0})$

Figure 9.1a

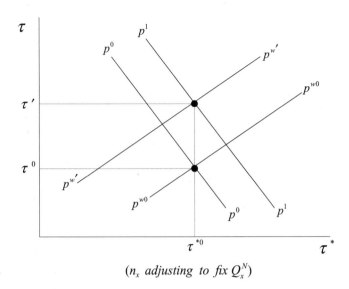

$(n_x$ adjusting to fix $Q_x^N)$

Figure 9.1b

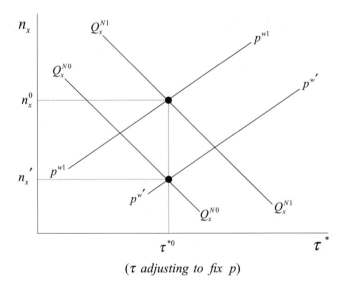

$(\tau$ adjusting to fix $p)$

Figure 9.1c

Q_x^N at its original level Q_x^{N0}. The movement from τ^0 to τ' induces the new world price $\tilde{p}^{w/}$, the new local price p^1, and an implied change in n_x from n_x^0 to n_x'. This movement can be decomposed into a movement along the original iso-local-price locus, labeled $p^0 \rightarrow p^0$, to the new iso-world-price locus, labeled $p^{w/} \rightarrow p^{w/}$, and then a movement along $p^{w/} \rightarrow p^{w/}$ to the new iso-local-price locus $p^1 \rightarrow p^1$.[3] In figure 9.1c, movements in n_x and τ^* are depicted, with τ adjusting to fix the local price at the new local price p^1. The movement from n_x' back to n_x^0 induces the new world price, $\tilde{p}^{w1}$, the new level of domestic import-competing output, Q_x^{N1}, and an implied change in τ from τ' to τ^1. This movement can be decomposed into a movement along the original iso-Q_x^N locus, labeled $Q_x^{N0} \rightarrow Q_x^{N0}$, to the new iso-world-price locus, labeled $p^{w1} \rightarrow p^{w1}$, and then a movement along $p^{w1} \rightarrow p^{w1}$ to the new iso-Q_x^N locus, labeled $Q_x^{N1} \rightarrow Q_x^{N1}$.[4] The structure we place on the objectives of the domestic government require only that the government values the implied income transfer associated with the induced drops in $\tilde{p}^w$ represented in figures 9.1b and c when p and Q_x^N are held fixed. How the domestic government feels about the associated changes in p and Q_x^N is left unrestricted.

9.3   The Purpose of a Trade Agreement

We next explore the nature of the inefficiency that arises in the absence of any international agreement between the home and foreign government. To accomplish this, we solve for the noncooperative policy choices of tariffs (τ and τ^*) and competition policy (n_x) across the domestic and foreign governments. The first-order conditions that define the home-government and foreign-government policy reaction curves can be written as

$$\left(\frac{\partial Q_x^N / \partial \tau}{dp / d\tau}\right) W_{Q_x^N} + W_p + \lambda W_{\tilde{p}^w} = 0, \tag{9.4}$$

$$\left(\frac{\partial Q_x^N / \partial n_x}{\partial \tilde{p}^w / \partial n_x}\right) W_{Q_x^N} = -\left[\tau W_p + W_{\tilde{p}^w}\right], \tag{9.5}$$

---

3. At each step, n_x adjusts to fix Q_x^N at Q_x^{N0}. This adjustment fixes the first argument in the function $\hat{p}^w(Q_x^N(n_x, \tau, \tau^*), \tau, \tau^*)$. Recalling that $\tilde{p}^w(n_x, \tau, \tau^*) \equiv \hat{p}^w(Q_x^N(n_x, \tau, \tau^*), \tau, \tau^*)$, it is evident that our restrictions on $\hat{p}^w$ imply that the iso-local-price and iso-world-price loci slope in the depicted manner.

4. At each step, τ adjusts to fix p at p^1, with τ rising from τ' to τ^1 as n_x rises from n_x' to n_x^0. Our restrictions on $\tilde{p}^w$ and Q_x^N then imply that the iso-world-price loci slope in the depicted manner. For simplicity, we depict the iso-Nash-output loci as negatively sloped.

$$W^*_{p^*} + \lambda^* W^*_{\tilde{p}^w} = 0. \tag{9.6}$$

The Nash equilibrium policy choices for the home and foreign governments require that each government be on its reaction curves, and hence noncooperative policy choices simultaneously solve (9.4) through (9.6). We denote the Nash policies by $(n^N_x, \tau^N, \tau^{*N})$.

It may now be seen that the fundamental inefficiency in the Nash equilibrium is insufficient trade volume. Governments are led to this inefficient outcome through their incentive to deny market access to foreign exporters so as to generate favorable movements in the world price. Put differently, as compared to the perfectly competitive setting analyzed in section 2.1.1, the choice of domestic competition policy and the possibility of imperfectly competitive firms operating in the domestic economy does not introduce a new source of international inefficiency.

The key point is that (9.4) and (9.5) may be combined to yield

$$\left(\frac{\partial Q^N_x / \partial n_x}{\partial \tilde{p}^w / \partial n_x} - \frac{\partial Q^N_x / \partial \tau}{\partial \tilde{p}^w / \partial \tau} \right) W_{Q^N_x} = \left[\frac{\tilde{p}^w}{\partial \tilde{p}^w / \partial \tau} \right] W_p. \tag{9.7}$$

Expression (9.7) implies that at the Nash equilibrium the home government is choosing its policies so that, for the given volume of imports demanded, the policy "mix" that delivers this volume of import demand (e.g., low τ and high n_x or high τ and low n_x) is efficient from a worldwide perspective. To see that this is implied by (9.7), note that market-access-preserving adjustments to n_x and τ (i.e., adjustments that preserve the volume of domestic import demand at the equilibrium world price) also preserve the equilibrium world price $\tilde{p}^w(n_x, \tau, \tau^*) \equiv \hat{p}^w(Q^N_x(n_x, \tau, \tau^*), \tau, \tau^*)$ according to (9.1). Given that p^* is a function of τ^* and $\tilde{p}^w$, these adjustments can have no impact on foreign welfare $W^*(p^*, \tilde{p}^w)$. But world-price-preserving adjustments to n_x and τ satisfy

$$\frac{dn_x}{d\tau}\bigg|_{d\tilde{p}^w = 0} = -\frac{\partial \tilde{p}^w / \partial \tau}{\partial \tilde{p}^w / \partial n_x}.$$

They can be shown to imply that

$$-\frac{dW/d\tau}{dW/dn_x} = -\frac{\partial \tilde{p}^w / \partial \tau}{\partial \tilde{p}^w / \partial n_x}$$

when (9.7) holds. Expression (9.7) therefore implies that at the Nash equilibrium, market-access-preserving adjustments to the mix of domestic policies can have no impact on domestic welfare either; that is, the domestic policy mix is efficient from an international perspective. Finally, that the level of market access implied by the domestic mix of policies and the foreign policy choice in the Nash equilibrium is inefficiently low can be shown following arguments analogous to those contained in Bagwell and Staiger (2001a) in the context of a competitive economy choosing domestic standards, once it is observed that (9.4) and (9.6) imply that $W_p < 0$ and $W_{p^*}^* > 0$ at the Nash equilibrium.[5]

Hence, we may conclude that when the domestic government chooses competition policy for its import-competing producers and both the domestic and foreign governments choose tariffs, the inefficiency associated with Nash choices is one of insufficient market access.

9.4   Trade Agreements and National Sovereignty

It now follows that efficient policy choices may be achieved along the same lines described in section 8.4 for the case of labor and environmental standards in competitive economies. Specifically, efficient policy choices can be achieved through negotiations over tariffs alone with the following two-step procedure. First, governments can negotiate over tariffs alone to achieve a desired level of trade volume and an equilibrium world price given the existing competition policy in the domestic country. And second, the domestic government may make unilateral adjustments to its tariff and competition policy, provided that these unilateral adjustments do not alter the market access it affords to foreign exporters. This second step can be accomplished with rules analogous to GATT's nonviolation nullification-or-impairment rules, as we described in section 8.4.

Figure 9.2 illustrates the case where, subsequent to tariff negotiations, the domestic government has incentive to set its competition policy at a level that is too stringent (i.e., n_x is too high) relative to the efficient level. When analyzing competition policy as applied to import-competing firms, this is the natural case to consider, since a country denies access to its markets and generates a negative terms-of-trade externality on foreign trading partners by allowing *too few*

---

5. To see that (9.4) implies $W_p < 0$ at the Nash equilibrium, observe that, using (9.5) and the relationship between $\bar{p}^w$ and $\hat{p}^w$, (9.4) may be rewritten as $W_p + \hat{\lambda} W_{\hat{p}^w} = 0$, where $\hat{\lambda} \equiv \dfrac{(\partial \hat{p}^w / \partial \tau)}{[dp(\tau, \hat{p}^w)/d\tau]}$. As $\hat{\lambda} < 0$ and $W_{\hat{p}^w} < 0$, it then follows that $W_p < 0$ at the Nash equilibrium. And as $\lambda^* < 0$ and $W_{\hat{p}^w}^* > 0$, it is direct that (9.6) implies $W_{p^*}^* > 0$ at the Nash equilibrium.

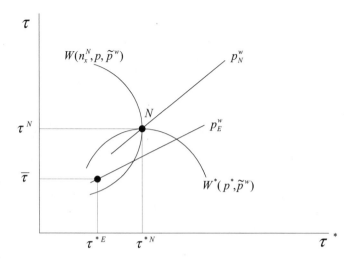

Figure 9.2a

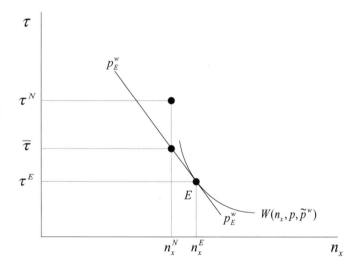

Figure 9.2b

mergers among its import-competing firms (see also note 6 below). To implement an efficient set of policies $(n_x^E, \tau^E, \tau^{*E})$ with negotiations over tariffs alone, the home and foreign government would negotiate in step one to the tariffs $(\bar{\tau}, \tau^{*E})$, where $\bar{\tau}$ is defined by $\tilde{p}^w(n_x^N, \bar{\tau}, \tau^{*E}) = \tilde{p}^w(n_x^E, \tau^E, \tau^{*E})$. Observe that $\bar{\tau}$ is the domestic tariff which, in combination with the Nash domestic competition policy n_x^N, would deliver the efficient level of domestic import demand (market access) at the efficient world price. The tariffs negotiated in step one, $(\bar{\tau}, \tau^{*E})$, are illustrated in figure 9.2a. Then, in step two, the domestic government is free to adjust its policy mix, so long as the (n_x, τ) pair that it unilaterally selects delivers the level of market access implied (at the efficient world price) by its tariff negotiations. But this implies that the domestic government chooses in step two its optimal (n_x, τ) pair along the (efficient) iso-world-price locus and, as figure 9.2b shows, this by construction leads the domestic government to select the efficient domestic policy pair, (n_x^E, τ^E). A nonviolation nullification-or-impairment rule such as that contained in the articles of the GATT can, in principle, provide the fixed-world-price constraint in step two that allows efficient policies to be achieved, and governments need never negotiate directly over competition policy.

The preceding discussion points to the following conclusion: in principle, a well-working nonviolation nullification-or-impairment rule can eliminate the need for governments to negotiate directly over the competition policy they apply to domestic producers in order to achieve efficient policy outcomes.[6] At the same time we caution that our analysis takes a very simplistic representation of competition policy. In other settings (R&D policy, e.g.), additional externalities may appear.

---

6. As with labor and environmental standards (see also note 10 to chapter 8) the reflection in GATT rules of the "targeting approach" logic as applied to international institutions that we describe here is not exact, and we discuss in Bagwell and Staiger (2001e) alterations in GATT rules that can strengthen this reflection. There we also consider the possibility of imperfect competition in an import-distribution sector, an assumption which is more in line with the allegations of the Kodak–Fuji case. We show that there is an incentive to adopt competition policy which is too lax (consistent with the US allegations against Japan) and that the inefficiency created by this incentive in principle can be addressed through nonviolation complaints.

10   Agricultural Export Subsidies

In this chapter we consider the treatment of export subsidies in GATT. Following Bagwell and Staiger (2001c), we give particular emphasis to subsidy disputes that are associated with agricultural goods. We first describe the key features of these disputes. Next we argue that the standard theoretical approaches to trade agreements fail to offer satisfactory interpretations of the agricultural disputes. We then present a model that generates strategic-trade policies in competitive industries, and we argue that this model offers an interpretation of the central features of the agricultural disputes. We close with some general reflections as to the treatment of export subsidies in GATT and now the WTO.

10.1   Agricultural Export Subsidies in GATT

How should export subsidies be treated in a trade agreement? Opinions vary. It is sometimes argued that export subsidies warrant encouragement, since they expand the volume of trade and enhance consumer welfare. According to this perspective, an importing country should send a "note of thanks" when a trading partner offers an export subsidy. But it is also sometimes argued that subsidies should be discouraged or even prohibited because they create "unfair" advantages. Advocates of this view hold that export subsidies work to distort market forces and foster inefficient patterns of trade.

In light of these conflicting views, it is not surprising that the treatment of subsidies in GATT is complex. GATT Article XVI states conditions under which export subsidies are prohibited for industrial products. At the same time important exceptions for "primary" products such as agricultural goods are allowed, so long as the subsidy received does not displace the exports of another member and thereby provide the recipient with "more than an equitable share of world export trade in that product." The language which accompanies the GATT agricultural exception is clearly ambiguous, and a number of disputes have arisen in connection with this exception.

Some of the most important disputes involve the United States and the European Community and concern the export of wheat flour. As Trebilcock and Howse (1999, p. 249) detail, in a 1958 wheat flour case, a GATT panel ruled against a French export subsidy. The panel held that the subsidy contributed to an increase in the French export market share and an associated displacement in the export market share of Australia (the complainant). However, in a wheat flour case of the early 1980s, a GATT panel ruled in favor of a European Community export subsidy. As Rhodes (1993, pp. 201–25) explains, the panel reached this decision, even though over the time period in question (1959–1981) the EC share of the world market grew considerably (from 29 to 75 percent) and the world market share for the United States (the complainant) fell sharply (from 27 to 9 percent). In this case the panel argued that over the time period in question it was difficult to attribute the market share changes to a particular export subsidy. After this setback the United States brought a complaint against the EC policy of subsidizing the export of pasta. At issue was whether pasta qualified as a "primary" product. The GATT panel gave a split decision, with the majority in favor of the US position. These cases accentuated a sense among member governments that agricultural trade policy should be brought more clearly and fully under the rules of GATT.

In the Uruguay Round, member governments thus accepted agricultural trade reform as a basic goal. Indeed, according to many (e.g., see Jackson 1997a, p. 314, and Rhodes 1993, p. 221) the single most important objective of the Uruguay Round was agricultural trade reform. GATT members, however, were deeply divided in their views as to the *extent* of reform that was needed. This division delayed considerably the completion of the Uruguay Round.[1] On one side of the debate, the United States held that agricultural export subsidies should be phased out. This position was endorsed as well by a group of countries known as the Cairns Group.[2] The European Community took the

---

1. See Croome (1995). Similar interpretations are offered by Low (1993), Oxley (1990), Preeg (1995), and Rhodes (1993).
2. The Cairns Group is a set of countries that are strong exporters in agricultural commodities. At the time of the Uruguay Round, this group was comprised of Argentina, Australia, Brazil, Canada, Chile, Colombia, Fiji, Hungary, Indonesia, Malaysia, New Zealand, the Philippines, Thailand, and Uruguay.

other side of the debate. It agreed to a principle of "progressive reduction in support" but argued against an outright prohibition of agricultural export subsidies.

Despite this division GATT members ultimately did achieve an
agreement. As Trebilcock and Howse (1999, p. 262) explain, in the
Uruguay Round Agreement on Agriculture, the exception granted
under GATT Article XVI to primary products is altered, so that member
governments from developed countries agree to reduce over a six-year
period by 36 percent the value of agricultural export subsidies and
by 21 percent the volume of agricultural products that receive such
subsidies.

10.2   Features of the Agricultural Disputes

The agricultural disputes are suggestive of a Prisoners' Dilemma
problem among exporting governments. According to this view, GATT
restrictions against export subsidies are attractive to exporting governments as a means to curb a mutually destructive subsidy war. To
develop this interpretation, we describe further the apparent motivations of governments at various stages in the disputes. We then identify four key features of the agricultural disputes.

After a GATT panel ruled in favor of the European Community in
the wheat flour dispute of the early 1980s, the United States retaliated
with its own wheat flour export-subsidization program in 1983. Rhodes
(1993, p. 215) explains the prevailing US view at that time:

... only if the United States matched the European Community subsidy for
subsidy, so traditional EC markets were lost in favor of US exporters, would
the community seriously reconsider agricultural trading methods.

The strategy did not produce the desired effect. As Boger (1984, p. 230)
details, the EC instead responded aggressively and expanded its subsidization efforts. The result was a subsidy war.

By the mid-1980s the costs of the subsidy war were unmistakable. In
the Uruguay Round negotiations, the United States and the Cairns
Group emphasized the costs of a mutually defeating subsidy war. As
Croome (1995, p. 73) reports, they sought to clarify and extend GATT
restrictions on agricultural export subsidies in order to curb these costs:

Almost all governments were increasingly conscious of the burden which subsidies placed on their national budgets and taxpayers, and of the risk that any
subsidy introduced to give a competitive advantage would only be matched

by other countries in (as the United States put it) "a self-defeating spiral." An Uruguay Round agreement that could in effect provide a mutual disarmament treaty for subsidies would serve the interests of all.

As suggested above, the United States and the EC both approached the Uruguay Round with a shared belief in the principle that a reduction of agricultural export subsidies might be mutually beneficial.[3] But they had different opinions as to the proper extent of any reduction.

Finally, any change in policy toward agricultural export subsidies would also interest those countries that primarily import agricultural products. Referring to a mostly African group of net food-importing countries, Croome (1995, p. 113) observes that they "... relied heavily on imports of grain and other products to feed their populations. They feared that an international agreement to cut export subsidies would result in higher and, for them, unaffordable world prices." Not surprisingly, some GATT members from countries that were net importers of agricultural products expressed concerns as to the desirability of restrictions on agricultural export subsidies.

With regard to agricultural export subsidies, the Uruguay negotiations thus included a mix of interests. One group of exporters (the United States and the Cairns Group) sought severe reductions. A second group of exporters (the EC) favored moderate reductions. Finally, a group of net food-importing countries feared the world-price consequences of a reduction.

In broad terms, this description of the agricultural disputes suggests that the exporting governments faced a Prisoners' Dilemma problem. In the absence of an effective agreement to restrain export subsidies, each government was tempted to subsidize its exporters, so as to create a competitive advantage in third-country markets. This incentive led to a mutually destructive subsidy war among exporting governments. These governments then understood that they could gain, if they were to cooperate and agree upon tighter GATT restrictions on export subsidies. Net food-importing countries, however, would lose if exporting governments were successful in this endeavor.

This general description points to four key features of the agricultural disputes. A first feature is that the disputants use export subsidies in order to compete for third-country export markets. A second

---

3. As Trebilcock and Howse (1999, p. 258) explain, as the "increasing cost of beggar-thy-neighbour subsidy wars" became evident, "the case for removing agricultural protection ... was accepted at the level of principle by both the United States and the European Union as a basic goal of the Uruguay Round negotiations."

feature is that exporting governments sought to cooperate by agreeing upon a reduction in export subsidies of agricultural products, although there were divergent views among GATT members as to the proper extent of the reduction. This feature reflects the Prisoners' Dilemma structure just described. A third feature is that the agricultural disputes emerge in markets that have competitive characteristics. In this respect, the agricultural disputes differ from other subsidy disputes (e.g., commercial aircraft), which involve oligopolistic markets. Finally a fourth feature is that political-economy issues are of particular relevance in agricultural markets.[4]

10.3 Theoretical Approaches

How are these experiences interpreted by standard theories? Consider first the traditional economic approach to trade agreements. As discussed in section 2.1.2, the traditional model involves two (large) countries that trade two goods in competitive markets. Each government chooses its respective trade-policy instruments in order to maximize national income. In a general equilibrium model such as that developed in section 2.1.1, the Lerner symmetry theorem ensures that the trade-policy decisions of each government can be summarized in terms of the export policies that it adopts. The optimal unilateral policy for a government is thus an export tax. Intuitively, with an export tax, a government restricts output in its competitive export sector and thereby generates and retains monopoly rents. This theory thus fails even to account for the potential appeal of an export-subsidization policy. As such, it cannot offer an interpretation of the first feature of the agricultural disputes.

Consider next the political-economy approach. Recall from section 2.1.3 that the distinguishing feature of the political-economy approach is that governments are motivated by both economic and political considerations. With this modification of the traditional economic approach, it becomes possible to rationalize a policy of export subsidization. If a government weighs heavily the welfare of its export sector, for example, then the government may choose to offer an export subsidy. But an important limitation remains. To see this, observe that

---

4. As Trebilcock and Howse (1999, pp. 252–54) observe, agricultural subsidies are often attributed to powerful farm lobbies, who in turn argue that agriculture warrants special support since this would promote national self-sufficiency, offset the unusual risks (e.g., weather) that farmers face, and preserve the rural way of life.

when a government subsidizes its exports, the world price falls, and some of the benefit of the export subsidy is thus received by foreign consumers. A government thus faces an exaggerated cost of stimulating its export sector. When the political-economy approach is recast in terms of export policies, the two governments therefore agree that a trade agreement should be designed to encourage export subsidization. But this stands in sharp contrast to the second feature listed above, whereby governments of exporting countries sought an agreement to *reduce* agricultural export subsidies.

We come now to the theory of strategic-trade policy. In the pioneering model of Brander and Spencer (1985), three key assumptions are imposed. First, the model has three countries and a "competing-exporters" structure: two countries export a common good to a third country. Second, export sectors are imperfectly competitive, in that each exporting country has a single exporter, where the two exporters compete in a Cournot fashion for third-country sales. Third, as in the traditional approach, governments maximize national income. Under these assumptions Brander and Spencer (1985) show that it is possible to rationalize both the potential appeal of export subsidies and the desire of exporting governments to reach an agreement to reduce such subsidies.

The basic intuition is easily summarized. An export subsidy is potentially appealing to an exporting government, since it represents a means through which the government may give its exporter a cost advantage and thereby shift profits in the subsequent Cournot competition. Of course, the other exporting government faces the same temptation. As a consequence a Prisoners' Dilemma problem arises between the exporting governments: they would each do better if an agreement were reached under which export subsidies were prohibited than if such an agreement were not reached and they were to "compete" with subsidies. Importantly, world welfare is higher when exporting countries compete in subsidies because the gain to consumers in the importing country more than offsets the losses experienced by the exporting countries.

Strategic-trade theory accounts well for the first two features of the agricultural disputes. Putting at center stage competition for third-country markets, it explains the potential appeal of export subsidies, and it also accounts for the desire of exporting governments to reach a subsidy-reduction agreement. The fourth feature also could be easily accommodated, since the theory could be naturally augmented to include political-economy motivations for governments. The key limitation of strategic-trade theory is that it fits poorly with the third feature of the agricultural disputes: strategic-trade theory is commonly understood to be applicable only for imperfectly competitive (Cournot) markets.[5] This understanding suggests that strategic-trade theory is better suited for the commercial aircraft than the agricultural market.

This discussion suggests a hybrid model. Following the traditional economic approach, we suppose that markets are competitive and that governments are cognizant of the terms-of-trade implications of their trade-policy selections. In keeping with the political-economy approach, we assume also that each government has a political interest in promoting the welfare of its export sector. Finally, as in the strategic-trade theory, we assume that there are three countries, where two exporting governments select export policies and all consumption occurs in a third importing country. As we show in Bagwell and Staiger (2001c) and confirm below, the hybrid model accounts for the four features listed above and therefore offers an interpretation of the agricultural disputes.

10.4 The Model of Agricultural Export Subsidies

We now develop the hybrid model. We present a partial equilibrium model of trade in competitive markets in which two countries export a homogeneous good to a third country.[6] Allowing that governments have both political and economic motivations, we then specify government preferences.

10.4.1 The Partial Equilibrium Model

In our three-country model, two identical countries, A and B, export a homogeneous good to country w, where all consumers reside. The export industries in countries A and B are perfectly competitive, and the governments of countries A and B each select specific export

---

5. For example, Brander (1995) and Helpman and Krugman (1989, p. 88) argue that imperfect competition is a defining characteristic for strategic-trade policy. Krugman and Obstfeld (1997) describe some important cases (the Japanese targeting of steel, the European support of aircraft, and the Japanese targeting of semiconductors) that illustrate the possible application of strategic-trade theory. These cases all involve highly oligopolistic markets.

6. Following the theory of strategic-trade policy, we present our findings in a partial equilibrium model. As we discuss below, our findings can also be developed in a general equilibrium setting.

subsidies. For simplicity, we assume that country w does not intervene in trade.

The competitive export industry in country A is described by a supply function $Q(p^A)$ and a profit function $\pi(p^A)$, where p^A denotes the price of the export in country A and where $\pi'(p^A) = Q(p^A)$. The competitive export industry in country B is described symmetrically, with supply and profit functions, $Q(p^B)$ and $\pi(p^B)$, respectively, where p^B denotes the price of the export in country B. In country w the demand function is given by $D(p^w)$, where p^w is the price of the good in country w. Throughout, we assume that supply slopes up and demand slopes down: $Q' > 0 > D'$.

Prices are constrained by market conditions. First, prices satisfy arbitrage conditions: $p^A = p^w + s^A$ and $p^B = p^w + s^B$, where s^A and s^B are the specific export subsidies in countries A and B, respectively. Second, prices must also satisfy a market-clearing condition:

$$D(p^w) = Q(p^A) + Q(p^B) \tag{10.1}$$

Together, these conditions yield the market-clearing price in country w, which we denote as $\tilde{p}^w(s^A, s^B)$. Under the slope assumptions just presented, it is straightforward to verify that $\tilde{p}^w(s^A, s^B)$ is decreasing in s^A and s^B. The market-clearing prices in countries A and B may now be expressed as $p^A(s^A, \tilde{p}^w(s^A, s^B)) = \tilde{p}^w(s^A, s^B) + s^A$ and $p^B(s^B, \tilde{p}^w(s^A, s^B)) = \tilde{p}^w(s^A, s^B) + s^B$. It is easily shown that p^A increases with s^A. An analogous observation applies for p^B. As before, to conserve notation, we use p^A and p^B to denote these local price functions.

Most of our arguments rely only on the general structure just described. It is, however, sometimes convenient to characterize solutions in closed form. We therefore impose the following specific assumption: for any price p, $Q(p) = p/2$, $\pi(p) = (p)^2/4$ and $D(p) = 1 - p$. Using this specific structure, we find that $\tilde{p}^w(s^A, s^B) = \frac{1}{2} - (s^A + s^B)/4$. From here it may be shown that trade is not prohibited from either exporter if $2 > \max\{s^B - 3s^A, s^A - 3s^B\}$. This condition holds in the equilibrium derived below.

Before proceeding, we note that the partial equilibrium model considered here also admits a general equilibrium interpretation. The supply and profit functions given above may be derived from an underlying production function of the form $Q = (L)^{1/2}$, where L is labor, when it is assumed that labor supply is infinitely elastic at a unitary wage. Likewise the demand function given above may be derived from an underlying representative-agent utility function of the form $U = (C$

$- C^2/2) + N$, where C and N denote the consumption of the traded good and a numéraire good respectively. Our partial equilibrium analysis is then appropriate provided that the marginal utility of income is fixed at one. This is the case if the numéraire good is sufficiently abundant in each country so that it is always consumed in positive amounts by each agent. Finally, we assume that a unit of labor produces a unit of the numéraire good, with trade in the numéraire good then determined by an overall trade balance requirement.

10.4.2 Government Preferences

Our next step is to represent political-economy influences and specify government preferences. To this end, we follow Baldwin (1987) and Grossman and Helpman (1994) and assume that exporting governments maximize profits less subsidy expenses, where profits are scaled by a parameter representing political-economy influences. For simplicity, we assume that importing government welfare is measured by consumer surplus. We may represent government welfare functions for the three countries as follows:

$$W^A(p^A, \tilde{p}^w) = \gamma_e \pi(p^A) - [p^A - \tilde{p}^w]Q(p^A), \tag{10.2}$$

$$W^B(p^B, \tilde{p}^w) = \gamma_e \pi(p^B) - [p^B - \tilde{p}^w]Q(p^B), \tag{10.3}$$

$$W^w(\tilde{p}^w) = \int_{\tilde{p}^w}^{1} D(p)dp, \tag{10.4}$$

where $\gamma_e \geq 1$ is a political-economy parameter. Under this representation, when $\gamma_e > 1$, the government is influenced by political-economy considerations.

In previous chapters we analyzed general equilibrium models and argued that the policies of one government are of interest to another government in so far as they affect the terms of trade. We have already noted that the partial equilibrium model analyzed here also admits a general equilibrium interpretation. We now observe that the equilibrium terms of trade (i.e., the world price) in this model is given by $\tilde{p}^w$.[7] From the previous discussion we may therefore anticipate the conclusion that inefficiencies arise when governments set policies in a unilateral fashion as they become motivated by the impact of their policies

---

7. By trade balance, country w must export the numeraire good, and the export price of this good is always unity. Furthermore the government of country w does not choose (discriminatory) import policies. Hence the terms of trade (i.e., the ratio of export prices on world markets) is given simply by $\tilde{p}^w$.

upon $\tilde{p}^w$. In support of this we observe from (10.1) and (10.2) through (10.4) that at fixed local prices, a change in the world price corresponds to an income transfer that has no effect on the combined welfare of the three governments.

10.5 The Purpose of Subsidy Agreements

With the model now specified, we offer a formal analysis of subsidy policy. To begin, we characterize the Nash subsidy that exporting governments would choose in the absence of an agreement. We then characterize the cooperative subsidy that these governments would prefer if they reached an agreement among themselves. Finally we characterize the subsidy that is efficient from the perspective of all three governments. After comparing these subsidy levels, we return to the agricultural disputes and offer a formal interpretation.

10.5.1 Nash Subsidies

In a Nash equilibrium, each exporting government sets its subsidy policy to maximize its objective function, taking as given the subsidy policy of the other exporting government. To characterize the export-subsidy reaction function for the government of country A, we fix s^B and maximize W^A with respect to s^A. The associated first-order condition can be expressed as

$$W_{p^A}^A + \lambda W_{\tilde{p}^w}^A = 0 \tag{10.5}$$

where $\lambda = [\partial \tilde{p}^w / \partial s^A]/[dp^A/ds^A] < 0$ reflects the impact of the subsidy on the terms of trade. Observe that the government of country A considers both the local- and world-price effects of a change in the level of the export subsidy. Let the government of country A's export-subsidy reaction function be denoted as $s^{AR}(s^B)$.

To further interpret the government of country A's optimal subsidy choice, we use (10.2) and rewrite the first-order condition in (10.5) as

$$\{Q(p^A)(\gamma_e - 1) - s^A Q'(p^A)\} + \lambda Q(p^A) = 0. \tag{10.6}$$

From (10.6) we see that when the government of country A increases its export subsidy, there are three effects on its welfare. First, the increased subsidy generates a higher local price in country A, and at a fixed volume of production the value to the government of country A

of the corresponding redistribution to its export industry is captured by the term $Q(p^A)(\gamma_e - 1)$. When $\gamma_e > 1$, this political-economy effect indicates a benefit from an increased export subsidy. Second, the local-price increase raises the volume of production and thereby raises subsidy expenses. This distortion effect describes a cost to an increased export subsidy, and it is captured by the term $s^A Q'(p^A)$. Finally, the increased export subsidy reduces the world price and thereby diminishes country A's terms of trade. This terms-of-trade effect also indicates a cost to an increased export subsidy, and it is captured by the term $\lambda Q(p^A)$. As the traditional model predicts, in the absence of a political-economy effect (i.e., when $\gamma_e = 1$), an export tax is optimal.

We now employ the specific assumptions of our model. We find that $\lambda = -1/3$. Solving (10.6), we further obtain that the export-subsidy reaction function may be expressed in closed-form as

$$s^{AR}(s^B) = \frac{(3\gamma_e - 4)(2 - s^B)}{3(8 - 3\gamma_e)}.$$

To interpret this expression, suppose that $s^B < 2$. This simply indicates that country B's export subsidy is not so large as to drive $\tilde{p}^w$ to zero when country A has no subsidy. Suppose, too, that $\gamma_e < 8/3$. This ensures that the second-order condition is satisfied. We may now observe that an export tax is optimal for the government of country A if political-economy effects are not large (i.e., $\gamma_e < 4/3$). But the optimal export policy is an export subsidy if political-economy considerations are important (i.e., $\gamma_e \in (4/3, 8/3)$). Finally, at a critical intermediate level for the political-economy parameter (i.e., $\gamma_e = 4/3$), the optimal policy is laissez faire, since the desire to subsidize for political-economy reasons is exactly offset by the desire to tax for terms-of-trade reasons.

Given the symmetry between countries A and B, we may find the Nash subsidy level, s^N, by solving $s^N = s^{AR}(s^N)$. Under the specific assumptions of our model, we find that the Nash subsidy level may be expressed in closed form as

$$s^N = \frac{3\gamma_e - 4}{10 - 3\gamma_e}. \tag{10.7}$$

In the Nash equilibrium, the exporting governments select export subsidies (taxes) if the political-economy parameter is sufficiently large (small); however, a laissez faire policy is adopted if the political-economy parameter is at the critical intermediate level.

10.5.2 Cooperative Subsidies

We now consider a different benchmark in which the governments of countries A and B "cooperate" through an agreement under which they choose s^A and s^B in order to maximize their combined welfare. To characterize the cooperative subsidies, we maximize $W^A + W^B$ with respect to s^A and s^B. For this program the first-order condition with respect to s^A is

$$W_{p^A}^A + \lambda \left[W_{\tilde{p}^w}^A + W_{p^B}^B + W_{\tilde{p}^w}^B \right] = 0. \tag{10.8}$$

It is interesting to compare (10.8) with (10.5). As this comparison reveals, cooperative exporting governments internalize the effects of one government's export subsidy on the welfare of the other. In particular, if the government of country A increases its export subsidy, then the domestic price in country B drops, and so profits in country B are reduced. Cooperative exporters recognize this profit-shifting externality. Noncooperative exporters do not.

Using the specific assumptions of the model, we find that the optimal cooperative export subsidy, s^C, is given by

$$s^C = \frac{\gamma_e - 2}{4 - \gamma_e}. \tag{10.9}$$

Thus the optimal cooperative policy may involve an export subsidy, but only if the political-economy parameter is quite large (i.e., $\gamma_e \in (2, 8/3)$). We may now use (10.7) and (10.9) to compare the Nash and cooperative policies, finding that the Nash subsidy is always higher:

$$s^N - s^C = \frac{4}{(10 - 3\gamma_e)(4 - \gamma_e)} > 0. \tag{10.10}$$

In other words, exporting governments reduce subsidies when they cooperate.

10.5.3 Efficient Subsidies

We last turn to consider efficient subsidies. To characterize the efficient subsidy policy, we choose s^A and s^B to maximize $W^A + W^B + W^w$. It is now useful to recall that a change in the world price $\tilde{p}^w$ amounts simply to an income transfer among the three governments. The associated first-order condition for s^A thus can be written as

$$W_{p^A}^A + \lambda W_{p^B}^B = 0. \tag{10.11}$$

It is instructive first to compare the efficiency condition (10.11) with the Nash condition (10.5). When the government of country A sets its policy in an efficient manner, it internalizes the negative externality that its subsidy has on profits in country B and the positive externality that its subsidy has for consumers in country w. As suggested above, the terms-of-trade improvement experienced by country-w consumers is precisely offset by the terms-of-trade deterioration experienced by countries A and B; therefore the government of country A ignores the terms of trade altogether when setting its policy efficiently. This clearly contrasts with the Nash condition (10.5) where the government of country A ignores the terms-of-trade implications of its policy only for the other governments.

Second, we may compare the efficiency condition (10.11) with the cooperative condition (10.8). When the government of country A sets its policy in a cooperative manner, it internalizes the negative externality that its subsidy has on profits in country B, but it does not internalize the positive externality that its subsidy engenders for consumers in country w through the implied improvement in country w's terms of trade. The government of country A therefore remains mindful of the terms-of-trade implications of its subsidy when setting its policy cooperatively.

Let us consider further the characterization of efficient subsidies. As (10.11) suggests, the symmetric efficient subsidy must satisfy

$$W_{p^A}^A = 0 = W_{p^B}^B. \tag{10.12}$$

Comparing (10.12) with (10.5), we see that the symmetric efficient subsidy level may be interpreted as the subsidy level that would be unilaterally optimal for an exporting government, if the government were not motivated by the terms-of-trade implications of its subsidy. In other words, whether or not governments have political considerations, the Nash subsidy level is inefficient if and only if governments are motivated by the terms-of-trade consequences of their trade policies. This confirms the conclusion anticipated above.

In analogy with our analysis in previous sections, where we consider import policies in a two-country general equilibrium model, we may refer to the (symmetric) subsidy level that satisfies (10.12) as the *politically optimal subsidy*. We thus confirm here that politically optimal policies remain efficient, when the analysis is extended to a three-country model of export policies.

Using the specific assumptions of the model, we now calculate the efficient subsidy, s^E. We find that the efficient subsidy is given as

$$s^E = (\gamma_e - 1)/(3 - \gamma_e) \geq 0. \tag{10.13}$$

Observe that an export subsidy is efficient if and only if political-economy effects exist. Using (10.7) and (10.13), we calculate that the efficient subsidy exceeds the Nash subsidy:

$$s^E - s^N = \frac{2}{(3 - \gamma_e)(10 - 3\gamma_e)} > 0. \tag{10.14}$$

Together, (10.10) and (10.14) imply that the efficient subsidy exceeds the Nash subsidy which in turn exceeds the cooperative subsidy. The total welfare of the three governments is thus higher when the exporting countries act noncooperatively than when they cooperate.

10.5.4 Illustration

Figure 10.1 illustrates our findings. In the southwest quadrant, the various policies are depicted for the case in which political-economy motivations are absent (i.e., $\gamma_e = 1$). Likewise the case in which political-economy considerations are important (i.e., $\gamma_e \in (4/3, 8/3)$) is represented in the northeast quadrant. The Nash policies are labeled as

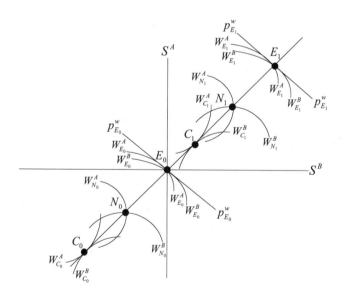

Figure 10.1

N_o and N_1 respectively. In both cases the Nash equilibrium is determined as the point where the iso-welfare contour of the government of country A (country B) is vertical (horizontal). No government is then able to increase its welfare with a unilateral policy change. The cooperative export policies are labeled as C_o and C_1. In both cases cooperative exporting governments agree to adjust their export policies so as to restrict export volumes from Nash levels. We observe further that when exporting governments cooperate, they agree on a pair of export policies at which their iso-welfare curves are tangent. Finally the efficient export policies are labeled as E_o and E_1. In both cases efficient export policies expand export volumes from their Nash levels. We observe further that these policies are determined by the point at which the iso-welfare contours of each exporting government are tangent to the iso-world-price locus.[8] But the iso-world-price locus also represents the iso-welfare contour for the importing government. Thus, when export policies are efficient, all three iso-welfare contours are tangent.

10.5.5 Interpretation

The hybrid model accounts for the four features of the agricultural disputes. The first feature is that governments use export subsidies when their exporters compete for third-country markets. To account for this feature, we recall (10.7) and observe that the Nash export subsidy is positive if political-economy effects are large. The second feature is that exporting governments seek an agreement to reduce export subsidies. The hybrid model accounts for this feature as well, since (10.10) indicates that export subsidies are reduced from Nash levels when exporting governments cooperate. Finally, the third and fourth features are also compatible with the hybrid model, since the model has competitive markets and politically motivated governments, respectively.

From the perspective of the model, the historical pattern of the agricultural disputes could be interpreted in the following way. The EC initially exercised a strategic export policy, and after the United States retaliated in kind, an outcome analogous to the Nash equilibrium of the model was induced.[9] Upon learning first-hand the costs of the

---

8. Recall that the world price, $\bar{p}^w(s^A, s^B)$, is decreasing in s^A and s^B. The iso-world-price locus thus takes a negative slope. Under our specific functional forms, this locus is linear.
9. We do not mean to imply that the EC subsidies were pursued only for strategic beggar-thy-neighbor reasons. Rather, the argument is simply that the EC subsidies were excessive from the perspective of the governments of exporting countries, since some of the cost of the program was borne by competing exporters from non-EC countries.

resulting subsidy war, the key exporting governments then sought to negotiate a reduction in agricultural export subsidies. This corresponds in the model to a movement by the governments of countries A and B from the high Nash subsidies to the lower cooperative subsidies. Naturally the governments of some net food-importing countries were concerned; likewise, in the model, the government of country w is harmed when subsidies are reduced. The model suggests further that such cooperation between exporting countries indeed diminishes global efficiency. The apparent purpose of an agreement to reduce subsidies is to advance the interests of exporting governments.

It is instructive to compare the hybrid model with the Brander-Spencer (1985) strategic-trade model. We note that the *ranking* of Nash, cooperative and efficient export subsidy levels is the same in each model. The hybrid model therefore preserves the essential Prisoners' Dilemma structure of the traditional strategic-trade model. The real difference between the two models concerns the means through which the traditional optimal export tariff is converted in *sign* into an export subsidy. In the model of Brander and Spencer (1985), export subsidies arise as a consequence of the Cournot interaction between imperfectly competitive firms.[10] By contrast, in the hybrid model, export subsidies are attributable to political concerns.

Finally, while the hybrid model accounts well for the central features of the agricultural disputes, the application of this model to the agricultural experience still may be questioned. We mention here three concerns. First, our symmetric model predicts that both the United States and the European Community would agree as to the desired extent of the reduction in export subsidies. But this is counterfactual. The actual experience suggests a model in which one exporting government (corresponding to the EC) weighs more heavily the negative effect of a reduced export subsidy for its agricultural sector than does the other exporting government (corresponding to the United States). We expect that this concern could be addressed with a modification of the hybrid

---

10. The export-subsidy prediction is, however, sensitive to the form of oligopolistic competition (Eaton and Grossman 1986; Maggi 1996) and the number of domestic firms (Dixit 1984). A strategic export subsidy is often more attractive when import-country consumers are uncertain as to the export's product quality (Bagwell 1991; Bagwell and Staiger 1989; Grossman and Horn 1988; Raff and Kim 1999). Finally, an exporting government also may have a strategic incentive to subsidize R&D (Spencer and Brander 1983), and this incentive is robust across a variety of forms of oligopolistic competition (Bagwell and Staiger 1992, 1994). Brander (1995) offers a survey of the strategic-trade literature.

model, under which the political-economy weight, χ_e, is higher for one exporting government than the other. Second, in some markets, the supply of a country's agricultural export is determined by a centralized national marketing board. The agricultural market then may have some imperfect-competition characteristics, and the competitive-markets assumption of the hybrid model may be inappropriate. Third, even if the competitive-markets assumption is accepted, if the *size* of the rents that are available for governments to "shift" with their export policies is small, then it would seem less likely that government behavior is well described by the hybrid model.

10.6   The Treatment of Export Subsidies

The discussion above was oriented around the agricultural disputes. These disputes are of undeniable importance. At the same time it is important also to extract the implications of our analysis for the treatment of export subsidies in GATT/WTO more generally. It is further useful to consider the possible implications of this analysis for the treatment of labor and environmental standards in export industries. We take up these remaining issues next.

At a general level, our analysis suggests that exporting governments may seek an agreement to limit export subsidies in order to curb the subsidy war that otherwise would occur. If exporting governments are successful in reaching such an agreement, then importing countries and the world as a whole may lose. From this perspective, GATT/WTO restrictions of export subsidies may correspond to a victory for exporting governments that comes at the expense of importing government— and world—welfare.[11] Our analysis thus calls into question the wisdom of GATT/WTO restrictions against export subsidies.

In making this claim, we emphasize that there is a fundamental difference between an agreement to reduce import tariffs and an agreement to reduce export subsidies. A tariff-liberalization agreement *expands* the volume of trade whereas a subsidy-reduction agreement *restricts* the volume of trade. Furthermore, as we argue throughout this book, when governments are able to manipulate the terms of trade, a

---

11. Under other assumptions, it is possible to identify special circumstances in which world welfare is greater when export subsidies are prohibited. Bagwell and Staiger (1997d) obtain this result in a model in which export subsidies influence entry into a "natural monopoly" export market, and Collie (1997) reaches a similar finding in a model in which strategic subsidies are financed by distortionary taxation.

trade agreement is valuable to the extent that its rules facilitate an expansion in the volume of trade. Rules that instead facilitate a reduction in trade volume warrant special scrutiny.

Finally, as Bagwell, Mavroidis, and Staiger (2002) argue, exactly analogous remarks apply with respect to the determination of labor and environmental standards in export industries. Each exporting government has a strategic incentive to lower its standard in order to give its exporters a competitive advantage. A Prisoners' Dilemma is thus suggested, whereby exporting governments lower standards in a mutually destructive way. The exporting governments then both gain if they reach an agreement under which standards in the export sector are raised. In the absence of any nonpecuniary externality, the importing government and the world as a whole may experience lower welfare if exporting governments are successful in raising standards.

11   The Practical Relevance of Terms-of-Trade Considerations

Our interpretation and evaluation of GATT relies heavily upon the political-economy approach. In other words, while we also highlight insights offered by the commitment approach, our workhorse model in this book is a (politically augmented) terms-of-trade model of trade agreements. It is therefore important for us to return to an issue that we raised in section 2.1.3: many economists are skeptical as to the practical relevance of terms-of-trade considerations for actual trade-policy negotiations. This skepticism seems to derive from four main objections. We now describe and assess these objections.

The first objection concerns the inherent plausibility of the terms-of-trade argument. As we discussed in section 2.1.3, the traditional presentation of the terms-of-trade argument for trade intervention involves a large and national-income-maximizing government that uses its tariff to manipulate the world price and thereby ensure that in the commercial trade across nations its exports command a greater volume of imports. Stated this way, the argument certainly sounds implausible. Relatedly, the plausibility of the theory may be questioned, in light of the fact that terms-of-trade considerations rarely receive explicit mention in actual trade-policy negotiations.

As we emphasized in section 2.1.3, however, the terms-of-trade argument is more plausible than the traditional presentation might suggest. First, the essential argument is that inefficient unilateral tariffs arise, because governments are tempted to shift the costs of their intervention onto one another. At a broad level, negotiators reason then in a manner consistent with the terms-of-trade theory if they are cognizant of the temptation to shift costs onto one another. And more specifically, if a partial-equilibrium perspective is taken, such cost-shifting clearly occurs provided only that some of the incidence of a government's tariff is borne by foreign exporters (i.e., the full tariff is not passed through to domestic consumers). When such cost-shifting does occur, it is plausible to expect that governments distort their policy choices, as they do not bear the whole cost of their decisions, and a role for a trade agreement is thus created.[1] Second, while it is true that trade-policy negotiators rarely mention the terms of trade, they do emphasize the market-access consequences of a trading partner's tariffs. As we argued at length in section 2.1.3, when a foreign trading partner raises its tariff, the loss in market access that home-country exporters experience is simply the "quantity effect" that accompanies the "price effect" of a deterioration in the home country's terms of trade.

A second objection questions the consistency of the main predictions of the terms-of-trade model with observed tariff patterns. For example, it is sometimes argued that the terms-of-trade theory is inconsistent with observed patterns because small countries often have high tariffs. Likewise it is sometime argued that the theory is inconsistent with the trade-policy choices of large countries (e.g., the United States), who set positive tariffs but do not seem to select "optimal tariffs."

But these criticisms are misguided. The traditional terms-of-trade theory of trade agreements is formalized under the joint hypotheses that governments (1) are motivated by terms-of-trade considerations, (2) are not motivated by political considerations, and (3) either interact noncooperatively (optimal tariffs) or cooperate through a trade agreement and reach the efficiency frontier (free trade). Yet the first hypothesis need not be bundled with the others. Thus a small country may set high tariffs because its government is politically motivated to redistribute income to its import-competing sector. And large countries may form a trade agreement and select low tariffs, precisely because they want to avoid the high (optimal) tariffs that otherwise would arise. Their cooperative tariffs may stop short of free trade, though, because

---

1. See, for example, Jackson (1989, p. 19) for a discussion of cost-shifting motives and GATT. He notes: "More subtle is the possibility that a national consensus could explicitly opt for a choice of policies that would not maximize wealth (in the traditionally measurable sense, at least), but would give preference to other non-economic goals. . . . It can be argued that when a nation makes an 'uneconomic' choice, it should be prepared to pay the whole cost, and not pursue policies which have the effect of unloading some of the burdens of that choice on to other nations. In an interdependent world, paying the whole cost is not often easy to accomplish." It is also relevant to note that, when reviewing escape clause cases, the US International Trade Commission routinely makes a "guesstimate" of the international incidence of the proposed tariff, that is, how much of the escape clause tariff will be *absorbed* by foreign producers, and how much will be *passed through* to US consumers. (We thank an anonymous reviewer for bringing this point to our attention).

of either enforcement difficulties that prevent perfect cooperation or political motivations that place free trade off the efficiency frontier. Finally, we have argued throughout the book that the (politically augmented) terms-of-trade theory provides a framework that yields implications that, in the main, are consistent with the observed GATT design and practice.

A third and related objection concerns the consistency of the predictions of the terms-of-trade model with the observed instruments of protection. As we discussed in chapter 10, the traditional two-country model of tariff selection does not account well for observed export-subsidization programs, such as for agricultural products. Yet we argue that a natural extension of the model, to allow for political motivations and competition between exporting governments for sales to consumers in third-country markets, offers an interpretation for observed agricultural subsidization practices and the associated agricultural trade disputes. The traditional static model of tariff selection also does not account well for the use of voluntary export restraints (VERs). As is well known, when an importing government requests a VER, the exporting government keeps all of the terms-of-trade gains that are associated with protection. Here, too, an interpretation can be offered, once the traditional model is extended. As we discussed in section 6.2.1, managed-trade policies have been used as "safeguard" instruments that assist governments in their attempts to achieve an enforceable trade agreement in a nonstationary world. From this perspective, the recent popularity of such policies reflect some practical weaknesses associated with GATT Article XIX, and with the changes adopted to this article with the formation of the WTO it is possible that the use of managed-trade policies will now decline.

The fourth and perhaps most serious objection directly questions the empirical relevance of the terms-of-trade theory. Are governments in fact able to improve their terms of trade with their trade-policy choices? And, if so, can they do so in a quantitatively significant fashion? These questions certainly warrant further empirical analysis. But strong affirmative presumptions already can be drawn from existing empirical work, as we now explain.

The hypothesis that governments can improve their terms of trade with their tariff choices is supported if a reduction in the domestic import tariff is not fully passed through as a reduced price for domestic consumers. It is therefore relevant to refer to the study of GATT negotiations by Kreinin (1961, p. 314), who finds that:

less than a third . . . of the tariff concessions granted by the United States were passed on to the US consumer in the form of reduced import prices, while more than two-thirds . . . accrued to the foreign suppliers and improved the terms of trade of the exporting nations.

Kreinin's study provides rather direct evidence that the effects of one country's tariff policy extend across national borders. Such findings are not limited to large industrialized countries. For example, Winters and Chang (1999, 2000) find substantial terms-of-trade effects associated with regional liberalization in Latin America under the Mercosur trade agreement and under Spain's accession to the European Union. In this regard it is also relevant to note that a large empirical literature exists that documents imperfect pass-through of exchange rate shocks. The survey of this literature by Goldberg and Knetter (1997) suggests that the degree of exchange rate pass-through averages about 60 percent. Presumably, if the cost increase to foreign exporters takes the form of a tariff increase as opposed to an exchange rate shock, then imperfect pass through would once again occur, confirming that some of the incidence of the import tariff is borne by foreign exporters. Empirical support for this presumption is offered by Feenstra (1995).[2]

Next empirical studies by Goldberg (1995) and Berry, Levinsohn, and Pakes (1999) strongly support the hypothesis that the terms-of-trade

---

2. In this context, it should be emphasized that even seemingly "small" countries may be able to impose some tariff incidence on foreign exporters. First, the analysis of Gros (1987) suggests that truly small countries may be difficult to find in practice, as even apparently small countries have some power over the terms of trade, provided that the industry is monopolistically competitive. Second, transportation costs encourage greater trade between proximate countries, and even between seemingly small countries some of the incidence of an import tariff can be passed onto exporters. For instance, adopting a gravity-model perspective to study the impacts of NAFTA, Anderson and van Wincoop (2001) find that even "small" countries such as Mexico can significantly affect their terms of trade with unilateral tariff changes. As another example, we note that Mexico brought a WTO case against Guatemala, whose government imposed an 89 percent tariff on imports of Mexican cement (e.g., Tuckman 1997). Apparently, in the context of the market for cement, Mexico does not regard the neighboring Guatemala as a small country.

At the same time, we also stress that the theory featured here does not require that all countries are able to alter the terms of trade. If in fact a country is small, then, of course, it would still benefit from joining the GATT/WTO, as it would thereby gain from the MFN tariff reductions extended to all GATT/WTO members by large countries. Indeed, the terms-of-trade theory of trade agreements indicates that small countries should be extended MFN treatment under GATT, and without a requirement that they offer reciprocal liberalization of their own. This is because the unilateral tariff policies of small countries impart no externality. To some extent this treatment is represented in GATT through MFN combined with the "principal supplier" rule (Dam 1970, p. 61) as it applies to reciprocal tariff negotiations.

effects of trade-policy choices can influence the national cost of intervention in quantitatively important ways. In both studies evidence is presented indicating that the terms-of-trade implications of the US decision in the 1980s to restrict automobile imports from Japan with VERs (rather than tariffs) increased substantially the cost to the United States of achieving the reduced import volumes. The study by Berry, Levinsohn and Pakes is of particular significance. They compare the actual VER policy with a hypothetical equivalent-tariff policy, calculating that the equivalent-tariff policy would have yielded revenue sufficient to turn what was a losing trade policy in terms of US national income into a policy that would have generated a net gain to the US national income of $12.5 billion. The study is relevant for the arguments developed in this book, since the only difference between the two policies is that they generate distinct world prices. The role of world prices in determining the incidence of the costs of intervention across trading partners lies at the core of the terms-of-trade theory of trade agreements.[3]

---

3. It may be tempting to infer that the decision of the United States to "give away" such an amount indicates that governments in fact do not care about the terms of trade, even when the associated implications for income are large. This inference, however, does not follow from the VER experience of the United States. Consistent with our discussion of VERs, a proper interpretation requires an awareness of the enforcement constraints that accompany a cooperative trade agreement. In particular, as Low (1993, p. 114) emphasizes, the relevant policy alternative for the United States was not a set of unilateral tariff increases (corresponding to the equivalent-tariff policy above), which surely would have incited a retaliatory "trade war" with Japan, but rather a set of tariff changes from the United States and Japan that were consistent with GATT rules.

12   Conclusion

We described recent work on the theory of trade agreements that speaks to the purpose and design of GATT. Our discussion unfolded in three steps. First, we examined the purpose of a trade agreement. In both the traditional economic and the political-economy approaches to the study of trade agreements, the problem for a trade agreement to solve is the excessive protection that arises in the absence of an agreement as a consequence of the terms-of-trade externality. Second, we considered the origin and design of GATT. We noted that the GATT/WTO is a rules-based institution whose origin can be traced to the disastrous economic performance that accompanied the high tariffs of the 1920s and 1930s. Finally, we discussed the theoretical literature that interprets and evaluates the institutional features found in GATT. We considered, in particular, whether GATT articles can be interpreted as offering negotiation rules that help governments undo the inefficient restrictions in trade that are caused by the terms-of-trade externality.

On the whole, our discussion suggests that the core principles of GATT indeed may be interpreted in this manner. Specifically, we reported findings that indicate that the principles of reciprocity and nondiscrimination work in concert to remedy the inefficiency created by the terms-of-trade externality. We also extracted a variety of predictions from the literature on enforcement and trade policy, and we argued that these predictions are broadly compatible with both the design of GATT and certain historical experiences in trade-policy conduct.

We also considered the treatment of new trade-policy issues. Here our evaluation of current GATT/WTO rules was more mixed. With regard to the treatment of preferential trading agreements, the corresponding theoretical models do not offer clear support for current GATT/WTO practice. At a positive level, however, the models do provide economic interpretations of recent GATT/WTO experiences associated with these issues. We argued as well that the policy debates that are associated with agricultural subsidization practices can be interpreted with strategic-trade theory—despite the competitive characteristics of the agricultural market. This suggests that efforts to reduce agricultural subsidies may offer gains to exporting countries at the expense of import-country and world welfare. Finally, we considered the treatment of labor/environment standards and of national standards with regard to competition policy, and suggested that such standards, in principle, could be brought into the GATT/WTO framework with only small adjustments to existing GATT/WTO rules and without any significant loss in national sovereignty.

Taken together, we interpret the results presented here as providing a strong presumption for the view that the GATT/WTO can be understood as an institution whose central design features make it well-equipped to help governments in their attempt to escape from a terms-of-trade-driven Prisoners' Dilemma. Hence this book offers support for the (politically augmented) terms-of-trade theory as an appropriate framework within which to interpret and evaluate the GATT/WTO.

We conclude by pointing to three promising directions in which future theoretical research might proceed. First, an open question concerns the extent to which GATT rules also serve to help governments correct additional inefficiencies (i.e., beyond the terms-of-trade externality) that are associated with unilateral trade-policy decisions. For example, as we discussed at several points, the unilateral trade-policy decisions of governments may be inefficient if governments face a domestic commitment problem with respect to their private sectors. Alternatively, frictions in the labor market or Keynesian rigidities may lead to unemployment, in which case tariff choices may serve to shift unemployment levels across trading partners. Whether or not GATT rules serve effectively to deal with these or other potential additional sources of inefficiency is an important topic for future research.[1]

Second, it is important to determine if GATT's principles constitute an effective approach to the host of new trade-policy issues with which the multilateral trading system must contend. We discussed this topic above in the context of some particular new trade-policy issues, but

---

1. Some empirical evidence that GATT rules do help governments make domestic commitments is provided in Staiger and Tabellini (1999).

there are many other new issues that also warrant attention. For example, interesting future work might consider the performance of GATT's principles when applied to the treatment of services, intellectual property rights and trade-related investment measures. Extensions of this nature are of particular importance as the scope of GATT (and now the WTO) extends beyond the traditional arena of tariff liberalization.[2]

Finally, while the government welfare function that we employed throughout is quite general, it does not capture all of the concerns that governments may wish to address through a trade agreement. We assumed that government preferences are captured as a general function of local and world prices, but other concerns, such as military security and political stability, are also of obvious importance, and particularly so in the context of regional integration initiatives.[3] The interaction between trade agreements and such broader objectives represents an interesting and challenging direction for future research.

---

2. For further discussion of the appropriate treatment of new trade-policy issues, see Hoekman and Kostecki (1995), Jackson (1997a, pp. 305–18), Trebilcock and Howse (1999), and articles in the volumes edited by Stern (1993) and Krueger (1998).

3. See Fernandez and Portes (1998) for further discussion along these lines.

A

Appendix to Chapter 2

We offer here simple proofs of the three observations reported in chapter 2. We also derive the characterization of the efficiency frontier reported there. Finally, we reinterpret the second observation in terms of market access.

PROPOSITION 2.1 Nash equilibrium tariffs are inefficient.

Proof To establish this first observation, we proceed by calculating the slope of the respective iso-welfare tariff loci. Observe that

$$\frac{d\tau}{d\tau^*}\bigg|_{dW=0} = -\left[\frac{\partial \tilde{p}^w/\partial \tau^*}{dp/d\tau}\right]\left[\frac{\tau W_p + W_{\tilde{p}^w}}{W_p + \lambda W_{\tilde{p}^w}}\right], \tag{A.1}$$

and

$$\frac{d\tau}{d\tau^*}\bigg|_{dW^*=0} = -\left[\frac{dp^*/d\tau^*}{\partial \tilde{p}^w/\partial \tau}\right]\left[\frac{W_{p^*}^* + \lambda^* W_{\tilde{p}^w}^*}{W_{p^*}^*/\tau^* + W_{\tilde{p}^w}^*}\right]. \tag{A.2}$$

From (2.4), (2.7), (2.8), (A.1), and (A.2), we may conclude that at the Nash tariff pair, $d\tau/d\tau^*|_{dW=0} = \infty > 0 = d\tau/d\tau^*|_{dW^*=0}$. Referring to the tangency condition (2.9), we see that the Nash tariff pair is inefficient. □

PROPOSITION 2.2 If a trade agreement generates greater than Nash welfare for the domestic and foreign governments, then the agreement must entail reciprocal trade liberalization.

Proof To establish this second observation, we must show that a negotiated tariff pair, (τ^0, τ^{*0}), induces welfare improvements for both the domestic and foreign governments relative to the Nash tariff pair, (τ^N, τ^{*N}), only if $\tau^0 < \tau^N$ and $\tau^{*0} < \tau^{*N}$. To this end, we suppose that $\tau^0 > \tau^N$ and prove that the foreign government then must lose. The other case where $\tau^{*0} > \tau^{*N}$ is analogous.

We consider first the impact of the tariff of one country on the welfare of the government of the other country. Observe that

$$\frac{dW}{d\tau^*} = \left[\tau W_p + W_{\tilde{p}^w}\right]\left[\frac{\partial \tilde{p}^w}{\partial \tau^*}\right] \tag{A.3}$$

and that

$$\frac{dW^*}{d\tau} = \left[W_{p^*}^*/\tau^* + W_{\tilde{p}^w}^*\right]\left[\frac{\partial \tilde{p}^w}{\partial \tau}\right]. \tag{A.4}$$

Recall that (2.7) and (2.8) respectively define the best-response functions for the domestic and foreign governments. Let these functions be denoted as $\tau^R(\tau^*)$ and $\tau^{*R}(\tau)$, respectively. Using (2.7), (2.8), (A.3), and (A.4), we consider the impact of the tariff of one country on the welfare of the government of the other country, when the latter is on its best-response function:

$$\frac{dW}{d\tau^*}\Big|_{\tau=\tau^R(\tau^*)} = [1 - \tau^R(\tau^*)\lambda]W_{\tilde{p}^w}\left[\frac{\partial \tilde{p}^w}{\partial \tau^*}\right] < 0 \tag{A.5}$$

and

$$\frac{dW^*}{d\tau}\Big|_{\tau^*=\tau^{*R}(\tau)} = \left[1 - \frac{\lambda^*}{\tau^{*R}(\tau)}\right]W_{\tilde{p}^w}^*\left[\frac{\partial \tilde{p}^w}{\partial \tau}\right] < 0, \tag{A.6}$$

where the inequalities in (A.5) and (A.6) follow from (2.4). Thus, along a government's best-response curve, its welfare is strictly decreasing in the tariff selected by the other government.

We may now establish the following:

$$W^*(p^*(\tau^{*0}, \tilde{p}_{00}^w), \tilde{p}_{00}^w) \le W^*(p^*(\tau^{*R}(\tau^0), \tilde{p}_{0R}^w), \tilde{p}_{0R}^w)$$
$$< W^*(p^*(\tau^{*R}(\tau^N), \tilde{p}_N^w), \tilde{p}_N^w) \equiv W^*(p^*(\tau^{*N}, \tilde{p}_N^w), \tilde{p}_N^w),$$

where $\tilde{p}_{00}^w \equiv \tilde{p}^w(\tau^0, \tau^{*0})$, $\tilde{p}_{0R}^w \equiv \tilde{p}^w(\tau^0, \tau^{*R}(\tau^0))$ and $\tilde{p}_N^w \equiv \tilde{p}^w(\tau^N, \tau^{*R}(\tau^N)) \equiv \tilde{p}^w(\tau^N, \tau^{*N})$. The first inequality follows since $\tau^{*R}(\tau^0)$ is the foreign government's best response to τ^0, and the second inequality uses (A.6) and our supposition that $\tau^0 > \tau^N$. Thus, the foreign government experiences a strict reduction in welfare from any change in tariffs that involves an increase in the domestic tariff from its Nash level, τ^N. $\square$

PROPOSITION 2.3 Politically optimal tariffs are efficient.

Proof To establish this third observation, we may use (2.11), (2.12), (A.1) and (A.2) and conclude that, at the politically optimal tariff pair, $d\tau/d\tau^* \mid_{dW=0} = -[\partial \tilde{p}^w/\partial \tau^*]/[\partial \tilde{p}^w/\partial \tau] = d\tau/d\tau^* \mid_{dW^*=0}$. Referring to the tangency condition (2.9), we see that the politically optimal tariff pair is efficient. □

As noted in the text, we may also establish the first and third observations by deriving a characterization of the efficiency frontier. We now provide this derivation.

PROPOSITION 2.4   A tariff pair is efficient if and only if

$$1 - AW_p = \frac{1}{1 - A^* W_{p^*}^*}.$$

Proof From (A.1) and (A.2), we see that (2.9) holds if and only if

$$\frac{[\partial \tilde{p}^w/\partial \tau^*]}{[dp/d\tau]} \frac{[\tau W_p + W_{\tilde{p}^w}]}{[W_p + \lambda W_{\tilde{p}^w}]} = \frac{[dp^*/d\tau^*]}{[\partial \tilde{p}^w/\partial \tau]} \frac{[W_{p^*}^* + \lambda^* W_{\tilde{p}^w}^*]}{[W_{p^*}^*/\tau^* + W_{\tilde{p}^w}^*]}. \tag{A.7}$$

From the definitions of A and A^*, we next observe that

$$1 - AW_p = [\lambda] \frac{[\tau W_p + W_{\tilde{p}^w}]}{[W_p + \lambda W_{\tilde{p}^w}]} \tag{A.8}$$

$$1 - A^* W_{p^*}^* = [\lambda^*] \frac{[W_{p^*}^*/\tau^* + W_{\tilde{p}^w}^*]}{[W_{p^*}^* + \lambda^* W_{\tilde{p}^w}^*]}. \tag{A.9}$$

We may thus rewrite (A.7) as $1 - AW_p = 1/[1 - A^* W_{p^*}^*]$. □

Finally, as noted in the text, the second observation may be recast in terms of market access. The formal result is as follows:

PROPOSITION 2.5   Beginning at the Nash equilibrium, a trade agreement generates greater than Nash welfare for the domestic and foreign governments only if each government secures additional market access from its trading partner.

Proof Suppose that the governments begin at the Nash tariff pair, (τ^N, τ^{*N}), and then negotiate a trade agreement that specifies a new tariff pair, (τ^0, τ^{*0}). Without loss of generality, suppose that the foreign government fails to secure additional market access from the domestic government through this negotiation. We will show that the foreign government then cannot achieve greater than Nash welfare under the trade agreement.

Under our supposition the foreign government confronts a domestic import demand function that is (weakly) shifted in at all world prices. The Marshall-Lerner stability conditions thus imply that the equilibrium world price, $\tilde{p}^w$, is (weakly) lower at (τ^0, τ^{*N}) than at (τ^N, τ^{*N}). Clearly, the foreign government cannot achieve greater than Nash welfare from a trade agreement if the domestic tariff remains at its Nash level. Suppose then that $\tau^0 \neq \tau^N$. Given our maintained assumption that the equilibrium world price is strictly decreasing in the domestic tariff, it follows that the equilibrium world price is strictly lower at (τ^0, τ^{*N}) than at (τ^N, τ^{*N}), and so $\tau^0 > \tau^N$. But we may now argue as in the proof of proposition 2, and establish thereby that the foreign government cannot achieve greater than Nash welfare. $\square$

B

Appendix to Chapter 5

We provide here further details for the multicountry general equilibrium model of trade. We then establish two of the characterizations of the efficiency frontier for the multicountry model that are reported in chapter 5. Finally, we extend our analysis to a many-good setting and consider in this context the potential for a bilateral opportunism problem.

B.1 The General Equilibrium Model: Further Details

The trade model is fully specified in section 5.2, except that the derivation of domestic tariff revenue and the resulting expressions for domestic quantities are not reported. Let $Q_i = Q_i(p)$ denote domestic production of product i, where $i \in \{x, y\}$, given the local relative price p. Likewise the domestic consumption of good i is determined as a function of the local relative price and domestic tariff revenue: $D_i(p, R)$ for $i \in \{x, y\}$. Next, using the definition for the domestic country's multilateral terms of trade given in (5.3), we implicitly define domestic tariff revenue as

$$R = [D_x(p, R) - Q_x(p)] \sum_{i=1,2} s_x^{*i}(p^{*1}, p^{*2}, p^{w1}, p^{w2}) \cdot [p - p^{wi}]$$

$$= [D_x(p, R) - Q_x(p)] \cdot [p - T],$$

or $R = R(p, T)$. We may now represent domestic consumption as $C_i(p, T) \equiv D_i(p, R(p, T))$. Home-country imports of x may be denoted as $M(p, T) \equiv C_x(p, T) - Q_x(p)$. Likewise home-country exports of y may be represented as $E(p, T) \equiv Q_y(p) - C_y(p, T)$.

B.2 The Efficiency Frontier: Characterizations

We next offer two propositions that further characterize the efficiency frontier. The first proposition relates to the discussion of renegotiation contained in section 5.3.2. After strengthening our basic assumptions slightly, we present a second proposition that relates to the discussion of bilateral opportunism found in section 5.3.1.

PROPOSITION 5.1 Politically optimal tariffs are efficient if and only if they conform to MFN.

Proof We first characterize the efficiency frontier. Define $\tilde{p}^{wj}(\tau^{*j}, \overline{W}^{*j})$ as the implied world price between the domestic country and foreign country j, when the government of foreign country j achieves welfare $\overline{W}^{*j}$ and sets its tariff at τ^{*j}. This price is defined implicitly by $W^{*j}(p^{*j}(\tau^{*j}, \tilde{p}^{wj}), \tilde{p}^{wj}) = \overline{W}^{*j}$. For simplicity, we assume that $\tilde{p}^{wj}(\tau^{*j}, \overline{W}^{*j})$ is a well-defined function of τ^{*j}. Observe that

$$\frac{\partial \tilde{p}^{wj}(\tau^{*j}, \overline{W}^{*j})}{\partial \tau^{*j}} = \frac{p^{*j} W_{p^{*j}}^{*j}}{W_{p^{*j}}^{*j} + \tau^{*j} W_{\tilde{p}^{wj}}^{*j}}. \tag{A.10}$$

Now fix the two foreign tariffs, τ^{*1} and τ^{*2}, and the two foreign welfare levels, $\overline{W}^{*1}$ and $\overline{W}^{*2}$. Using the implied world price function just derived, a complete set of world and foreign local prices is thus determined. By (5.3), a value for the domestic multilateral terms of trade is also implied:

$$\overline{T}(\tau^{*1}, \tau^{*2}, \overline{W}^{*1}, \overline{W}^{*2}) \equiv T(p^{*1}(\cdot), p^{*2}(\cdot), \tilde{p}^{w1}(\cdot), \tilde{p}^{w2}(\cdot)), \tag{A.11}$$

where $p^{*j}(\cdot) \equiv p^{*j}(\tau^{*j}, \tilde{p}^{wj}(\cdot))$ and $\tilde{p}^{wj}(\cdot) \equiv \tilde{p}^{wj}(\tau^{*j}, \overline{W}^{*j})$. With world prices and foreign local prices defined in this way, we next impose the market-clearing requirement, (5.6), that implies a value for the domestic local price. We denote this price as $\overline{p}(\tau^{*1}, \tau^{*2}, \overline{W}^{*1}, \overline{W}^{*2})$. The domestic local price in turn implies values for the domestic tariffs, since $\overline{p}(\cdot) = \tau^j \tilde{p}^{wj}(\cdot)$ where $\overline{p}(\cdot) \equiv \overline{p}(\tau^{*1}, \tau^{*2}, \overline{W}^{*1}, \overline{W}^{*2})$.

Given this construction, the equilibrium domestic welfare level may be written as a function of the foreign tariffs and welfare levels: $W(\overline{p}(\cdot), \overline{T}(\cdot))$ where $\overline{T}(\cdot) \equiv \overline{T}(\tau^{*1}, \tau^{*2}, \overline{W}^{*1}, \overline{W}^{*2})$. Therefore, if we fix foreign welfare levels and choose foreign tariffs to maximize domestic welfare, then a point on the efficiency frontier is generated. The first-order conditions are

$$W_p + \overline{\lambda}^{*j} W_T = 0 \qquad \text{for } j = 1, 2, \tag{A.12}$$

where $\overline{\lambda}^{*j} \equiv [\partial \overline{T}/\partial \tau^{*j}]/[\partial \overline{p}/\partial \tau^{*j}]$.

We now prove the proposition. Suppose that a set of tariffs are politically optimal. By (5.7) and (A.12), they are efficient if and only if $\partial \overline{T}/\partial \tau^{*j} = 0$ for $j = 1, 2$. Using (5.3) and (A.11), we find that

$$\frac{\partial \overline{T}}{\partial \tau^{*j}} = \frac{1}{M}\left\{\left[\frac{\partial E^{*j}}{\partial p^{*j}}\frac{dp^{*j}}{d\tau^{*j}} + \frac{\partial E^{*j}}{\partial p^{wj}}\frac{\partial \tilde{p}^{wj}(\cdot)}{\partial \tau^{*j}}\right][\tilde{p}^{wj}(\cdot) - \overline{T}(\cdot)] + E^{*j}\frac{\partial \tilde{p}^{wj}(\cdot)}{\partial \tau^{*j}}\right\}. \qquad \text{(A.13)}$$

By (A.10), political optimality implies $\partial \tilde{p}^{wj}(\cdot)/\partial \tau^{*j} = 0$. Thus, by (A.13), political optimal tariffs are efficient if and only if

$$\frac{\partial \overline{T}}{\partial \tau^{*j}} = \frac{1}{M}\left[\frac{\partial E^{*j}}{\partial p^{*j}}\frac{dp^{*j}}{d\tau^{*j}}\right][\tilde{p}^{wj}(\cdot) - \overline{T}(\cdot)]. \qquad \text{(A.14)}$$

With political optimality implying $\partial \tilde{p}^{wj}(\cdot)/\partial \tau^{*j} = 0$, it follows that at politically optimal tariffs $dp^{*j}/d\tau^{*j} = \partial p^{*j}/\partial \tau^{*j} = -p^{*j}/\tau^{*j} < 0$, and hence the righthand side of (A.14) is zero if and only if tariffs also conform to MFN. □

We develop next a second characterization of the efficiency frontier for the multicountry model. In particular, we provide a proposition that confirms the depiction of the efficiency frontier offered in figure 5.1. This proposition is thus related to the discussion of bilateral opportunism presented in section 5.3.1.

To begin, we represent government welfare in reduced form as a direct function of tariffs. Let $\hat{W}(\tau) \equiv W(p, T)$ and $\hat{W}^{*i}(\tau) \equiv W^{*i}(p^{*i}, \tilde{p}^{wi})$, where $\tau \equiv (\tau^1, \tau^2, \tau^{*1}, \tau^{*2})$ and all prices and terms of trade are evaluated at their market-clearing levels. Next, as indicated in note 5 of chapter 5, we strengthen our basic assumptions slightly so as to focus on tariffs for which externalities can be unambiguously signed. Specifically, we consider tariffs that rest on the efficiency frontier at a point where (1) each government would prefer to unilaterally raise its tariff, (2) each government experiences a welfare reduction when its export good is confronted with a higher tariff from a trading partner, and (3) foreign government i is pleased when either the home government raises its tariff on the exports of foreign country j or foreign government j raises its tariff on the exports of the home country. These relationships follow directly from the multicountry model detailed in section 5.2, so long as government welfare at the initial tariffs is sufficiently sensitive to the terms-of-trade change that an adjustment in tariffs would imply.

Formally, we may capture the additional structure with the following assumptions. We restrict attention to efficient tariffs for which, for $i, j = 1, 2$ and $i \neq j$:

1. $\partial \hat{W} / \partial \tau^i > 0$ and $\partial \hat{W}^{*i} / \partial \tau^{*i} > 0$

2. $\partial \hat{W} / \partial \tau^{*i} < 0$ and $\partial \hat{W}^{*i} / \partial \tau^i < 0$

3. $\partial \hat{W}^{*i} / \partial \tau^{*j} > 0$ and $\partial \hat{W}^{*i} / \partial \tau^j > 0$.

This additional structure is easily motivated. In essence, we focus on the set of efficient trade agreements that are suggested by the nature of GATT tariff bindings. The fundamental legal commitment associated with GATT bindings is that governments agree not to raise their tariffs *above* bound levels. It would be difficult to reconcile the value that governments evidently place on such commitments with points on the efficiency frontier that did not satisfy assumptions 1 and 2. Furthermore, from the multicountry model detailed in section 5.2, it follows that condition 3 is implied by condition 2. This can be seen by noting that the impact of a change in τ^{*j} or τ^j on the welfare of foreign country i travels through $\tilde{p}^{wi}$, as does the impact on the welfare of foreign country i of a change in τ^i. Our assumptions relating tariffs to equilibrium world prices are then sufficient to establish that condition 2 implies condition 3.

At an efficient set of tariffs, no one government can gain from an adjustment in the tariff vector, without simultaneously reducing the welfare of at least one other government. An efficient vector of tariffs, $\tau_e \equiv (\tau_e^1, \tau_e^2, \tau_e^{*1}, \tau_e^{*2})$, must therefore solve the following program:

PROGRAM W   *Choose τ to maximize $\hat{W}(\tau)$*

s.t. $\hat{W}^{*i}(\tau) \geq \hat{W}^{*i}(\tau_e)$ for $i = 1, 2$.

We can now confirm the relationships illustrated in figure 5.1:

PROPOSITION 5.2   Given an efficient vector of tariffs, for $i, j = 1, 2$ and $i \neq j$, we must have that

$$-\frac{\partial \hat{W} / \partial \tau^{*i}}{\partial \hat{W} / \partial \tau^i} > -\frac{\partial \hat{W}^{*i} / \partial \tau^{*i}}{\partial \hat{W}^{*i} / \partial \tau^i} > 0 > -\frac{\partial \hat{W}^{*j} / \partial \tau^{*i}}{\partial \hat{W}^{*j} / \partial \tau^i}.$$

Proof To establish this characterization, we refer to figure 5.1. Under the additional structure imposed above, the iso-welfare curve for the home-country government must be positively sloped. The iso-welfare curve of the government of foreign country i is likewise positively sloped. By contrast, the iso-welfare curve for the government of foreign country j is negatively sloped. It remains to show that the home-government welfare curve is steeper than that of foreign government i at the efficient point. Equivalently, we must show that an efficient tariff vector leaves a lens in which the governments of the home country and foreign country i could experience welfare gains, where the lens lies below the iso-welfare curve of the government of foreign country j.

We first hypothesize the opposite possibility, in which the iso-welfare curve of the home government is flatter than that of the government of foreign country i at the efficient point. By this hypothesis, there exists a lens above the efficient tariff vector in which the governments of the home country and foreign country i could enjoy welfare gains. More-over, when these governments impose higher tariffs on each other's exports, foreign country j experiences a terms-of-trade gain, and under the additional structure that we impose, this results in a welfare improvement for the government of this country. All three govern-ments would thus gain by adjusting τ^i and τ^{*i} upward so as to move into the lens. The hypothesis of an upward lens thus contradicts the assumption of an efficient tariff vector.

We second hypothesize that there is no lens: the iso-welfare curves of the governments of the home country and foreign country i are tangent at the point at which they intersect the iso-welfare curve of the government of foreign country j. This arrangement fails to solve Program W as well, but a more involved alteration of tariffs is now required to produce Pareto improvements. For example, raising τ^i and τ^{*i} along the iso-welfare curve of foreign country i will cause the home-country government to experience a second-order welfare loss, while generating a first-order welfare benefit for the government of foreign country j. Adjustments to τ^j and τ^{*j} can then be found that ensure gains for all three governments.

Formally, by the second (tangency) hypothesis, the welfares of the governments of the home country and foreign country j can be increased while maintaining the welfare of the government of foreign country i if we adjust tariffs according to the following procedure: (1) increase τ^i and τ^{*i} so as to preserve $\hat{W}^{*i}$, thereby creating a second-order loss (first-order gain) for $\hat{W}$ ($\hat{W}^{*j}$), (2) raise τ^j and lower τ^{*j} so as to preserve $\hat{W}^{*i}$, thereby creating a first-order gain (first-order loss) for $\hat{W}$ ($\hat{W}^{*j}$), and (3) ensure that the first adjustment is large as compared to the second, thereby creating a net gain for $\hat{W}^{*i}$. Specifically, with sub-scripts denoting partial derivatives, it suffices to pick tariff changes that satisfy:

$$d\tau^{*i} = \varepsilon^i > 0, \quad d\tau^i = -\left[\frac{\hat{W}^{*i}_{\tau^{*i}}}{\hat{W}^{*i}_{\tau^i}}\right]\varepsilon^i > 0, \quad d\tau^{*j} = -\varepsilon^j < 0,$$

$$d\tau^j = \left[\frac{\hat{W}^{*i}_{\tau^{*j}}}{\hat{W}^{*i}_{\tau^j}}\right]\varepsilon^j > 0,$$

where

$$\frac{\varepsilon^i}{\varepsilon^j} > \frac{\left[\hat{W}^{*j}_{\tau^j}\big/\hat{W}^{*j}_{\tau^i}\right]\left[\hat{W}^{*j}_{\tau^{*j}}\big/\hat{W}^{*j}_{\tau^j} - \hat{W}^{*i}_{\tau^{*j}}\big/\hat{W}^{*i}_{\tau^j}\right]}{\left[\hat{W}^{*j}_{\tau^{*i}}\big/\hat{W}^{*j}_{\tau^i} - \hat{W}^{*i}_{\tau^{*i}}\big/\hat{W}^{*i}_{\tau^i}\right]} > 0.$$

The hypothesis of a tangency thus also contradicts the assumption of an efficient tariff vector.

One possibility remains: if the vector of tariffs is efficient, then the lens indeed must lie below the iso-welfare curve of the government of foreign country j, so that $-[\partial\hat{W}/\partial\tau^{*i}/\partial\hat{W}/\partial\tau^i] > -[\partial\hat{W}^{*i}/\partial\tau^{*i}/\partial\hat{W}^{*i}/\partial\tau^i]$. This is the case depicted in figure 5.1. □

B.3   Many Goods

We now consider briefly the extension of our multicountry findings to a many-good setting. For our purposes the novel feature of this setting is that there are many relative world prices even when MFN is imposed (i.e., under MFN, there are $n - 1$ relative world prices in an n-good world). Here we briefly explore the implications of this new feature for the bilateral opportunism problem.

To make our points as simply as possible, we restrict our attention to MFN environments and consider the addition of a third good z to our two-good multicountry model. We suppose that, like good y, good z is exported by the home country to each of its two foreign trading partners. For the home country, there are now two local relative prices, $p_1 \equiv p_x/p_y$ and $p_2 \equiv p_z/p_y$; furthermore, with tariffs restricted to conform to MFN, there are also two world relative prices, $p_1^w \equiv p_x^w/p_y^w$ and $p_2^w \equiv p_z^w/p_y^w$. Local relative prices for foreign country i are similarly denoted by $p_1^{*i} \equiv p_x^{*i}/p_y^{*i}$ and $p_2^{*i} \equiv p_z^{*i}/p_y^{*i}$ for $i = 1, 2$. By Lerner's symmetry theorem, we may represent the home-country tariff policy with the ad valorem trade taxes t_x and t_z, with $t_z > 0$ ($t_z < 0$) denoting an export subsidy (tax). Letting $\tau_x \equiv (1 + t_x)$ and $\tau_z \equiv (1 + t_z)$, we may then represent home local prices in terms of world prices and tariffs: $p_1 = \tau_x p_1^w \equiv p_1(\tau_x, p_1^w)$ and $p_2 = \tau_z p_2^w \equiv p_2(\tau_z, p_2^w)$. Similarly, for foreign country i, we represent tariff policy with the ad valorem trade taxes t_x^{*i} and t_z^{*i} for $i = 1, 2$, with $t_x^{*i} > 0$ ($t_x^{*i} < 0$) denoting an export subsidy. With $\tau_x^{*i} \equiv (1 + t_x^{*i})$

and $\tau_z^{*i} \equiv (1 + t_z^{*i})$, we may then write $p_1^{*i} = \tau_x^{*i} p_1^w \equiv p_1^{*i}(\tau_x^{*i}, p_1^w)$ and $p_2^{*i} = \tau_z^{*i} p_2^w \equiv p_2^{*i}(\tau_z^{*i}, p_2^w)$ for $i = 1, 2$. As these expressions indicate, local prices are determined once tariffs and world prices are given.

As in our two-good model each country's production, consumption, import, and export quantities are determined once tariffs and world prices (and hence local prices) are given. Under a set of tariffs satisfying MFN, and for $i = 1, 2$, the balanced-trade conditions are given by

$$p_1^w M_x(p_1, p_2, p_1^w, p_2^w) = p_2^w E_z(p_1, p_2, p_1^w, p_2^w) + E_y(p_1, p_2, p_1^w, p_2^w), \quad \text{(A.15)}$$

$$p_1^w E_x^{*i}\left(p_1^{*i}, p_2^{*i}, p_1^w, p_2^w\right)$$
$$= p_2^w M_z^{*i}\left(p_1^{*i}, p_2^{*i}, p_1^w, p_2^w\right) + M_y^{*i}\left(p_1^{*i}, p_2^{*i}, p_1^w, p_2^w\right). \quad \text{(A.16)}$$

Equilibrium world prices, $\tilde{p}_1^w(\tau_x, \tau_z, \tau_x^{*1}, \tau_z^{*1}, \tau_x^{*2}, \tau_z^{*2})$ and $\tilde{p}_2^w(\tau_x, \tau_z, \tau_x^{*1}, \tau_z^{*1}, \tau_x^{*2}, \tau_z^{*2})$, are then determined by the x and z market-clearing conditions:

$$M_x(p_1, p_2, p_1^w, p_2^w) = \sum_{i=1,2} E_x^{*i}\left(p_1^{*i}, p_2^{*i}, p_1^w, p_2^w\right),$$
$$E_z(p_1, p_2, p_1^w, p_2^w) = \sum_{i=1,2} M_z^{*i}\left(p_1^{*i}, p_2^{*i}, p_1^w, p_2^w\right). \quad \text{(A.17)}$$

As before, market clearing in the y market is assured by (A.15), (A.16), and (A.17). Summarizing, with their selections of tariffs, governments determine the equilibrium world prices, and this in turn implies the equilibrium values for all local prices and quantities.

Finally, we extend our representation of government preferences to the three-good case. Under MFN this representation takes the form of $W(p_1, p_2, \tilde{p}_1^w, \tilde{p}_2^w)$ for the home government and $W^{*i}(p_1^{*i}, p_2^{*i}, \tilde{p}_1^w, \tilde{p}_2^w)$ for foreign government $i = 1, 2$. As in our two-good model we suppose that with local prices held fixed, each government strictly prefers an improvement in its terms of trade: $W_{\tilde{p}_1^w}(p_1, p_2, \tilde{p}_1^w, \tilde{p}_2^w) < 0$, $W_{\tilde{p}_2^w}(p_1, p_2, \tilde{p}_1^w, \tilde{p}_2^w) > 0$, and $W_{\tilde{p}_1^w}^{*i}(p_1^{*i}, p_2^{*i}, \tilde{p}_1^w, \tilde{p}_2^w) > 0$; $W_{\tilde{p}_2^w}^{*i}(p_1^{*i}, p_2^{*i}, \tilde{p}_1^w, \tilde{p}_2^w) < 0$ for $i = 1, 2$. In addition we now assume that these world price movements are valued by governments for their monetary implications alone. With this additional structure, we rule out the possibility that a government might care about the level of a particular world price for reasons, such as "national status," that are independent of its revenue consequences.

We are now ready to establish three results. Starting with an initial MFN-efficient tariff vector, we show first that reciprocity in combination with MFN continues to eliminate the opportunities for two countries to form a bilateral agreement in which they gain for terms-of-trade reasons. In the two-good case, this followed directly from the observation that in the presence of MFN, reciprocity fixes $\tilde{p}^w$. With more than two goods, individual world prices may change even when reciprocity is satisfied. However, we now establish that the permissible changes in world prices that result from the negotiations can have no direct welfare consequences for the negotiating governments.

To see this, suppose that the governments of the home country and foreign country i were to consider further negotiations starting from a set of MFN-efficient tariffs for the three governments. Denoting by a prime (') the new magnitudes to which these governments negotiate, reciprocity may be defined in terms of the following restrictions on the outcome of their negotiations:

$$\tilde{p}_1^w[M_x' - M_x] = [E_y' - E_y] + \tilde{p}_2^w[E_z' - E_z], \tag{A.18}$$

$$\tilde{p}_1^w\left[E_x^{*i'} - E_x^{*i}\right] = \left[M_y^{*i'} - M_y^{*i}\right] + \tilde{p}_2^w\left[M_z^{*i'} - M_z^{*i}\right]. \tag{A.19}$$

Utilizing the balanced-trade conditions that must hold before and after the bilateral negotiations, and the equilibrium conditions subsequent to the bilateral negotiations, we can rewrite the reciprocity restrictions as

$$[\tilde{p}_1^{w'} - \tilde{p}_1^w]M_x' - [\tilde{p}_2^{w'} - \tilde{p}_2^w]E_z' = 0, \tag{A.20}$$

$$[\tilde{p}_1^{w'} - \tilde{p}_1^w]E_x^{*1'} - [\tilde{p}_2^{w'} - \tilde{p}_2^w]M_z^{*1'} = 0, \tag{A.21}$$

$$[\tilde{p}_1^{w'} - \tilde{p}_1^w]E_x^{*2'} - [\tilde{p}_2^{w'} - \tilde{p}_2^w]M_z^{*2'} = 0. \tag{A.22}$$

Clearly, these conditions are met when both $\tilde{p}_1^w$ and $\tilde{p}_2^w$ are unchanged as a result of the bilateral negotiations. These conditions may also be satisfied when both $\tilde{p}_1^w$ and $\tilde{p}_2^w$ are changed as a result of the bilateral negotiations, but all of the permissible world price changes share a special feature. Specifically, (A.20), (A.21), and (A.22) imply that in combination with the new local prices, the new world prices must deliver the same tariff revenue to each country as would have been delivered if these new local prices had been combined with the old world prices.[1] As a consequence the permissible changes in world

---

1. This can be seen by adding and subtracting p_1' (p_2') inside the first (second) bracket of (A.20), adding and subtracting $p_1^{*1'}$ ($p_2^{*1'}$) inside the first (second) bracket of (A.21), and adding and subtracting $p_1^{*2'}$ ($p_2^{*2'}$) inside the first (second) bracket of (A.22), and then rearranging these expressions.

prices that result from bilateral negotiations under reciprocity can have no direct welfare consequences for the negotiating governments. In this way reciprocity and MFN continue to eliminate the opportunities for countries to disrupt an MFN-efficient multilateral trade agreement for terms-of-trade advantages in a many-good world, just as these tandem rules did in the two-good case.

We now come to the second result: with many goods there arises an additional problem of bilateral opportunism. This new problem of bilateral opportunism is conceptually distinct from the terms-of-trade problem, and it is related instead to the desire to achieve mutually advantageous changes in local prices through a bilateral negotiation. The point is simply that while the permissible changes in world prices that result from bilateral negotiations under reciprocity can have no direct welfare consequences for the negotiating governments, these world price changes may nevertheless have indirect welfare effects through the local-price movements that they make possible. It may therefore be possible that, starting from a set of MFN-efficient tariffs for all three governments, the home government and that of foreign country i could undertake bilateral negotiations to lower their tariffs in accordance with MFN and subject to reciprocity in a way that yielded mutually beneficial changes in local prices, of course at the expense of foreign country j.[2]

Our third result is to establish that under MFN and reciprocity, the potential for opportunistic bilateral negotiations in a many-good world is nevertheless limited, in the sense that it arises only at certain points on the efficiency frontier. To see this, note that beginning from any set of MFN-efficient tariffs, a necessary condition for the home government and that of foreign country i to gain from a bilateral agreement is that world prices do in fact change as a result of their negotiations (since otherwise no welfare is appropriated from foreign country j). In this case the three restrictions (A.20), (A.21), and (A.22) implied by reciprocity may be combined, together with the balanced trade condition, to yield:

---

2. For example, suppose that, owing to the bargaining power of foreign country j, the government of foreign country i had failed through multilateral negotiations to secure a mix of imports from the home country that were tilted away from one of its most politically sensitive sectors. In this case the government of foreign country i might, through further bilateral negotiations with the home government, be able to "worsen" the mix of imports that foreign country j receives, and thereby achieve a more favorable import mix for itself while still satisfying reciprocity.

$$\frac{M_y^{*1'}}{E_y'} = \frac{M_y^{*2'}}{E_y'} = \frac{M_z^{*1'}}{E_z'} = \frac{M_z^{*2'}}{E_z'} = \frac{E_x^{*1'}}{M_x'} = \frac{E_x^{*2'}}{M_x'}. \tag{A.23}$$

Hence, whenever reciprocity is satisfied and world prices also change, we may represent the restriction of reciprocity as contained in (A.20), (A.21), and (A.22) by the equivalent conditions (A.20) and (A.23).

Condition (A.23) is illuminating. It says that if the home government and that of foreign country i succeed in altering world prices in a reciprocity-consistent fashion as a result of their bilateral negotiation, then the resulting world trade patterns must satisfy a strong "proportionality" condition so that the fraction of home-country exports of good y and of good z that each foreign country accepts is identical across countries and across goods (with three countries, this fraction is $\frac{1}{2}$), and is the same as the fraction of home-country imports of good x that each foreign country supplies. Such a condition would be satisfied automatically in equilibrium in a two-country world (where each fraction would be one).[3] But with three countries, condition (A.23) imposes an additional restriction (beyond A.20) on the local-price combinations that are attainable when bilateral negotiations alter world prices but still satisfy reciprocity.

Whether the feasible combinations of local prices consistent with these restrictions can provide mutual welfare improvements for the two governments will depend on circumstances. For example, if countries had negotiated to a point on the efficiency frontier at which the proportionality condition implied by (A.23) was initially satisfied, then the restriction that this condition must also be satisfied after bilateral negotiations which alter world prices might not be so severe, and an opportunistic bilateral negotiation might well be feasible under MFN and reciprocity. But if the point on the efficiency frontier to which countries had initially negotiated implied trading patterns that were sufficiently far away from satisfying the restriction in (A.23), then this requirement is likely to severely undermine the attractiveness of further bilateral negotiations. In such circumstances there is unlikely to be a serious problem of bilateral opportunism if the rules of MFN and reciprocity are applied.

---

3. As may be confirmed by inspection, in a two-country world (A.20), (A.21), and (A.22) collapse to a single condition as well.

Hence, by providing a solution to the terms-of-trade-driven bilateral opportunism problem, the tandem rules of MFN and reciprocity can be viewed as solving the most pervasive problem associated with bilateral opportunism in a many-good environment. More speculatively, we suggest that the opportunities for bilateral opportunism that remain in a many-good world even in the presence of MFN and reciprocity, while fairly limited, might signify an additional role for the nullification-or-impairment rule in providing a second line of defense against this problem.

References

Anderson, Kym, and Richard Blackhurst, eds. 1993. *Regional Integration and the Global Trading System.* New York: St. Martin's Press.

Anderson, James, and Eric van Wincoop. 2001. Borders, trade and welfare. NBER Working Paper 8515. October.

Bagwell, Kyle. 1991. Optimal export policy for a new-product monopoly. *American Economic Review* 81: 1156–69.

Bagwell, Kyle, and Robert W. Staiger. 1989. The role for export subsidies when product quality is unknown. *Journal of International Economics* 27: 69–89.

Bagwell, Kyle, and Robert W. Staiger. 1990. A theory of managed trade. *American Economic Review* 80: 779–95.

Bagwell, Kyle, and Robert W. Staiger. 1992. The sensitivity of strategic and corrective R&D policies in battles for monopoly. *International Economic Review* 33: 795–816.

Bagwell, Kyle, and Robert W. Staiger. 1994. The sensitivity of strategic and corrective R&D policies in oligopolistic industries. *Journal of International Economics* 36: 133–50.

Bagwell, Kyle, and Robert W. Staiger. 1995. Protection and the business cycle. NBER Discussion Paper 5168. July.

Bagwell, Kyle, and Robert W. Staiger. 1996. Reciprocal trade liberalization. NBER Discussion Paper 5488. March.

Bagwell, Kyle, and Robert W. Staiger. 1997a. Collusion over the business cycle. *Rand Journal of Economics* 28: 82–106.

Bagwell, Kyle, and Robert W. Staiger. 1997b. Multilateral tariff cooperation during the formation of customs unions. *Journal of International Economics* 42: 91–123.

Bagwell, Kyle, and Robert W. Staiger. 1997c. Multilateral tariff cooperation during the formation of free trade areas. *International Economic Review* 38: 291–319.

Bagwell, Kyle, and Robert W. Staiger. 1997d. Strategic export subsidies and reciprocal trade agreements: The natural monopoly case. *Japan and the World Economy* 9: 491–510.

Bagwell, Kyle, and Robert W. Staiger. 1998. Will preferential agreements undermine the multilateral trading system? *Economic Journal* 108: 1162–82.

Bagwell, Kyle, and Robert W. Staiger. 1999a. An economic theory of GATT. *American Economic Review* 89: 215–48.

Bagwell, Kyle, and Robert W. Staiger. 1999b. Regionalism and multilateral tariff cooperation. In John Piggott and Alan Woodland, eds., *International Trade Policy and the Pacific Rim*, London: Macmillan, pp. 157–85.

Bagwell, Kyle, and Robert W. Staiger. 2000a. Multilateral trade negotiations, bilateral opportunism and the rules of GATT/WTO. Mimeo. University of Wisconsin, Madison.

Bagwell, Kyle, and Robert W. Staiger. 2000b. Shifting comparative advantage and accession in the WTO. Mimeo. University of Wisconsin, Madison.

Bagwell, Kyle, and Robert W. Staiger. 2001a. Domestic policies, national sovereignty and international economic institutions. *Quarterly Journal of Economics* 116: 519–62.

Bagwell, Kyle, and Robert W. Staiger. 2001b. Reciprocity, non-discrimination and preferential agreements in the multilateral trading system. *European Journal of Political Economy* 17: 281–325.

Bagwell, Kyle, and Robert W. Staiger. 2001c. Strategic trade, competitive industries and agricultural trade disputes. *Economics and Politics* 13: 113–28.

Bagwell, Kyle, and Robert W. Staiger. 2001d. The WTO as a mechanism for securing market access property rights: Implications for global labor and environmental issues. *Journal of Economic Perspectives* 15: 69–88.

Bagwell, Kyle, and Robert W. Staiger. 2001e. Competition policy and the WTO. Mimeo. University of Wisconsin, Madison. August.

Bagwell, Kyle, Petros C. Mavroidis, and Robert W. Staiger. 2002. It's a question of market access. *American Journal of International Law* 96: 56–76.

Baldwin, Richard. 1987. Politically realistic objective functions and trade policy. *Economic Letters* 24: 287–90.

Baldwin, Richard. 1995. A domino theory of regionalism. In Richard Baldwin, P. Haaparnata, and J. Kiander, eds., *Expanding Membership of the European Union*. Cambridge: Cambridge University Press, pp. 25–53.

Baldwin, Richard, and Anthony Venables. 1995. Regional economic integration. In G. Grossman and K. Rogoff, eds., *Handbook of International Economics*, vol. 3. Amsterdam: North Holland, pp. 1597–644.

Baldwin, Robert. 1985. *The Political Economy of U.S. Import Policy*. Cambridge: MIT Press.

Beckett, Grace. 1941. *The Reciprocal Trade Agreements Program*. New York: Columbia University Press.

Bernheim, B. Douglas, and Michael D. Whinston. 1990. Multimarket conduct and collusive behavior. *Rand Journal of Economics* 21: 1–26.

Berry, Stephen, Levinsohn, James, and Ariel Pakes. 1999. Voluntary export restraints on automobiles: Evaluating a trade policy. *American Economic Review* 89: 400–30.

Bhagwati, Jagdish. 1988. *Protectionism*. Cambridge: MIT Press.

Bhagwati, Jagdish. 1990. Aggressive unilateralism: An overview. In J. Bhagwati and H. T. Patrick, eds., *Aggressive Unilateralism: America's 301 Trade Policy and the World Trading System*. Ann Arbor: University of Michigan Press, pp. 1–45.

Bhagwati, Jagdish. 1991. *The World Trading System at Risk*. Princeton: Princeton University Press.

Bhagwati, Jagdish. 2002. Introduction: The unilateral freeing of trade versus reciprocity. In J. Bhagwati, ed. *On Going Alone: The Case for Relaxed Reciprocity in Freeing Trade*. Cambridge: MIT Press, pp. 1–29.

Bhagwati, Jagdish, and Arvind Panagariya. 1996. "Preferential trading areas and multilateralism—strangers, friends, or foes? In J. Bhagwati and A. Panagariya, eds., *The Economics of Preferential Trade Agreements*, Washington: AEI Press, pp. 1–78.

Bhagwati, Jagdish, David Greenaway, and Arvind Panagariya. 1998. Trading preferentially: Theory and policy. *Economic Journal* 108: 1128–48.

Boger III, William H. 1984. The United States–European Community agricultural export subsidy dispute. *Law and Policy in International Business* 16: 213–30.

Bond, Eric W., and Jee-Hyeong Park. 2002. Gradualism in trade agreements with asymmetric countries. *Review of Economic Studies*, forthcoming.

Bond, Eric W., and Costas Syropoulos. 1996a. Trading blocs and the sustainability of inter regional cooperation. In M. Canzoneri, W. Ethier, and V. Grilli, eds., *The New Transatlantic Economy*. Cambridge: Cambridge University Press, pp. 118–41.

Bond, Eric W., and Costas Syropoulos. 1996b. The size of trading blocs: market power and world welfare effects. *Journal of International Economics* 40: 411–37.

Bond, Eric W., Costas Syropoulos, and Alan A. Winters. 1996. Deepening of regional integration and external trade relations. CEPR Discussion Paper 1317.

Brainard, Lael. 1994. Last one out wins: Trade policy in an international exit game. *International Economic Review* 35: 151–72.

Brander, James. 1995. Strategic trade policy. In G. M. Grossman and K. Rogoff, eds., *Handbook of International Economics*, vol. 3, Amsterdam: North-Holland, pp. 1395–1455.

Brander, James, and Barbara Spencer. 1985. Export subsidies and market share rivalry. *Journal of International Economics* 18: 83–100.

Brock, William A., and Stephen P. Magee. 1978. The economics of special interest politics. *American Economic Review* 68: 246–50.

Caplin, Andrew, and Kala Krishna. 1988. Tariffs and the most-favored-nation clause: A game-theoretic approach. *Seoul Journal of Economics* 1: 267–89.

Carmichael, C. 1987. The control of export credit subsidies and its welfare consequences. *Journal of International Economics* 23: 1–19.

Caves, Richard A. 1976. Economic models of political choice: Canada's tariff structure. *Canadian Journal of Economics* 9: 278–300.

Chisik, Richard. 2002. Gradualism in free trade agreements: A theoretical justification. *Journal of International Economics*, forthcoming.

Choi, Jay Pil. 1995. Optimal tariffs and the choice of technology: Discriminatory tariffs vs. the "most favored nation" clause. *Journal of International Economics* 38: 143–60.

Collie, David R. 1997. Bilateralism is good: Trade blocs and strategic export subsidies. *Oxford Economic Papers* 49: 504–20.

Coneybeare, John AC. 1987. *Trade Wars: The Theory and Practice of International Commercial Rivalry*. New York: Columbia University Press.

Croome, John. 1995. *Reshaping the World Trading System: A History of the Uruguay Round*. Geneva: World Trade Organization.

Culbert, Jay. 1987. War-time Anglo-American talks and the making of GATT. *World Economy* 10: 381–407.

Dam, Kenneth W. 1970. *The GATT: Law and International Economic Organization*. Chicago: University of Chicago Press.

Devereux, Michael. B. 1997. Growth, specialization and trade liberalization. *International Economic Review* 38: 565–85.

Dixit, Avinash. 1984. International trade policy for oligopolistic industries. *Economic Journal* 94 (suppl.): 1–16.

Dixit, Avinash. 1987. Strategic aspects of trade policy. In Truman F. Bewley, ed., *Advances in Economic Theory: Fifth World Congress*. New York: Cambridge University Press.

Dixit, Avinash. 1996. *The Making of Economic Policy: A Transaction-Cost Politics Perspective*. Cambridge: MIT Press.

Dixit, Avinash, Gene M. Grossman, and Elhanan Helpman. 1997. Common agency and coordination: General theory and application to government policy making. *Journal of Political Economy* 105: 752–69.

Eaton, Jonathan, and Gene M. Grossman. 1986. Optimal trade and industrial policy under oligopoly. *Quarterly Journal of Economics* 51: 383–406.

Ederington, Josh. 2001. International coordination of trade and domestic policies. *American Economic Review* 91: 1580–93.

Enders, Alice. 1996. The role of the WTO in minimum standards. In van Dijck and Faber, eds., *Challenges to the New World Trade Organization*. The Hague: Kluwer Law International.

Enders, Alice. 1997. The origin, nature and limitations of reciprocity in GATT 1947. Mimeo.

Ethier, Wilfred. 1998a. Regionalism in a multilateral world. *Journal of Political Economy* 106: 1214–45.

Ethier, Wilfred. 1998b. The new regionalism. *Economic Journal* 108: 1149–61.

Ethier, Wilfred. 2000. Reciprocity, nondiscrimination and a multilateral world. Mimeo. University of Pennsylvania.

Feenstra, Robert. 1980. Monopsony distortions in an open economy: A theoretical analysis. *Journal of International Economics* 10: 213–35.

Feenstra, Robert, and Jagdish Bhagwati. 1982. Tariff seeking and the efficient tariff. In J. Bhagwati, ed., *Import Competition and Response*. Chicago: University of Chicago Press.

Feenstra, Robert. 1995. Estimating the effects of trade policy. In G. M. Grossman and K. Rogoff, eds., *The Handbook of International Economics*, vol. 3. Amsterdam: North-Holland.

Fernandez, Raquel, and Jonathan Portes. 1998. Returns to regionalism: An analysis of non-traditional gains from regional trade agreements. *World Bank Economic Review* 12: 197–220.

Fernandez, Raquel, and Dani Rodrik. 1991. Resistance to reform: status-quo bias in the presence of individual-specific uncertainty. *American Economic Review* 81: 1146–55.

Financial Times. 2000. Taxing the WTO to the Limit. Editorial, September 4.

Findlay, Ronald, and Stanislaw Wellisz. 1982. Endogenous tariffs, the political economy of trade restrictions and welfare. In J. Bhagwati, ed., *Import Competition and Response*. Chicago: University of Chicago Press.

Flam, Harry, and Elhanan Helpman. 1987. Industrial policy under monopolistic competition. *Journal of International Economics* 22: 79–102.

Freund, Caroline. 2000a. Multilateralism and the endogenous formation of preferential trade agreements. *Journal of International Economics* 52: 359–76.

Freund, Caroline. 2000b. Spaghetti regionalism. Board of Governors of the Federal Reserve System Discussion Paper 680. September.

Freund, Caroline. 2000c. Different paths to free trade: The gains from regionalism. *Quarterly Journal of Economics* 115: 1317–41.

Freund, Caroline, and John McLaren. 1999. On the dynamics of trade diversion: Evidence from four trade blocs. Board of Governors of the Federal Reserve System, International Finance Discussion Papers 637. June.

Furusawa, Taiji, and Edwin Lai. 1999. Adjustment costs and gradual trade liberalization. *Journal of International Economics* 49: 333–61.

Gilligan, Michael. 1997. *Empowering Exporters: Reciprocity, Delegation and Collective Action in American Trade Policy*. Ann Arbor: University of Michigan Press.

Goldberg, Penny Koujianou, and Michael M. Knetter. 1997. Goods prices and exchange rates: What have we learned? *Journal of Economic Literature* 35: 1244–72.

Goldberg, Penny Koujianou. 1995. Product differentiation and oligopoly in international markets: The case of the U.S. automobile industry. *Econometrica* 63: 891–951.

Green, Edward J., and Robert H. Porter. 1984. Noncooperative collusion under imperfect price information. *Econometrica* 52: 87–100.

Grimwade, Nigel. 1996. *International Trade Policy: A Contemporary Analysis*. London: Routledge.

Gros, Daniel. 1987. A note on the optimal tariff, retaliation and the welfare loss from tariff wars in a framework with intra-industry trade. *Journal of International Economics* 23: 357–67.

Grossman, Gene M., and Elhanan Helpman. 1994. Protection for sale. *American Economic Review* 84: 833–50.

Grossman, Gene M., and Elhanan Helpman. 1995a. Trade wars and trade talks. *Journal of Political Economy* 103: 675–708.

Grossman, Gene M., and Elhanan Helpman. 1995b. The politics of free trade agreements. *American Economic Review* 85: 667–90.

Grossman, Gene M., and Henrik Horn. 1988. Infant-industry protection reconsidered: The case of informational barriers to entry. *Quarterly Journal of Economics* 103: 767–87.

Grossman, Gene M., and Giovanni Maggi. 1998. Free trade vs. strategic trade: A peek into Pandora's box. In R. Sato, R. Ramachandran, and K. Mino, eds., *Global Competition and Integration* Dordrecht: Kluwer Academic.

Gruenspecht, Howard K. 1988. Dumping and dynamic competition. *Journal of International Economics* 25: 225–48.

Helpman, Elhanan, and Paul R. Krugman. 1989. *Trade Policy and Market Structure*. Cambridge: MIT Press.

Herter, Christian. 1961. Statement before the Joint Economic Committee of the Congress of the United States, December 4–14, pp. 8–13.

Hillman, Arye L. 1982. Declining industries and political-support protectionist motives. *American Economic Review* 72: 1180–87.

Hoekman, Bernard, and Michel Kostecki. 1995. *The Political Economy of the World Trading System: From GATT to WTO*. Oxford: Oxford University Press.

Horn, Henrik, and James Levinsohn. 2001. Merger policies and trade liberalization. *Economic Journal* 111: 244–76.

Horn, Henrik, and Petros C. Mavroidis. 2001. Economic and legal aspects of the most-favored nation clause. *European Journal of Political Economy* 17: 233–79.

Hudec, Robert E. 1990. *The GATT Legal System and World Trade Diplomacy*, 2nd ed. New York: Praeger.

Hull, Cordell. 1948. *The Memoirs of Cordell Hull*. London: Hodder and Stoughton.

Jackson, John. 1969. *World Trade and the Law of GATT*. New York: Bobbs-Merrill.

Jackson, John. 1997a. *The World Trading System*, 2nd ed. Cambridge: MIT Press.

Jackson, John. 1997b. Dispute settlement in the WTO: Policy and jurisprudential considerations. Mimeo. University of Michigan.

Johnson, Harry G. 1953–54. Optimum tariffs and retaliation. *Review of Economic Studies* 1: 142–53.

Kemp, M. C., and H. Y. Wan. 1976. An elementary proposition concerning the formation of customs unions. *Journal of International Economics* 6: 95–97.

Kennan, John, and Raymond Reizman. 1988. Do big countries win tariff wars? *International Economic Review* 29: 81–85.

Klimenko, Mikhail, Garey Ramey, and Joel Watson. 2000. Recurrent trade agreements and the value of external enforcement. Mimeo.

Kovenock, Dan, and Marie Thursby. 1992. GATT, dispute settlement and cooperation. *Economics and Politics* 4: 151–70.

Kreinin, Mordechai. 1961. Effect of tariff changes on the prices and volume of imports. *American Economic Review* 51: 310–24.

Krishna, Pravin. 1998. Regionalism and multilateralism: A political economy approach. *Quarterly Journal of Economics* 113: 227–51.

Krishna, Pravin, and Devashish Mitra. 1999. Reciprocated unilateralism: A political economy perspective. Mimeo. Brown University.

Krueger, Anne O., ed. 1998. *The WTO as an International Organization*. Chicago: University of Chicago Press.

Krugman, Paul R. 1991a. The move toward free trade zones. In *Policy Implications of Trade and Currency Zones, A Symposium Sponsored by The Federal Reserve Bank of Kansas City*, Jackson Hole, Wyoming, August 22–24.

Krugman, Paul R. 1991b. Is bilateralism bad? In E. Helpman and A. Razin, eds., *International Trade and Trade Policy*. Cambridge: MIT Press.

Krugman, Paul R. 1997. What should trade negotiators negotiate about? *Journal of Economic Literature* 35: 113–20.

Krugman, Paul R., and Maurice Obstfeld. 1997. *International Economics: Theory and Policy*, 4th ed., Reading, MA: Addison-Wesley.

Lapan, H. E. 1988. The optimal tariff, production lags, and time consistency. *American Economic Review* 78: 395–401.

League of Nations. 1933. *Reports Approved by the Conference on July 27th, 1933, and Resolutions Adopted by the Bureau and the Executive Committee*. Geneva: League of Nations.

League of Nations. 1942. *Commercial Policy in the Interwar Period: International Proposals and National Policies*. Geneva: League of Nations.

Levy, Phil. 1997. A political economic analysis of free trade agreements. *American Economic Review* 87: 506–19.

Limao, Nuno. 2000. Trade policy, cross-border externalities and lobbies: Do linked agreements enforce more cooperative outcomes? Mimeo. University of Maryland. November.

Limao, Nuno. 2001. Are preferential trade agreements with non-trade objectives a stumbling block for multilateral liberalization. Mimeo. University of Maryland.

Low, Patrick. 1993. *Trading Free: The GATT and U.S. Trade Policy*. New York: Twentieth Century Fund Press.

Ludema, Rodney. 1991. International trade bargaining and the most-favored nation clause. *Economics and Politics* 3: 1–20.

Maggi, Giovanni. 1996. Strategic trade policy with endogenous mode of competition. *American Economic Review* 86: 237–58.

Maggi, Giovanni. 1999. The role of multilateral institutions in international trade cooperation. *American Economic Review* 89: 190–214.

Maggi, Giovanni, and Andres Rodriguez-Clare. 1998. The value of trade agreements in the presence of political pressures. *Journal of Political Economy* 106: 574–601.

Magnusson, Paul. 2000. This tax break could trigger a trade war. *Business Week*, September 4, pp. 103–104.

Maskin, Eric, and David Newberry. 1990. Disadvantageous oil tariffs and dynamic consistency. *American Economic Review* 80: 143–56.

Matsuyama, Kiminori. 1990. Perfect equilibria in a trade liberalization game. *American Economic Review* 80: 480–92.

Mavroidis, Petros C. 2000. Remedies in the WTO legal system: Between a rock and a hard place. *European Journal of International Law* 11: 763–813.

Mayer, Wolfgang. 1981. Theoretical considerations on negotiated tariff adjustments. *Oxford Economic Papers* 33: 135–53.

Mayer, Wolfgang. 1984. Endogenous tariff formation. *American Economic Review* 74: 970–85.

Mayer, Wolfgang. 1994. Optimal pursuit of safeguard actions over time. In A. Deardorff and R. Stern, eds., *Analytical and Negotiating Issues in the Global Trading System*. Ann Arbor: University of Michigan Press.

McCalman, Phillip. 2002. Multilateral trade negotiations and the most-favored nation clause. *Journal of International Economies* 57: 151–76.

McLaren, John. 1997. Size, sunk costs, and Judge Bowker's objection to free trade. *American Economic Review* 87: 400–20.

McLaren, John. 2002. A theory of insidious regionalism. *Quarterly Journal of Economics* 117: 571–608.

McMillan, John. 1986. *Game Theory in International Economics*. New York: Harwood.

McMillan, John. 1989. A game-theoretic view of international trade negotiations: Implications for developing countries. In J. Whalley, ed. *Developing Countries and the Global Trading System*, vol. 1. London: Macmillan.

Mill, John Stuart. 1844. *Essays on Some Unsettled Questions of Political Economy*. London: Parker.

Mitra, Devashish. 1999. Endogenous lobby formation and endogenous protection: A long-run model of trade policy determination. *American Economic Review* 89: 1116–34.

Olson, Mancur. 1965. *The Logic of Collective Action*. Cambridge: Harvard University Press.

Ostry, Sylvia. 1997. *The Post–Cold War Trading System: Who's on First?* Chicago: Twentieth Century Fund, University of Chicago Press.

Oxley, Alan. 1990. *The Challenge of Free Trade*. New York: St. Martin's Press.

Panagariya, Arvind. 2000. Preferential trade liberalization: The traditional theory and new developments. *Journal of Economic Literature* 38: 287–331.

Petersmann, Ernst-Ulrich. 1997. *The GATT/WTO Dispute Settlement System: International Law, International Organizations and Dispute Settlement*. London: Kluwer Law International.

Pomfret, Richard E. 1997. *The Economics of Regional Trading Agreements*. Oxford: Oxford University Press.

Preeg, Ernest H. 1970. *Traders and Diplomats*. Washington: Brookings Institute.

Preeg, Ernest H. 1995. *Traders in a Brave New World: The Uruguay Round and the Future of the International Trading System*. Chicago: University of Chicago Press.

Raff, Horst, and Y.-H. Kim. 1999. Optimal export policy in the presence of informational barriers to entry and imperfect competition. *Journal of International Economics* 49: 99–123.

Rhodes, Carolyn. 1993. *Reciprocity, U.S. Trade Policy, and the GATT Regime*. Ithaca, NY: Cornell University Press.

Riezman, Raymond. 1991. Dynamic tariffs with asymmetric information. *Journal of International Economics* 30: 267–83.

Romalis, John. 2001. NAFTA's impact on North American trade. Mimeo. September.

Rotemberg, Julio J. and Garth Saloner. 1986. A supergame-theoretic model of price wars during booms. *American Economic Review* 76: 390–407.

Ruggiero, Renato. 1995. Speech at Harvard University, October 16, 1995. Available at WTO Web site: *http://www.wto.org/wto/pressrel/press25.html*.

Schwartz, W. F., and Alan O. Sykes. 1997. The economics of the most favored nation clause. In J. S. Bhandani and A. O. Sykes, eds., *Economic Dimensions in International Law: Comparative and Empirical Perspectives*, Cambridge: Cambridge University Press, pp. 43–79.

Scitovsky, Tibor. 1942. A reconsideration of the theory of tariffs. *Review of Economic Studies* 9: 89–110.

Spagnolo, Giancarlo. 1999. On interdependent supergames: Multimarket contact, concavity and collusion. *Journal of Economic Theory* 89: 127–39.

Spagnolo, Giancarlo. 2000. Issue linkage, delegation, and international policy cooperation. Mimeo. Stockholm School of International Economics.

Spencer, Barbara, and James Brander. 1983. International R&D Rivalry and industrial strategy. *Review of Economic Studies* 50: 707–22.

Srinivasan, T. N. 1996. International trade and labour standards from an economic perspective. In P. van Dijck and G. Faber eds., *Challenges to the New World Trade Organization*. The Hague: Kluwer Law International.

Staiger, Robert W. 1995a. International rules and institutions for trade policy. In G. M. Grossman and K. Rogoff, eds., *The Handbook of International Economics*, vol. 3. Amsterdam: North-Holland.

Staiger, Robert W. 1995b. A theory of gradual trade liberalization. in A. Deardorff, J. Levinsohn, and R. Stern, eds., *New Directions in Trade Theory*. Ann Arbor: University of Michigan Press.

Staiger, Robert W., and Guido Tabellini. 1987. Discretionary trade policy and excessive protection. *American Economic Review* 77: 823–37.

Staiger, Robert W., and Guido Tabellini. 1989. Rules and discretion in trade policy. *European Economic Review* 33: 1265–77.

Staiger, Robert W., and Guido Tabellini. 1999. Do GATT rules help governments make domestic commitments? *Economics and Politics* 11: 109–44.

Stern, Robert M. ed. 1993. *The Multilateral Trading System: Analysis and Options for Change*. Ann Arbor: University of Michigan Press.

Syropoulos, Constantinos. 2000. Optimum tariffs and retaliation revisited: How country size matters. Mimeo. Florida International University.

Telser, Lester G. 1980. A theory of self-enforcing agreements. *Journal of Business* 53: 27–44.

Tornell, Aaron. 1991. On the ineffectiveness of made-to-measure protectionist programs. In E. Helpman and A. Razin, eds., *International Trade and Trade Policy*. Cambridge: MIT Press.

Torrens, Robert. 1844. *The Budget: On Commercial Policy and Colonial Policy*. London: Smith, Elder.

Trebilcock, Michael J., and Robert Howse. 1999. *The Regulation of International Trade*, 2nd ed., London: Routledge.

Tuckman, Johanna. 1997. Central Americans start to act together. *Financial Times*, July 9, p. 4.

Tyson, Laura D. 2001. The new laws of nations. *New York Times* oped, July 14.

Viner, Jacob. 1924. The most-favored-nation clause in American commercial treaties. *Journal of Political Economy* 32: 101–29. Reprinted in J. Viner (1951) *International Economics*, Chapter 1, Glencoe, IL: Free Press.

Viner, Jacob. 1931. The most-favored-nation clause, index. sevenka handelsbanken: Stockholm. Reprinted as chapter 5 of *International Economics*, Glencoe, IL: Free Press, 1951.

Viner, Jacob. 1936. Comments on the improvement of commercial relations between nations. In *The Improvement of Commercial Relations between Nations and the Problem of Monetary Stabilization*. Paris: Carnegie Endowment-International Chamber of Commerce Joint Committee.

Viner, Jacob. 1950. *The Customs Union Issue*. New York: Carnegie Endowment for International Peace.

Whalley, John. 1985. *Trade Liberalization among Major World Trading Areas*. Cambridge: MIT Press.

Winters, L. Alan. 1996. Regionalism versus multilateralism. Policy Research Working Paper 1687. World Bank, Washington, DC.

Winters, L. Alan, and Won Chang. 1999. How regional blocs affect excluded countries: The price effects of MERCOSUR. CEPR Discussion Paper 2179, June.

Winters, L. Alan, and Won Chang. 2000. Regional integration and the prices of imports: An empirical investigation. *Journal of International Economics* 51: 363–77.

WTO. 1995a. *Analytical Index: Guide to GATT Law and Practice*, vol. 2. Geneva: World Trade Organization.

WTO. 1995b. *Regionalism and the World Trading System*. Geneva: World Trade Organization.

WTO. 1998. Communication from the United States. Working Group on the Interaction between Trade and Competition Policy. March 26. Geneva.

WTO. 2001. *Annual Report 2001*. Geneva: World Trade Organization.

Yi, Sang-Seung. 1996. Endogenous formation of customs unions under imperfect competition: Open regionalism is good. *Journal of International Economics* 41: 153–77.

Index